CDL Test Preparation Guide

Everything You Need to Know

CDL Test Preparation Guide

Everything You Need to Know

Alice Adams

Van O'Neal

THOMSON

DELMAR LEARNING   Australia   Canada   Mexico   Singapore   Spain   United Kingdom   United States

THOMSON
DELMAR LEARNING

CDL Test Preparation Guide: Everything You Need To Know
Alice Adams and Van O'Neal

Contributor:
Kevin Lewis
Vice President of Driver Programs,
American Association of Motor Vehicle Administrators

Vice President, Technology
Professional Business Unit:
Gregory L. Clayton

Product Development Manager:
Kristen L. Davis

Product Manager:
Kimberley Blakey

Editorial Assistant:
Jason Yager

Director of Marketing:
Beth A. Lutz

Marketing Manager:
Brian McGrath

Marketing Coordinator:
Jennifer Stall

Director of Production:
Patty Stephan

Production Manager:
Andrew Crouth

Content Project Manager:
Kara A. DiCaterino

Art Director:
Robert Plante

Library of Congress Cataloging-in-Publication Data
Adams, Alice.
  CDL test preparation guide : everything you need to know / Alice Adams and Van O'Neal.
    p. cm.
  Includes index.
  ISBN 1-4180-3847-4
  1. Truck driving--United States. 2. Truck drivers--Licenses--United States. I. O'Neal, Van.
  II. Title.
  TL230.3.O54 2006
  629.28'44076--dc22
                                    2006035604

NOTICE TO THE READER

Publisher does not warrant or guarantee any of the products described herein or perform any independent analysis in connection with any of the product information contained herein. Publisher does not assume, and expressly disclaims, any obligation to obtain and include information other than that provided to it by the manufacturer.

The reader is expressly warned to consider and adopt all safety precautions that might be indicated by the activities herein and to avoid all potential hazards. By following the instructions contained herein, the reader willingly assumes all risks in connection with such instructions.

The publisher makes no representation or warranties of any kind, including but not limited to, the warranties of fitness for particular purpose or merchantability, nor are any such representations implied with respect to the material set forth herein, and the publisher takes no responsibility with respect to such material. The pub-

Contents

Preface

When you pass the Commercial Driver's License (CDL) examination, you become a member of one of this country's most important professions.

Professional drivers supply each and every citizen of this country with many of their basic needs.

The saying, "If you've got it, a trucker brought it!" applies to everyone, from the city to the countryside. Each consumer item the American public needs and uses every day is available because it was loaded onto a truck and delivered to docks, warehouses, and stores around the country.

This book was written to help you pass the CDL examination. More important, it was written so that you will be "the expert" when it comes to trucks, driving skills, and the responsibilities of a professional driver.

As you review this book, keep in mind the legions of men and women who have paved the way for today's professional drivers. Also remember that as a professional driver, you have entire communities counting on you to do your best job, to make deliveries on time, and to maintain security and safety for every load on every road you travel.

America's quality of life depends on you, your knowledge of the laws, and your driving skills. Delivering items—from emergency medical supplies to Halloween candy—is the everyday responsibility of professional drivers. They take this responsibility seriously—and so should you.

We, the authors, welcome you to this highly skilled and respected profession and wish you all the best in your truck driving career.

PART

I

The Basics

1 Welcome to the New Millennium of Professional Driving

When you get your CDL (Commercial Driver's License), you have the opportunity to enter a profession much different than the one professional drivers found two decades ago (see Figure 1-1). The changes made in the transportation industry during the last quarter-century have created an environment of increased professionalism and continuing opportunity.

Here's what one retired driver had to say about his tenure in trucking from 1948 to 1980:

I was lucky. I worked for a carrier who tried to stay at the forefront of the industry, so when something new was available, we were usually the first to get it, but we still had trucks we held together with baling wire. And until the last years I worked, there wasn't the emphasis on safety that there is now.

In the old days, getting a load delivered was everything—and that still holds true today, except the driver's health and well-being also plays a role now. Back then—when I first started driving—I drank a lot of coffee and drove a lot of hours I probably shouldn't have, just to be on time.

And back then, I usually felt like the Lone Ranger out on the road. Dispatchers today have some empathy. But when I first started, their word was law—no ifs,

Figure 1-1 Professional truck driving has changed over the decades for the better.

ands, or buts. I remember wanting to come home so I could be with my wife while she had our first kid. But delivering that load came first, so I got home a few days after the baby was born.

When we got CB radios, now that was a positive change. We only called home once a week because long-distance could eat up your paycheck in a hurry. With the CB, we could communicate with other drivers instead of going hundreds of miles and having the only conversation be with the waitress at a restaurant at what eventually became a truck stop—though back then such places consisted of a couple of gas pumps and a "greasy spoon" type of café, which is probably why I have trouble with my stomach even today.

Truck drivers today will find a totally different environment when they go to work, and today's carriers are continuing to find ways to improve the driver's quality of life. Technology has made paperwork almost a thing of the past. Today's driver is knowledgeable about computers, wireless communications, and other technology that not only makes their job easier but also makes the work safer and more secure.

Next Stop: Great Opportunity!

Trucking is one of this country's most important industries. Without trucks, people's quality of life declines. Without trucks, costs skyrocket. Trucks move food, furniture, books, clothing, automobiles, refrigerators, and medicine.

Currently, there are more than 9.6 million people driving and supporting the transportation industry in the United States. Together these workers generate more than $372 billion a year hauling 6.7 billion tons of freight.

The trucking industry uses more than 4.5 million trailers and more than 1.7 million tractors as they travel over 118 billion miles every year.

Trucks include step van delivery vehicles, straight trucks, tractor trailers, doubles, and triples. Trucks also pay more than $28 billion in federal and state highway user taxes and more than 38 percent of all federal highway taxes that go to pay for those roads.

In the United States, there are now approximately 458,000 trucking companies.

Some have only one truck, whereas others use thousands of vehicles to do business. About 88 percent of these companies can be classified as small businesses, while others are large, publicly traded firms or closely held businesses, including partnerships and sole proprietorships owning only one or two tractors and trailers.

A serious driver shortage has plagued the industry for years and to solve this problem, trucking companies are offering better pay, better equipment, more benefits, and bonus programs to attract and keep good drivers (see Figure 1-2). Compensation runs $22,000 to $26,000 per year for starting drivers and an average of $36,000 for more experienced drivers.

To qualify for an intrastate driving job you must be 18 years of age or older and 21 years of age or older for an interstate driving job. You must also have a valid CDL. To qualify for one, a driver must be 18 years of age or older. CDL Drivers must be able to pass a complete Department of Transportation physical every two years and may not have suffered the loss of a hand, arm, foot, or leg, and should not have any other physical defect that interferes with safe driving.

Anyone who has been diagnosed with diabetes, requiring routine insulin injections, cannot drive a commercial motor vehicle in interstate commerce but certainly can work in any other capacity within the industry.

Figure 1-2   A serious shortage has created more opportunities for professional drivers.

Drivers must be able to speak and write English well enough to communicate with law enforcement authorities and the general public. Some companies have additional educational requirements.

The industry has strict regulations against the use of alcohol or drugs prior to or while operating any commercial vehicle. Negative results (clean) on alcohol and drug screenings are often a condition of employment.

Drivers may not have a felony conviction involving the use of a motor vehicle, or have been charged with a crime involving drugs, driving under the influence of drugs or alcohol, or a hit-and-run accident resulting in an injury or death.

Men and women who have passed the CDL and who meet the requirements to become professional drivers have seen doors open for additional responsibilities, increasingly higher pay, and respected positions within the companies for which they work. It is not unusual to find vice-presidents and CEOs of transportation companies who began as drivers in this challenging and rewarding industry.

What You Need to Know About the Profession

When carriers have been asked to name the skills new drivers lack, most say new people are coming into the profession with no clue about how the transportation industry operates.

To give you an idea of professional driving today, here are some frequently asked questions about the transportation industry:

Q. Are there driving jobs where I can be home every night?

A. Absolutely, and many of these jobs provide a tremendous foundation for your professional driving career. "Local" or "regional" carriers usually cover about a 200-mile radius from their home base, which makes it fairly easy for a driver to take a load, deliver it, and return home in the same day.

The drawbacks these jobs offer: some don't pay as well as over-the-road jobs, but drivers *are* home every night or, at the most, every second night.

Q. If I take an over-the-road job, how long will I be away from home at one time?

A. Depending on the company, some work will have drivers home every two weeks, whereas other assignments will put you on the road for as long as three weeks out of every four.

Q. Do any companies allow my spouse or partner to come with me over the road?

A. Many companies allow wives to travel with their husbands. And many companies have liberal policies so that a driver's children (age 12 and over) can travel with them over summer vacations or Christmas break. A few companies even have policies where a pet can travel with the driver.

Q. Are there opportunities for women as professional drivers?

A. Absolutely! Today, professional driving schools report that a large percentage of each class—12 to 15 percent—is female and that more women are taking jobs on the road. Some companies, as you'll read later on, are buying trucks with automatic transmissions so that more women will drive, while other firms train a driver's spouse, partner, or significant other to drive so that couples can drive in teams.

Q. What if my wife or husband has to stay home with the kids? How do I communicate with them?

A. Many of the major carriers offer special hotlines so that your wife or husband can contact you immediately if they need to talk or if there's a problem. Some companies give phone cards so you can call home more often. In the "old days," drivers might have been allowed one long-distance call home at company expense. Today, thanks to QualComm, the Internet, and cell phones, drivers can talk to families and friends every night of the week, and "phone home" programs are more popular than ever before.

Q. What if there's a special event that requires my attendance at home?

A. Some companies—but not all—do everything possible to get drivers home when they need to be there for weddings, funerals, graduations, the birth of a child, and other special occasions. Drivers also help each other out by offering to take loads so that their comrades can be home for family events. Some companies actually guarantee that their drivers will be home for special occasions, even if it means flying them back at company expense.

Q. What about banking, getting paid, and paying my bills while I'm on the road?

A. Some companies make it possible to see each paycheck, via the Internet, even if the driver has direct deposit. This tells the driver how much is going into his or her bank account. Drivers with partners sometimes allow the partners to take care of their bills for them. However, with the advent of laptop computers, Internet banking, and automatic bill-pay services offered by some banks, paying monthly bills has become easier for over-the-road drivers.

Q. What about a laptop computer? Do I need one if I go over-the-road?

A. Actually, there are a couple of options here. Some companies provide on-board computers with the ability to receive and send e-mails. However, drivers who use their own laptops or hand-held computers prefer their privacy. Some drivers also report success with sending and receiving e-mail over their cell phones. Other companies also provide drivers with the option of being paid on a check card system through the fuel card provider. This allows drivers to have access to their money, or a prescribed portion, similar to a check card system.

Q. How much can I expect to make as a professional driver?
A. The typical average salary for an entry-level driver starts at $35,000. Drivers who work hard can make anywhere from $40,000 to $60,000 depending on how long they stay out on the road. Like any other profession, what you make as a professional driver depends on how hard you work and how much you do.

Welcome to the new millennium of transportation. The success of the industry depends on you, the driving professional (Figure 1-3). Many men and women have gone before you, making certain their fellow Americans had what was needed for comfortable lifestyles. Those dedicated drivers established a tradition of reliability, expertise behind the wheel, courtesy on the highways, and professional service.

They have passed the torch. Now it's your turn!

Figure 1-3 The success of the transportation industry depends on you, the driving professional.

2 Everything You Need to Know About the CDL—Before You Start Studying

At one time or another, you have had to study for a test. Whether you have been out of school for two years or twenty, studying for your CDL will require two things: (1) a plan to study regularly, and (2) sticking to that plan.

We suggest dividing the eighteen chapters of this study guide into comfortable chunks of information. You may want to cover a chapter a week, or you may decide to spend two weeks on each chapter. Either way, no matter how much time you have to study, make a study plan and stick to it!

How to Get the Most Out of Your Study Time

Most learners get more out of studying for short periods of time. Don't try to "cram" for the CDL over a few days.

Decide now how much time you can study—three times a week, five times a week, or more. Study for 30 minutes, take a break, and then study for another 30 minutes. Study at your own pace and you'll be surprised at how fast the time flies.

Most people learn best by reading information and then writing it down (see Figure 2-1).

Figure 2-1 Studying for the CDL takes planning and persistence.

ROAD SENSE

Read each chapter and highlight the most important information. Then go back and write down what you have highlighted. This way you automatically review the information twice.

After reading, highlighting, and taking notes on each chapter, you'll find ten review questions at the end of the chapter. These are to help you make sure you've absorbed the important information contained therein. Read each question and mark your answer. Then check them. If you need more study in one area, go back and reread that section of information.

One week before taking the exam, revisit the highlighted chapters, read over your notes, take the sample final exams—and you should be ready to go.

See how easy it is?

A. Read the book, highlighting the most important information.
B. Go back over each chapter and write down the highlighted information.
C. Take the test at the end of the chapter/check answers. Review material that is not clear to you.
D. Before taking the CDL exam, review chapters and take sample exams at the end of the book.

Now, let's get busy!

What Is the CDL and Why Is It Important?

The Commercial Driver's License (CDL) grants the holder permission to legally operate certain vehicles, including:

- Vehicles with a Gross Vehicle Weight Rating (GVWR) of 26,001 pounds or more
- Trailers with GVWR of 10,001 pounds or more
- Vehicles carrying placarded hazardous materials
- Vehicles (buses) with a capacity of sixteen or more people (including driver)

What CDL Classification Should You Choose?

This really is a simple choice. The CDL classifications are divided into three categories:

Class A—Combination

All tractor-trailer drivers must have a Class A CDL if the trailer GVWR (amount of weight for which the vehicle was designed) is 10,001 pounds or more. So, when you

Figure 2-2 Class A vehicles.

add the weight of the tractor, the Gross Combination Vehicle Weight Rating (GCVWR) is 26,001 pounds or more.

If you plan to pull double or triple trailers, you must have a Class A CDL.

In certain states, if a tow-truck operator tows vehicles that have a GVWR of 10,001 pounds or more, or if the GCVWR of the tow truck and the towed vehicle is 26,001 pounds or more, a Class A CDL may be required. Check with your state Drivers License Division (DLD) for specific requirements. Figure 2-2 shows Class A vehicles.

Class B—Heavy Straight Truck or Bus

If you plan to operate a large straight truck or bus with a GVWR of 26,001 pounds or more, you need a Class B CDL. You may pull a trailer as long as the GVWR is not more than 10,000 pounds. Articulated buses are in this category but may also be a Class A vehicle if pulled by a separate power unit. Figure 2-3 shows Class B vehicles, while Figure 2-4 shows types of buses.

Class C—Small Vehicles

A person who drives a minibus, car, small van, or any other vehicle may require a Class C CDL, depending on the type of cargo, not the weight.

- If you are transporting hazardous materials requiring hazardous materials (HazMat) placards, you need a Class C or higher CDL, no matter how small or how heavy the vehicle is.
- If you operate a small vehicle designed to carry more than sixteen people, including yourself (the driver), you will need a Class C CDL. Figure 2-5 shows some types of Class C vehicles.

Figure 2-3 Straight line trucks (Class B).

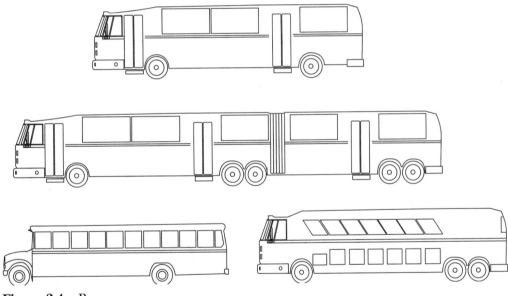

Figure 2-4 Buses.

Figure 2-5 Class C vehicles.

What the CDL Test Looks Like

The CDL test is divided into two parts—the Knowledge Tests and the Skills Tests.

The Knowledge Tests

The Knowledge Tests are written tests. Contact the DLD in your state of legal residence to find out when and where the Knowledge Tests are given, how much time they take to complete, and the costs. You must normally answer 80 percent of the questions correctly to pass the Knowledge Tests; however, your jurisdiction may have a higher passing score than established by the federal requirements. You should contact your local motor vehicle office to find out what the passing score is for your jurisdiction.

ROAD SENSE

The DMV (Department of Motor Vehicles) is where you get your vehicle licensed, not always where you take the tests

There are eight Knowledge Tests. Three that test general knowledge and five that test specialized knowledge areas. These five tests are known as Endorsement Tests:

The General Knowledge Test

All CDL applicants must take the General Knowledge Test. It reviews general safety rules for driving a commercial vehicle carrying various types of cargo.

The General Knowledge Test is made up of fifty true-false or multiple-choice questions, the latter type having three or four possible answers. You must have forty correct answers to pass. After passing the General Knowledge Test, you are eligible to take the Skills Tests, unless the vehicle you will be driving while taking the Skills Tests requires one of the following endorsements:

- **Combination Vehicle Test**—for articulated vehicles or if you plan to pull a trailer. The Combination Vehicle Test is made up of approximately twenty questions. You must correctly answer sixteen to pass.

- **Air Brakes Test**—for operators of any vehicle equipped with air brakes (road test required). This test must be taken if you plan to drive any commercial vehicle equipped with air brakes. If you take the Skills Test in a vehicle without air brakes or if you fail the air brakes test, your CDL will indicate you are not qualified to drive a vehicle with air brakes. There are approximately twenty-five true-false or multiple-choice questions on this test. You must correctly answer twenty to pass.

ROAD SENSE
To receive the Class A CDL, you must pass the General Knowledge Test and the Combination Vehicle Test.

Endorsement Tests (Five)

Endorsement Tests are dependent on the type of vehicle you will be driving. Each Endorsement Test covers knowledge of a specific type of commercial vehicle, including:

- **Passenger Vehicles (Bus)**—needed by operators of all motor vehicles designed to transport sixteen or more people, including the driver.

- **Tanker**—for operators of vehicles transporting liquids or gas in bulk.

- **Double or Triple Trailers**—for operators of vehicles pulling two or three trailers. This endorsement requires a Class A CDL.

- **Hazardous Materials (HazMat)**—for operators of vehicles transporting hazardous materials. Must be trained and retested every two years. You must also be 21 years or older for a HazMat Endorsement. Applicants for a HazMat endorsement must have their fingerprints taken and pass a background check required by the Transportation Security Administration. Your local motor vehicle department will provide information to you on the procedures and costs involved with the background check.

- **The School Bus Endorsement**—for operators of school buses. The operator must also have a passenger endorsement if the vehicle is designed to transport sixteen or more people, including the driver.

What Do the Endorsement Tests Look Like?
When you pass an Endorsement Test, your CDL will carry a special marking (or endorsement), indicating you are qualified to drive a particular commercial vehicle.

- **The Passenger Vehicle Endorsement Test**—has approximately twenty questions, sixteen of which must be correctly answered for a passing grade.

- **The Tanker Endorsement Test**—is made up of approximately twenty questions, and sixteen correct answers are required to pass.

- **The Doubles and Triples Endorsement Test**—has approximately twenty multiple choice questions, and you must correctly answer sixteen to pass.

- **The Hazardous Materials Endorsement Test**—is made up of approximately thirty multiple-choice questions. You must correctly answer twenty-four to pass.

- **The School Bus Endorsement Test**—contains twenty questions, sixteen of which must be answered correctly.

It is best to take all the Endorsement Tests while the material is fresh in your mind. In addition, prospective employers look for applicants with all endorsements. And you never know when you will need an additional endorsement.

The Skills Tests

Three types of Skills Tests must be taken in the state of your legal residence and in a representative vehicle of the type you wish to operate. These tests are usually given by appointment only, so an examiner can be scheduled. Contact the DLD in your home state for more information.

- **The Pre-Trip Inspection Test**—is given to see if you know whether the vehicle is safe to drive. On this test, you may be asked to do a pre-trip inspection of your vehicle and/or explain to the examiner what you would inspect and why. Some states require only a written pre-trip test. However, the main reason for a complete pre-trip inspection before each trip is to ensure that you, the driver, are operating a safe piece of equipment.

- **The Basic Control Skills Test**—evaluates your basic skills in controlling the vehicle. The test involves exercises including moving the vehicle forward, backing up, and making turns. You will be scored on how well you stay within boundaries (marked with lines or cones) and how many pullups (stopping and remaneuvering to the correct position) you make as you park your vehicle.

- **The Road Test**—evaluates your ability to drive safely in a variety of on-the-road situations. The test course includes left and right turns, intersections, railroad crossings, curves, up and down grades, rural or semi-rural roads, city multi-lane streets, and expressway driving. You will be scored on specific tasks, including turns, merging into traffic, lane changes, and speed control as well as signaling, spotting hazards, and lane positioning. You will also be scored on how well you "start and stop" the vehicle, as well as your shifting, braking, and clutching.

The Commercial Vehicle Safety Act of 1986

The United States Congress passed the Commercial Vehicle Safety Act of 1986 (CMVSA/86) to increase highway safety. Among other things, the act requires all fifty states meet the same minimum standards in testing and licensing of all commercial drivers. These standards require that all commercial motor vehicle (CMV) drivers must pass the required tests and obtain the CDL.

The reason for this requirement is to ensure that anyone operating a CMV has the skills and knowledge required to operate it safely on the highway.

Therefore, all professional drivers must take the CDL Knowledge Tests as well as appropriate Skills Tests (by driving the vehicles they are being licensed for with an examiner).

What You Need to Know About the CMVSA/86

1. As of April 1, 1992, it is illegal to drive a commercial vehicle without a CDL. If you do so, you may be fined up to $5,000 or jailed for breaking this law.
2. Commercial drivers may have only one license. The fine for having more than one license can be up to $5,000 or possible jail time. Your CDL must be issued by the state of your legal residence.

3. If you are an experienced commercial driver and have a safe driving record, you may not need to take the Skills Test to transfer your CDL another state. Check with the local licensing authority or the Department of Motor Vehicles (DMV) to verify your state's requirements.

4. Testing and licensing of all commercial drivers is required.

5. All commercial drivers are required to report all moving violations to their employers and to their state of legal residence within 30 days of conviction. Drivers must also report license suspensions, revocations, cancellations, or disqualifications before the end of the business day on which the driver receives notification. This notification is required, whether you are driving a commercial vehicle or an automobile when the violation occurred. This does not include parking violations.

6. When applying for any commercial driving job, commercial drivers must give information about all driving jobs held over the past ten years to the new employer.

7. All states will share information about CDL drivers via a universal computerized database.

8. Your employer cannot allow you to drive any commercial vehicle if you have more than one license or if your CDL has been suspended or revoked. The penalty for doing so is a $5,000 fine or jail time for your employer.

9. You will lose your CDL for at least one year if:
   - You drive a commercial vehicle while using alcohol or other controlled substances.
   - You leave the scene of an accident involving the vehicle you are driving.
   - If you use a commercial vehicle to commit a felony.

10. You will lose your CDL:
    - For at least two months if you have had two serious traffic violations involving a commercial vehicle within a three-year period.
    - For at least four months for three serious violations within a three-year period.
    - For one year for a first offense of driving under the influence of alcohol (Blood Alcohol Concentration [the BAC limit] is 0.04 percent or more). If your BAC is less than 0.04 percent and there is any detectable alcohol in the bloodstream, you will be taken out of service for 24 hours.
    - For life if you have a second offense of driving after using alcohol or other controlled substances.

11. "Serious violations" include excessive speed, reckless driving, and traffic offenses committed in connection with fatal traffic accidents.

12. Individual states may add to this list and their penalties may be more severe.

13. Your state may have additional rules, which you must know and obey.

OTR SAFETY

A 180-pounds person consuming two drinks will have a BAC of 0.04 percent, so drinking two beers may cause you to lose your CDL—a high price to pay!

Table 2-1
Penalties for Violations – FMCSR Sec. 383.51

If a driver operates a motor vehicle and is convicted of:	For a first conviction or refusal to be tested while operating a CMV, a person required to have a CDL and a CDL holder must be disqualified from operating a CMV for:	For a first conviction or refusal to be tested while operating a non-CMV, a CDL holder must be disqualified from operating a CMV for:
(1) Being under the influence of alcohol as prescribed by state law.	1 year	1 year
(2) Being under the influence of a controlled substance.	1 year	1 year
(3) Having an alcohol concentration of 0.04 or greater while operating a CMV.	1 year	Not applicable
(4) Refusing to take an alcohol test as required by a State or jurisdiction under its implied consent laws or regulations as defined in §383.72 of this part.	1 year	1 year
(5) Leaving the scene of an accident.	1 year	1 year
(6) Using the vehicle to commit a felony other than a felony described in paragraph (b)(9) of this table.	1 year	1 year
(7) Driving a CMV when, as a result of prior violations committed operating a CMV, the drivers CDL is revoked, suspended, or canceled, or the driver is disqualified from operating a CMV.	1 year	Not applicable
(8) Causing a fatality through the negligent operation of a CMV, including but not limited to the crimes of motor vehicle manslaughter, homicide by motor vehicle and negligent homicide.	1 year	Not applicable
(9) Using the vehicle in the commission of a felony involving manufacturing, distributing, or dispensing a controlled substance.	Life—not eligible for 10-year reinstatement	Life—not eligible for 10-year reinstatement

Table 2-1
(continued)

For a first conviction or refusal to be tested while operating a CMV transporting hazardous materials required to be placarded under the Hazardous Materials Regulations (49 CFR part 172, subpart F), a person required to have a CDL and CDL holder must be disqualified from operating a CMV for:	For a second conviction or refusal to be tested in a separate incident of any combination of offenses in this table while operating a CMV, a person required to have a CDL and a CDL holder must be disqualified from operating a CMV for:	For a second conviction or refusal to be tested in a separate incident of any combination of offenses in this table while operating a non-CMV, a CDL holder must be disqualified from operating a CMV for:
3 years	Life	Life
3 years	Life	Life
3 years	Life	Not applicable
3 years	Life	Life
3 years	Life	Life
3 years	Life	Life
3 years	Life	Not applicable
3 years	Life	Not applicable
Life—not eligible for10-year reinstatement	Life—not eligible for10-year reinstatement	Life—not eligible for10-year reinstatement

Disqualification for serious traffic violations. A list of the offenses and the periods for which a driver must be disqualified, depending upon the type of vehicle the driver is operating at the time of the violation as follows.

Table 2-2
Disqualification for Serious Traffic Violation – FMCSR Sec. 383.51

If a driver operates a motor vehicle and is convicted of:	For a second conviction of any combination of offenses in this table in a separate incident within a 3-year period while operating a CMV, a person required to have a CDL and a CDL holder must be disqualified from operating a CMV for:	For a second conviction of any combination of offenses in this table in a separate incident within a 3-year period while operating a non-CMV, a CDL holder must be disqualified from operating a CMV, if the conviction results in the revocation, cancellation, or suspension of the CDL holder's license or non-CMV driving privileges, for:
(1) Speeding excessively, involving any speed of 24.1 kmph (15 mph) or more above the posted speed limit.	60 days	60 days
(2) Driving recklessly, as defined by state or local law or regulation, including but not limited to offenses of driving a motor vehicle in willful or wanton disregard for the safety of persons or property.	60 days	60 days
(3) Making improper or erratic traffic lane changes.	60 days	60 days
(4) Following the vehicle ahead too closely.	60 days	60 days
(5) Violating state or local law relating to motor vehicle traffic control (other than a parking violation) arising in connection with a fatal accident.	60 days	60 days
(6) Driving a CMV without obtaining a CDL.	60 days	Not applicable
(7) Driving a CMV without a CDL in the driver's possession.[1]	60 days	Not applicable
(8) Driving a CMV without proper class of CDL and/or endorsements for the specific vehicle group being operated for the passengers or type of cargo being transported.	60 days	Not applicable

[1]Any individual who provides proof to the enforcement authority that issued the citation, by the date the individual must appear in court or pay any time for such a violation, that the individual held a valid CDL on the date the citation was issued, shall not be guilty of this offense.

Table 2-2
(continued)

For a third or subsequent conviction of any combination of offenses in this table in a separate incident within a 3-year period while operating a CMV, a person required to have a CDL and a CDL holder must be disqualified from operating a CMV for:	For a third or subsequent conviction of any combination of offenses in this table in a separate incident within a 3-year period while operating a non-CMV, a CDL holder must be disqualified from operating a CMV, if the conviction results in the revocation, cancellation, or suspension of the CDL holder's license or non-CMV driving privileges, for:
120 days	120 days
120 days	120 days
120 days	120 days
120 days	120 days
120 days	120 days
120 days	Not applicable
120 days	Not applicable
120 days	Not applicable

Disqualification for railroad-highway grade crossing offenses. A list of the offenses and the periods for which a driver must be disqualified, when the driver is operating a CMV at the time of the violations as follows.

Table 2-3
Disqualification for Railroad-Highway Grade Crossing Offenses – FMCSR Sec. 383.51

If a driver is convicted of operating a CMV in violation of a federal, state or local law because:	For a first conviction a person required to have a CDL and a CDL holder must be disqualified from operating a CMV for:	For a second conviction of any combination of offenses in this table in a separate incident within a 3-year period a person required to have a CDL and a CDL holder must be disqualified from operating a CMV for:	For a third or subsequent conviction of offenses in this table in a separate incident within a 3-year period a person required to have a CDL and a CDL holder must be disqualified from operating a CMV for:
(1) The driver is not required to always stop, but fails to slow down and check that tracks are clear of an approaching train.	No less than 60 days	No less than 20 days	No less than 1 year
(2) The driver is not required to always stop, but fails to stop before reaching the crossing, if the tracks are not clear.	No less than 60 days	No less than 20 days	No less than 1 year
(3) The driver is always required to stop, but fails to stop before driving onto the crossing.	No less than 60 days	No less than 20 days	No less than 1 year
(4) The driver fails to have sufficient space to drive completely through the crossing without stopping.	No less than 60 days	No less than 20 days	No less than 1 year
(5) The driver fails to obey a traffic control device or the direction of an enforcement official at the crossing.	No less than 60 days	No less than 20 days	No less than 1 year
(6) The driver fails to negotiate a crossing because of insufficient undercarriage clearance.	No less than 60 days	No less than 20 days	No less than 1 year

Disqualification for violating out-of-service orders. A list of the offenses and periods for which a driver must be disqualified when the driver is operating a CMV at the time of the violation as follows.

Table 2-4
Disqualification for Violating Out-of-Service Orders – FMCSR Sec. 383.51

If a driver operates a CMV and is convicted of:	For a first conviction while operating a CMV, a person required to have a CDL and a CDL holder must be disqualified from operating a CMV for:	For a second conviction in a separate incident within a 10-year period while operating a CMV, a person required to have a CDL and a CDL holder must be disqualified from operating a CMV for:	For a third or subsequent conviction in a separate incident within a 10-year period while operating a CMV, a person required to have a CDL, and a CDL holder must be disqualified from operating a CMV for:
(1) Violating a driver or vehicle out-of-service order while transporting non-hazardous materials.	No less than 90 days or more than 1 year	No less than 1 year or more than 5 years	No less than 3 years or more than 5 years
(2) Violating a driver or vehicle out-of-service order while transporting hazardous materials required to be placarded under part 172, subpart F of this title, or while operating a vehicle designed to transport 16 or more passengers, including the driver.	No less than 180 days or more than 2 years	No less than 3 years or more than 5 years	No less than 3 years or more than 5 years

The Motor Carrier Safety Improvement Act of 1999

The purposes of the act are to:

1. Establish a Federal Motor Carrier Safety Administration (FMCSA) and
2. Reduce the number and severity of large-truck involved crashes through CMV and driver inspections and carrier compliance reviews, stronger enforcement, expedited completion of rules, sound research, and effective CDL testing, record keeping, and sanctions.

What You Need to Know About the MCSIA/99:

1. It established the (effective January 1, 2000) within the Department of Transportation.
2. The act creates *new* one-year disqualifying offenses for (1) driving a CMV with a revoked, suspended, or canceled CDL, or driving while disqualified, and (2) conviction for causing a fatality through the negligent or criminal operation of a CMV. Lifetime disqualification is *required* for multiple violations or convictions.
3. Drivers may also be disqualified for up to 30 days if their operation of a CMV would create an imminent hazard.
4. The list of serious traffic violations for which a CDL holder can be disqualified is expanded to include:
   - Driving a CMV without obtaining a CDL.
   - Driving a CMV without a CDL in possession.
   - Driving without a required endorsement.
5. The federal medical qualification certificate must be made part of the CDL requirements. This will be addressed in a future rulemaking by FMCSA.
6. The act requires states to:
   - Request a driver's record from all states that have issued a driver's license to the applicant within the past ten years before issuing or renewing a CDL.
   - Include information on the underlying violation when reporting disqualification, revocation, suspension, or cancellation of a CDL.
   - Include information on all violations of motor vehicle traffic control laws committed by CDL holders in the driver's record.
   - Record information on traffic violations received from other states in a driver's record. States may not allow information on violations to be masked or withheld from the CDL holder's record.
   - Notify the licensing state of violations by CDL holders within ten days after violations are committed. This is a 2008 MCSIA requirement. The current requirement is 30 days until September 30, 2008. After 9/30/2008, the requirement is ten days.
7. States may not issue special licenses or permits to CDL holders.
8. Before issuing any motor vehicle operator's license, a state must check the National Driver Register and the Commercial Driver's License Information System (CDLIS).

Let's Review

Read each question and all of the answers provided. Place the letter of the correct answer in the space provided or write your answers on a separate piece of paper so you can use these questions again as you review for the CDL. Once you have answered all the questions, check your answers against the answer key that follows.

_____ 1. The penalty for being convicted twice for driving under the influence of alcohol or controlled substances is losing your CDL for:
(A) 120 days
(B) The rest of your life
(C) Until the company allows you to return to the road
(D) Three years

_____ 2. The Commercial Motor Vehicle Safety Act of 1986 (CMVSA/86) required that all states:
(A) License all commercial vehicle drivers
(B) Allow doubles and triples to operate on state highways
(C) Charge tolls for all commercial vehicles
(D) None of the above

_____ 3. If a commercial vehicle driver is stopped and his or her blood alcohol concentration is found to be 0.04 percent or higher, the driver will be:
(A) Ticketed
(B) Given a warning
(C) Arrested for driving under the influence
(D) Reported to their employer

_____ 4. If you are planning to drive a vehicle equipped with air brakes, you must:
(A) Take the Skills Test in a vehicle equipped with air brakes
(B) Pass the Air Brakes Knowledge Test
(C) Earn the Air Brakes Endorsement
(D) All of the above

_____ 5. The MCSIA/99 expands the list of serious traffic violations for which a CDL holder can be disqualified to include:
(A) Driving a CMV without obtaining a CDL
(B) Driving a CMV without a CDL in possession
(C) Driving without a required endorsement
(D) All of the above

_____ 6. If you do not obtain a CDL and are stopped by authorities while driving a commercial vehicle, you will be fined:
(A) $5,000　　(C) $15,000
(B) $10,000　　(D) None of the above

_____ 7. If you are convicted of a moving violation, the CMVSA/86 requires you to notify your employer within:
(A) 24 hours　　(C) Two weeks
(B) 30 days　　(D) 21 days

_____ 8. The Class A CDL grants the holder:
(A) The right to legally operate vehicles with a GVWR of 26,001 pounds or more
(B) The right to operate trailers with a GVWR of 10,001 pounds or more
(C) The ability to operate straight trucks
(D) All of the above

_____ 9. A BAC of 0.04 percent can be achieved in a 180-lb. person by:
(A) Drinking six beers　　(C) Drinking one beer
(B) Drinking two beers　　(D) Drinking one wine cooler

_____10. True or False: When applying for any commercial driving job, the driver must give information about all driving jobs held over the past ten years to the new employer.

Answers to Let's Review

1. B; 2. A; 3. C; 4. D; 5. D; 6. A; 7. B; 8. D; 9. B; 10. True.

Terms You Need to Know

The following terms have been taken from Chapter 2. Review them.
If you see any you are not sure of, check the definition in the Glossary at the end of the book:

Air brakes

BAC

CMVSA/86

Doubles endorsement

Hazardous materials

Knowledge test

MCSIA/99

Placard

Pre-trip inspection

Pullups

School bus

Skills test

Tanker

Triples

3 | What You Can Expect on the Test

If you plan to obtain a CDL, you will be required to pass both knowledge and skills tests before your jurisdiction issues you a CDL.

The knowledge and skills tests you will be given will cover information and skills you already know. If you have studied the CDL manual and practiced your driving skills, you should be prepared to take, and pass, these tests (see Figure 3-1).

CDL Knowledge Tests

Depending on your jurisdiction, the General Knowledge Test you take will be made up of fifty true-false or multiple-choice questions, the latter having three or four possible answers. This test covers basic knowledge that all commercial drivers need to know. The testing model in use in a majority of the jurisdictions utilizes multiple-choice questions with either three or four answers. You must have a minimum of forty correct answers to pass. All of the information you need to pass the CDL knowledge test can be found in your jurisdictional CDL driver's manual.

Depending on your jurisdiction, you will either take a paper-based test, where you mark the correct answers on a score sheet, or take a computer-based test, where you select the correct answer on a computer screen.

Figure 3-1 Studying this manual, along with practicing your driving skills, will help you prepare to take and pass your CDL exam.

After passing the General Knowledge Test, you are eligible to take the Skills Test, unless the vehicle you will be driving while taking the Skills Test requires one or more specialized endorsements.

The CDL Endorsement Knowledge Tests consist of twenty to thirty questions each. These tests cover knowledge of a specific commercial vehicle or knowledge area. Again, the testing model in use in a majority of the jurisdictions utilizes multiple-choice questions with either three or four answers. You must correctly answer at least 80 percent of the questions to pass each test. All of the information you need to pass the CDL Endorsement Tests can be found in your jurisdictional CDL driver's manual.

Note: Even though federal regulations have set 80 percent as a minimum passing score for all CDL knowledge and endorsement tests, your jurisdiction may have a higher minimum passing score. Be sure to ask your Department of Motor Vehicles what their passing requirements are for all tests you wish to take.

CDL Skills Tests

The CDL Skills Tests determine your skills as a professional driver. When you arrive at the testing location (either a jurisdictional testing facility or a third-party testing location), you will:

- Perform a pre-trip inspection of your vehicle.
- Perform basic control skill maneuvers.
- Perform a road test.

Normally, the Skills Tests are given in the order shown in the preceding list. In some jurisdictions, however, the basic control skills are performed during the road test.

The CDL examiner will provide you with instructions prior to beginning each part of the Skills Test. During the Skills Tests the examiner will not have you perform any unsafe or illegal maneuvers. If you have questions or don't understand what the examiner is asking you to do, be sure to ask for clarification!

Skills Test Models

The American Association of Motor Vehicle Administrators has developed several skills test "models" which the jurisdictions may use in their CDL testing program. The first model, developed in the early 1990s, is the one in use by many jurisdictions today. It provides directions for:

- Performing a complete vehicle inspection
- Performing skills exercises consisting of:
  - Forward stop
  - Straight line backing
  - Alley dock
  - Jackknife parallel park (driver side)
  - Jackknife parallel park (conventional)

- ◆ Right turn
- ◆ Backward serpentine
- Performing a road test.

In late 2005, a new testing model was released that made numerous changes to the old testing model and made the Skills Tests more realistic by modifying the basic skill exercises performed. The changes made include:

- Vehicle inspection
  - ◆ Performing a partial or full vehicle inspection based upon jurisdictional desires
- Basic skill exercises
  - ◆ Elimination of forward stop, right turn, and backward serpentine exercises
  - ◆ Modification of the parallel park exercises to require the full vehicle be within the parking space. Jackknifing of the tractor will no longer be permitted.
  - ◆ Modification of the alley dock exercise to eliminate the 45-degree setup and require a 90-degree setup to begin the exercise.
  - ◆ New skill exercises to replace those deleted.
    - ◗ Offset backing to right
    - ◗ Offset backing to left
- Road test
  - ◆ The number of scored items throughout the test was increased.

You will need to contact your DMV to determine what skills exercises you will need to perform during your CDL exam.

Tips for Passing the CDL

Read through this information before beginning your review. It will help you take the tests and accurately measure your areas of strength and weakness.

The following are some suggestions to help you pass the written CDL tests. Each of the test questions will be either true-false or multiple choice, the latter type usually having three or four possible answers. Only one will be correct. (See Figure 4-1.)

ROAD SENSE
Read the question. Then read it again.

First, answer all questions where you are 100 percent certain you know the answer.

- When you answer a question, don't go back and change it. Chances are, your first impression is usually right.
- If your test sheet will be graded by a machine, and you do change an answer, completely erase the old answer before marking the new answer.

Figure 4-1 Passing the CDL requires reading, studying what you've read, and asking questions about those areas you don't understand.

- As you go through the test, make certain you're marking the right question with the right answer.
- Sometimes you can find a question further down the page that will give you the answer to a question or will help you fill in the blanks for a question you're not sure you know.
- If the right answer does not come to you immediately, narrow down the choices.

ROAD SENSE

Never leave a blank, because a blank will count as an incorrect answer. At least put down something—wild guesses sometimes are right!

Most states give written CDL tests. Some use computers, where you read the question and then push button A, B, C, or D to indicate your answer.

If one chapter gave you problems, go back and scan the chapter. If you highlighted information as you read, go back over all the highlighted information.

Some people like to review major chapters, others may take practice quizzes. Many will highlight as they study and then review the highlighted areas afterward.

Practice Tests and Review

Read through this information before beginning your review. It will help you take the tests and accurately measure your areas of strength and weakness. The following is a suggestion to help you pass the written CDL tests:

- Each of the test questions will be either true-false or multiple choice, the latter type usually having three or four possible answers. Only one is right.

The following are some of the most frequently asked questions by CDL applicants. Read through them carefully to make certain you are aware of this information.

Q. How do I arrange to take the CDL tests?
A. This process depends on the state where you are taking the test. You can get the best information from the local branch of the state department of transportation. You can almost always take the written Knowledge Test on a walk-in basis—you don't need an appointment. However, in many states, you *must* have an appointment to take the Skills Test.

Q. How much does it cost to take the CDL?
A. The costs differ from state to state. Call your local Department of Transportation.

Q. Where will I take the CDL tests?

A. You will almost always take the written test at the Department of Motor Vehicles driver's license stations. Some of the stations, however, will not be equipped to conduct the Skills Test. In this case, the Department of Motor Vehicles will tell you where the Skills Tests are conducted.

Q. How old do I have to be when I take the CDL tests?

A. In most states, CDL applicants must be 21 years of age to take the CDL General Knowledge and Skills Tests. In a few states, drivers between 18 and 21 years of age can apply for a Restricted CDL, which limits them to driving within that state only.

Q. How long do I have to take the CDL tests?

A. Usually, there are no time limits, but check with your local Department of Motor Vehicles to make certain this is the case in your state. In any case, make certain to give yourself enough time to complete the test.

Q. What identification and other documents do I need to bring when I take the CDL tests?

A. If you already have a CDL and are going in for renewal, make sure your medical card has not expired. If it has, you'll need to get a Department of Transportation physical—and many states require that you have it before you apply for your CDL.

   You should also take a driver's license or some type of photo ID and your Social Security card. If you are testing for endorsements—particularly the Tank and Hazardous Materials Endorsements—some states require other documents, licenses, and certificates. Check with the Department of Motor Vehicles for specifics.

Q. Is there any way I could take an oral test rather than a written one?

A. Some states offer these. Find out if they are available from the Department of Motor Vehicles. You will probably need to make an appointment.

Q. What is a passing grade on the CDL Knowledge Test?

A. Federal law states you must score 80 percent or better to pass the CDL Knowledge Test. Your state may require an even higher score to pass the CDL. Ask about your state's requirements when you call to make an appointment to take the test.

Q. Are there any suggestions about taking the Skills Test?

A. Just one: Listen carefully to the examiner's instructions—make sure you understand them. If you don't understand what the examiner wants you to do, ask for more information. If you ask the examiner to restate the instructions or to explain what he or she wants, it will not be held against you . . . and it won't cost you any points.

Q. Are there any last words of advice?

A. We don't want to sound like your third grade teacher, but . . .

- Read slowly and carefully—know exactly what the question is asking.
- Write neatly—so anybody can read your writing.
- Don't leave any blanks. Give it your best guess if you just don't know.
- Don't make any marks—other than marking your answers on the answer sheet.

- Ask questions—such as what kind of pencil is required? What grade average is required? Don't be pesky, but find out what you need to know to be comfortable taking the test.

Q. What tools should I take for the Skills Test?
A. For the inspection, take a flashlight, tire pressure gauge, tire tread depth gauge, and a pair of gloves.

Q. Will the examiner provide a vehicle if I don't have one?
A. No state and no CDL examiner will provide a vehicle. You must bring your own—no ifs, ands, or buts.

Q. What else will help me do my best on the tests?
A. Study, prepare, and one last thing . . . be organized on the day of the test. Know where the DMV is. Don't be rushed. Get a good night's sleep.

Testing Formats

True/False

Usually written in the form of statements, we often think true/false test questions are the easiest type of testing. Wrong!

ROAD SENSE

In a true/false test, you must check to see if all parts of the statement or question are true.

If one part is false, the entire statement is false and should be marked "false" even though the majority of the statement is true. Look for words like "always," "never," "complete," and "all." When you see these words in the test, read the statement several times. Whatever the answer, it should cover the entire statement, not just part of it.

Multiple Choice

A favorite of testers and those taking the test, multiple choice questions are easier to deal with if you follow these seven steps:

1. Read the question.
2. Read the question and the first answer. Does this combination make a true statement? If not, go to the next choice.
3. Generally, only one combination makes a true statement.
4. If more than one answer appears true, use the process of elimination or make a "smart guess" by eliminating those answers you absolutely know to be wrong. Does a remaining answer have the word "every," "always," "all," or

"never"? Remember—it's rare that something is *always* or *never* the case. That narrows the choice.

5. If you are left with two possible answers, a "wild" guess gives you a fifty-fifty chance of getting the answer right.

6. If an answer is much shorter or much longer than the others, it is often the correct answer.

7. When one of the choices is "all of the above," choose this answer only if you are convinced that all the answer choices are correct. It may be that only one answer completes a true statement with the question.

ROAD SENSE

There may be questions where none of the possible combinations makes a true statement. Be careful and make sure no answer choice is correct before choosing "none of the above."

Matching

When you are asked to match one item with another, look at the instructions carefully.

You may be asked to match the first list of terms with a second list of definitions.

Or you may be asked to match a heading in one list with several items in the second.

First, know what you are being asked to do. If there are an equal number of items in each list, you probably are being asked to make a one-to-one match. If there are more items in one list, expect to have some leftovers or items with more than one match. Then, follow these steps:

1. Scan the two lists quickly—make any matches that are obvious.
2. As you match, you may want to mark through those choices you've used.
3. Next, take the remainder of each list and try to answer each heading with what you know—then check the other list to find anything close.
4. Make all the matches you can—skip the ones for now that you can't answer at all.
5. For the terms you just can't match, line them up with the remaining choices and pick the best match.

ROAD SENSE

If you're taking the Skills Test for a Class A CDL, you must take the Skills Test in a Class A vehicle. If you plan to take the Air Brakes Endorsement and don't want the air brakes restriction on your CDL, you need to have air brakes on your vehicle.

ROAD SENSE

Be positive. Watch your coffee/tea/caffeine intake. The same goes for chocolate. Be positive—make positive statements about the test—and yourself.

ROAD SENSE

Be committed—be responsible for studying and reviewing. Be committed about doing a good job so you can get on with your career plans . . . and the next exciting chapter of your life.

5 The CDL Skills Test

You must perform the Skills Test in a vehicle that is representative of the type you plan to drive. If you plan to obtain a Class A CDL, you will be asked to take the Skills Test in the tractor-trailer or truck model you will be using on the job. If you plan to operate a bus, you must take the Skills Test in the type of bus you plan to operate. (See Figure 5-1.)

What Is the Skills Test?

Just as its name implies, this examination will test your skills as a professional driver. It is divided into three parts:

- **The Pre-Trip Inspection Test**—A test to determine if you know how to correctly conduct an inspection of your vehicle. It will also test your ability to determine if the vehicle is safe to drive.
- **The Basic Control Skills Test**—A test to show the examiner if you can safely back, park, and judge vehicle length. You will be directed to move the vehicle forward and backward in an area defined by cones or other barriers.
- **The CDL Road Test**—An actual driving test where you will go on the road to test your ability to safely handle the vehicle in a variety of traffic and road conditions. The test will include turns, curves, intersections, urban and rural driving, railroad grade crossings, and other traffic situations.

Note: If you're applying for a Class C CDL, your jurisdiction may waive the road test portion of the skills test.

Note: For the Basic Control Skills Test and the Road Test, you will be required to take the test in the same vehicle as the type of CDL for which you are applying.

Figure 5-1   Before drivers can receive their CDL, they must first pass the Skills Test.

General Information About the Skills Test

1. The Skills Test is normally scheduled by the jurisdiction. You should contact the Department of Motor Vehicles to make an appointment.
2. Procedures differ by state—contact your state Department of Motor Vehicles to find out where the test is conducted, the costs for the tests, what tests are offered, and when.
3. Some states use third-party examiners, so the test may be held at a trucking school or trucking company.
4. The Skills Test is designed to thoroughly test your driving skills. It isn't easy, so don't take your Skills Test without preparing and practicing.

The Pre-Trip Inspection

Before going to take your Skills Test, you should do a thorough pre-trip inspection of your vehicle. (See Figure 5-2.) This will keep you from getting to the examiner's station and discovering a defect in the vehicle there. If that happens, the examiner will not allow you to use that vehicle for the road test—which means you will lose your appointment time and will have to reschedule another appointment several weeks later.

To do a good job on the pre-trip inspection, bring the following with you:

- A tire pressure gauge
- A tread depth gauge

Figure 5-2   Take the time to properly perform the pre-trip inspection at the start of your exam.

- A tire "billy"-tire "checker"
- Wheel chocks
- A shop rag (to clean lights and reflectors)
- Gloves
- Vehicle registrations
- Proof of insurance (in certain states)
- Any applicable permits to operate in the state
- Your current driver's license

When you arrive at the testing center, the examiner will give you instructions similar to the following:

During this test, you will be examined in three areas—a vehicle inspection test, a basic control skills test, and an on-the-road driving test. For the vehicle inspection test, you will be asked to perform a thorough inspection of the vehicle. You may be asked to perform a partial vehicle inspection or a complete vehicle inspection. For the basic control skills test, you will do backing and parking exercises. And for the road test, we will go out on the road for a trip that will last 30 to 45 minutes.

At all times when you are behind the wheel during this test, you are in charge of the vehicle. I will never ask you to do something that is either unsafe or illegal.

I will give you instructions as we go along. If you have any questions, please ask. If you don't understand a direction, ask me for more information.

When it is time to begin the pre-trip inspection, the examiner will say:

Please conduct a complete and thorough inspection of the vehicle. You may use the Vehicle Inspection Memory Aid from the driver's manual if you want to use it. As you do the inspection, point out or touch the things you are inspecting and explain what you're looking for as you inspect them. If you do not do so, you may not receive credit for that item.

Note: *If your jurisdiction utilizes the partial vehicle inspection, the examiner will give you directions regarding the specific area of the vehicle to inspect.*

Start by inspecting the engine compartment. Then climb into the cab and start the engine. After you have done the startup checks in the cab, turn off the engine and do the rest of the inspection. Do you have any questions? Then, go ahead and start the vehicle inspection.

The keys to doing a proper pre-trip inspection are:

- Do it all the time.
- Practice.
- Know all the systems and components.

Practice your pre-trip inspection and do it the same way each time. By doing the pre-trip inspection this way, you'll develop a rhythm or routine. If you miss checking something, you'll know it because you'll feel "off" or "off rhythm."

Practice until you have the routine down to the minute. It will usually require 45 to 60 minutes.

When you're taking the pre-trip inspection test, the examiner will normally ask you to do it in the following manner:

- Inspect the engine compartment.
- Start the engine and perform the in-vehicle checks.
- Shut down the engine and perform the external inspection.

It is possible that the examiner will have you check only one side of the vehicle, because if you can do one side correctly, then you'll know how to do the other one as well. However, if there are items that are unique to the other side of the vehicle, mention those to the examiner.

On a straight truck or tractor-trailer, it will be left to the examiner's choice which side he or she wants checked. A bus will be inspected on the passenger-door side only.

If you have a cab-over vehicle, the examiner will not require you to jack up the cab. However, if you are not able to check an item due to the cab not being raised, tell the examiner you are not able to check that part and just tell him or her what you would normally look for—this will give you credit for having checked that item.

While doing the inspection, the examiner will be taking notes, but don't get paranoid about what he or she is writing down—don't be in a hurry, and don't be nervous.

As you perform your pre-trip inspection, call out what you are inspecting and what you are going to be looking for in that area. Here's an example: "I'm checking the wheel, lugs, and nuts. I'll be looking for any cracks, any rust—which could indicate a loose nut—or any missing lugs or nuts." If the examiner doesn't know what you're checking or what you're looking for, you may not get credit for it. Go slowly and be precise. Prove to the examiner that you know what you're doing.

Review the Seven-Step Pre-Trip Inspection

- **Step One: Approach the vehicle**—As you walk toward the vehicle, look for signs of damage, leaks, and whether the vehicle is leaning. Then, check the surrounding area for any hazards.
- **Step Two: Check the engine compartment**—Check all components: fluid levels, wiring, belts, hoses, steering controls, front brakes, the suspension, and so on.
- **Step Three: Start the engine and check the cab interior**—With the transmission in neutral (or in park if it is an automatic transmission), apply the brakes, depress the clutch, and start the engine. Check all gauges and controls and all emergency equipment. Make certain you have the vehicle registration (this is part of your inspection).
- **Step Four: Turn off the engine and check the lights**—Check headlights (both low and high beams) and four-way flashers on the front of the vehicle. Then, turn off the headlights and flashers and turn on all marker/clearance lamps and the right-turn signal.
- **Step Five: Complete a walkaround inspection**—Beginning at the driver's side of the cab, begin checking all items—lights, fuel tanks, wheels, mirrors, coupling devices, the suspension, air line connections and air lines, brakes, doors, and so on. Each axle must be inspected thoroughly. (See Figure 5-3.)
- **Step Six: Check the signal lights**—Turn off all body lights; turn on brake lights and the left-turn signal. Then, get out and check them.
- **Step Seven: Start the engine and check the brake system**—You're almost done now. Turn off all lights and perform a brake check. If you have air brakes, remember to turn your engine off before pumping the brakes to check your low air pressure warning light/signal.

The way to pass your pre-trip inspection test is to do the following:

1. Practice—until you can complete your pre-trip inspection in about 45 to 60 minutes.

WALKAROUND SEQUENCE

1. Left Side of Cab Area
2. Front of Cab Area
3. Right Side of Tractor Area
4. Right Saddle Tank Area
5. Coupling System Area
6. Right Rear Tractor Wheels Area
7. Rear of Tractor Area
8. Front of Trailer Area
9. Right Side of Trailer Area
10. Right Rear Trailer Wheels Area
11. Rear of Trailer Area
12. Left Rear Trailer Wheels Area
13. Left Side of Trailer Area
14. Left Saddle Tank Area

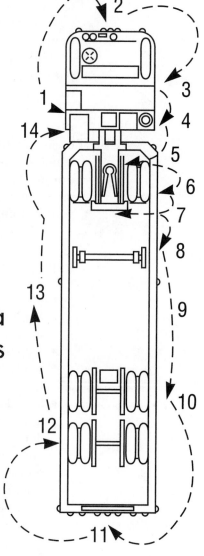

Figure 5-3   Pre-trip Walk-Around Sequence.

2. Be consistent. Use the same routine to do your pre-trip inspection every time.
3. Study all the information on pre-trip inspections.
4. Be certain the examiner knows what you're inspecting and what you'll be looking for in each area.
5. Be prepared. Check the truck before you go to the examining station. Take a tire pressure gauge, tread depth gauge, wheel chocks, shop rag, gloves, your driver's license, and all registrations and permits.

Note: Do all of the required brake checks.

Some states have added a simulated downgrade question. This is usually done after the vehicle inspection and before you go out on the road test. However, it may also be done during the road test. In this question, the examiner will ask you to simulate going down a long downgrade. The examiner will ask you what you would do. You must tell the examiner:

- "I would test my brakes before beginning the downhill."
- "I would downshift to the proper gear before I start."
- "I would not clutch or shift while going down the grade."
- "I would check my mirrors constantly."
- "I would use light, steady braking pressure."

Mention each of these steps—each one is important!

The Basic Control Skills Test

Q. Why is this test given?

A. Basically, this test is to determine whether or not you can operate and control a truck safely and on the road with other traffic.

The examiner can ask you to complete two different sets of six exercises. Which six exercises a jurisdiction employs is based upon which testing model they are using. See Chapter 3 for additional information on what exercises each model contains. You will be asked to perform as few as three of them, all six, or some number in between. The examiner will be looking to see if you can judge the length of your vehicle and its position in relationship to other boundaries. You will have time to practice before you are tested. Learn and practice all of the exercises ahead of time. The exercises are:

- Model 1
  - Right turn
  - Backward serpentine
  - Jackknife parallel park (driver side)
  - Jackknife parallel park (passenger side)
  - 45-degree alley dock
  - Straight-line backing—forward stop line

- Model 2 (new)
  - Straight-line back
  - Offset back to left (see Figure 5-4)
  - Offset back to right (see Figure 5-5)
  - Parallel park (driver side)—full vehicle in parking space
  - Parallel park (passenger side)—full vehicle in space
  - 90-degree alley dock

Veteran examiners have this to say about this test:

People who are confident in their skills do very well.

Some people get nervous—too nervous. So practice until you know you've got it down to a science.

The Basic Control Skills Test comes after the pre-trip inspection and before the road test. At some test sites, examiners prefer to start the road test and then, along the way, will have you stop and do the Basic Control Test exercises.

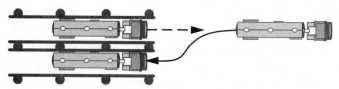

Figure 5-4   Offset backing to the left.

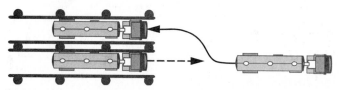

Figure 5-5   Offset backing to the right.

Q. What can I expect from the Basic Control Tests?
A. The examiner will tell you this:

This is a test that is made up of a series of basic control moves. Try not to go over any lines or hit any cones or dividers—which represent our boundaries. Remember it is better to do a pull-up than it is to drive over a boundary.

As we do each exercise, I will give you directions—and when you finish the exercise, sound your horn and set your brakes to let me know you've completed the maneuver. If you see me raise my arm with my palm facing you, stop your vehicle.

After the examiner provides these instructions, you will begin the Basic Control Skills Test.

Straight-Line Backing

The examiner will tell you: *Drive forward through the alley and stop with your front bumper as close as possible to the painted line at the end without going past the line and without leaning out of the window or the door. You may stop only once—and I will wave you forward when I get to the end of the alley.*

When this maneuver is completed, the examiner will provide the following instructions: *Now, back your vehicle down the alley, avoid touching either side of the alley and stop with your front bumper even with the stop line at the end of the alley.* (See Figure 5-6.)

Note: The new testing model no longer has the two-foot stop box as part of the scoring criteria. The examiner will indicate to you when you should stop your vehicle and begin backing down the alley.

Hints to Help
- When you pull forward, go slowly. Keep your vehicle straight and centered between the boundaries or the sides of the alley.
- When you stop, do so gently and deliberately—how you stop your vehicle counts in the exercise, so do it smoothly.
- Remember, stopping within two feet of the stop line is just as important as backing down the alley without touching the sides.
- The alley length is 100 feet and the width between boundaries is 12 feet.

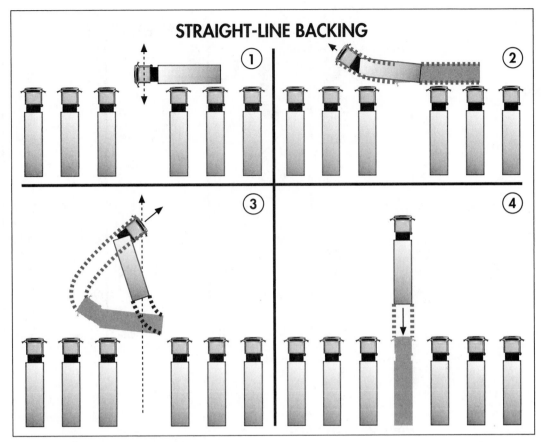

Figure 5-6   Straight-line backing.

Parallel Parking

The examiner will start the exercise:

(For tractor-trailers)—*Drive by the parking spot and back the trailer into it. You are only required to get the trailer into the space. Try to get your trailer as close as possible to the rear and to the curb without striking any boundaries or crossing the lines. You may jackknife your trailer, but get the trailer into the space. When you see me wave you forward, start the exercise. Sound your horn and set your brakes when you have completed it.* (See Figure 5-7.)

Hints to Help
- The parking space will be ten feet longer than the trailer.
- The width of the parking space is 12 feet.
- To pass, get the trailer within 18 inches of the rear stop line and as close to the curb (really a painted line) as possible.
- Practice makes passing this test easier.

Note: *The new testing model requires that the entire vehicle be within the parking space. Jackknifing of the tractor is no longer permitted. In order to accomplish this, the parking space has been enlarged to be 15 feet longer than the entire vehicle. The rear stop box has also been eliminated.*

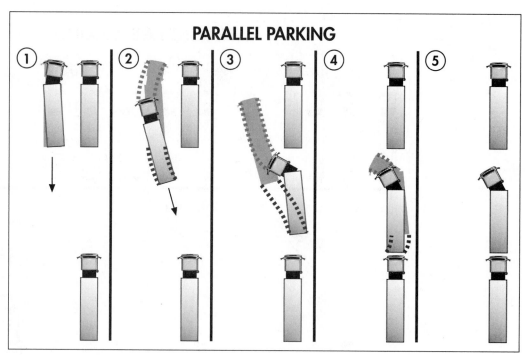

Figure 5-7 Parallel parking.

Alley Dock Exercise

For this exercise, the examiner will say:

Drive by the entrance to the alley with the alley on your left side. Kick your truck to a 45-degree angle. Stop and back into it. When you are straight, attempt to get as close to the back of the alley as possible, but don't back past it. I will stand near the entry to the alley. When I wave you forward, you may begin the exercise. Sound your horn and set your brakes when you've completed the maneuver.

Hints to Help

- Go past the entrance to the dock.
- As the middle of the tractor passes the entrance, make a hard right by turning the steering wheel.
- Use soft braking throughout the maneuver—and go slowly.
- Use the lowest reverse gear.
- Head toward the cone on a 45-degree angle and stay left of the cone.
- Stop when the truck and trailer are straight and at a 45-degree angle to the dock.
- Begin backing slowly—making minor adjustments with the steering wheel to keep from over correcting.
- Watch the trailer swing!
- Stop within two feet of the rear of the alley.
- Once the vehicle's rear passes the clearance line, you are within two feet of the back of the alley.
- Stay within all boundaries.

Note: The new testing model eliminates the 45-degree cone. The new exercise requires you to position your vehicle parallel to an outer boundary before beginning your backing exercise.

The exercise also requires the entire vehicle be straight within the alley and be within three feet of the back of the alley when completing the exercise.

The Right Turn

This exercise is included to simulate a right turn at an intersection and to test your ability to make a right turn safely.

The examiner will say: *Drive forward and make a right turn around the cone, trying to bring your rear wheels as close as possible to the cone without hitting it. I will wave you forward from the cone.* (See Figure 5-8.)

Hints to Help

- To make a successful right turn, stay toward the center of the street but in your lane.
- As you pass the turn, begin to turn to the right. The turn will be determined by how much your vehicle off-tracks—and a tractor-trailer will off-track much more than a small straight truck.
- Get your right rear tires as close to the cone as possible without touching it—you'll lose points if you touch the cone *or* swing too far out.
- Before going for your test, practice turning with the vehicle you will drive for the test.
- Go slowly.
- Don't touch or drive over any boundaries.
- After turning, continue forward until the vehicle is straight, and then wait for further instructions.

Note: The new testing model has eliminated this exercise. See the following for new exercise descriptions.

Backward Serpentine

The total distance of this course is 270 feet and the distance between the traffic cones is the length of your vehicle. The distance from the traffic cones to either outside boundary is 35 feet and the total distance from boundary to boundary is 70 feet.

The instructor will say:

I will adjust the distance between the cones for your vehicle. When I signal, move forward, driving along the right side of the row of cones. Stop when your entire vehicle is past the third cone, then back up in a serpentine in this diagram until you back past the first cone. Try not to touch any cones or allow any part of your vehicle to pass over any cone, and keep your vehicle within the painted boundaries.

Hints to Help

- If you get to a point where you are going to hit a cone, stop and reposition the vehicle by pulling forward.
- Each pull-up costs you points, but it's much better to pull up than to hit a cone.
- Don't cross any boundary lines.
- Practice, practice, practice!
- Go slowly.

Note: The new testing model has eliminated this exercise. See the following for new exercise descriptions.

MAKING A RIGHT TURN

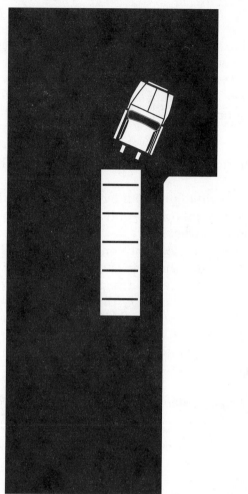

- Assume Proper Speed and Position

- Shift into Proper Gear

- Begin Turn When Cab Is Halfway Past Corner

- Watch Right Mirror During Turn

Figure 5-8   Making a right turn.

New Skills Exercises

The new testing model has two new skills exercises: offset back to the left and offset back to the right. If your jurisdiction is using the new testing model, the examiner will give you directions similar to:

Drive forward (straight ahead) to the boundary line ahead. Stop your vehicle, and then back your vehicle into the opposite lane until the front of your vehicle has passed the first set of cones. Please set your parking brake and sound your horn when you have completed the exercise. Do you have any questions?

Hints to Help

- If you get to a point where you are going to hit a cone, stop and reposition the vehicle by pulling forward.
- Each pull-up costs you points, but it's much better to pull up than to hit a cone.

- Don't cross any boundary lines.
- Practice, practice, practice!
- Go slowly.

The CDL Road Test

Two parts down and one—the fun part—to go. The Road Test will determine if you can safely drive your vehicle in actual over-the-road situations and conditions.

The CDL Road Test will require approximately 30 to 45 minutes and will involve a number of road conditions and maneuvers, such as right turns, left turns, various grades, railroad crossings, two-lane country roads, commercial areas, and interstate highways.

If the road condition is not available, the examiner may ask you what you would do in certain driving situations. In these roadside simulations, the examiner will give you instructions to set up the situation and then ask you describe what you would do in that particular case.

The examiner will never ask you to do anything that is unsafe or that may cause an accident. But, you are the driver—the individual responsible for the vehicle and its safety. So, if the examiner asks you to do something that you are not entirely comfortable doing, you can ask questions or even politely refuse to follow the instruction.

However, you must have a reason why you are refusing.

The examiners will not try to cross you up or trick you, but they are only human and sometimes all of us make mistakes. Again, politely explain why you feel that what the examiner is asking is unsafe.

On the CDL Road Test, here are some of the instructions you will hear:

During this test, I will give directions for maneuvers as far in advance as possible. As we're driving, I may point out a location and ask you to pretend it is the top of a steep hill or maybe a railroad crossing. I will then ask you to go through the motions of what you would do if it were a real railroad crossing or steep grade. And at the same time you're going through the motions, tell me what you are doing and why.

During the test, I will not give you trick directions or instructions to do something illegal or unsafe. During the test, I will also be marking the test form, but don't let this make you uncomfortable, because a mark does not mean you've done something wrong.
Just concentrate on your driving.

Q. What happens if I have an accident during the test?

A. You get an automatic failing grade—so study for the Road Test and practice, and study for the General Knowledge Test by answering the several tests in that chapter.

On the Road Test, if you make a mistake or two, don't worry. The examiner mainly wants to see if you can handle a commercial vehicle safely. A few minor glitches won't set you up to fail.

Q. During the CDL Road Test, what will the examiner be looking for?

A. The examiner will be checking the following:

1. Starting and stopping

- Do you do these maneuvers smoothly without jerking or bouncing?

2. Shifting

- Do you shift without grinding gears or jerking the vehicle?
- Do you use the clutch and double-clutch?

3. Engine control

- Do you maintain proper revolutions per minute without overspeeding or lugging?
- If you're driving a new engine that shifts at a lower rpm, point this out to the examiner.

4. Proper following distance

- Do you maintain a safe following distance at all times?

5. Turn signals

- Do you signal in advance of a lane change or turn?
- Do you turn off the turn signal immediately after the maneuver?

6. Proper setup

- When making turns, is your vehicle in the correct position?

7. Intersections

- Do you move into the intersection cautiously? Are you prepared to stop?
- Do you turn your head to check for approaching vehicles or foot traffic?
- Do you stop within the stop lines?
- Do you keep your transmission in neutral and your foot off the clutch at traffic lights and stop signs?
- Do you stop at the stop line and then slowly move ahead?

8. Transmission control

- Is your truck in gear at all times—no coasting to a stop and no coasting through a turn?

9. Braking

- Do you brake smoothly, using the brake pedal—never the hand valve?
- Do you check the mirrors when braking to see if anyone is following too closely?

10. Traffic signs and traffic control

- Do you always observe speed limits and all traffic control devices, including stop lights, stop signs, and so on?

11. Curves

- Do you slow down to negotiate a curve? Never allow a truck to lean while going through a curve.

12. Interstate driving

- Do you stay in the far right lane except when moving to the left to allow traffic to enter the freeway from an on-ramp or to pass a slow vehicle?

- Do you check mirrors often?
- Do you merge smoothly?
- you use turn signals when merging and changing lanes and then turn them off promptly after the turn is made?
- Do you look 12 to 15 seconds ahead?
- Is your vehicle centered in your lane?

13. Upgrades

   - Do you maintain correct rpm and downshift when appropriate?
   - Can you start up an upgrade without rolling back?
   - When stopped, do you turn on your four-way flashers?

14. Downgrades

   - Do you maintain speed using a lower gear and steady, light braking?
   - Do you check your brakes before beginning a long downgrade?
   - Do you check the mirrors for signs of the brakes overheating?

15. Turns

   - Do you signal in advance of a turn and turn off your signal as soon as the turn is completed?
   - Do you stay in your lane?
   - Are both hands on the wheel when turning?
   - Do you stay in the same gear—no shifting—on a turn?

16. Railroad crossings

   - Do you look left and right and then look left and right again?
   - Do you roll down your window to listen?
   - If you are hauling HazMat cargo or passengers, do you stop at least 15 feet from the tracks—and no more than 50 feet?
   - Do you shift gears while crossing the track?

17. Underpasses and bridges

   - Do you check all bridge weight signs and height clearances? (Once you've cleared an underpass, the inspector may want to know the clearance on the underpass or height or weight limit. Be sure to look.)

Avoid These Bad Habits!

When taking the CDL Road Test:

- Don't forget to put on your seatbelt.
- Don't drive with one hand on the wheel.
- Don't exceed speed limits.
- Don't allow the vehicle to roll forward or backward when stopped.
- Don't forget to slow down and look both ways at an intersection or railroad crossing.
- Use turn signals, but don't forget to turn them off.

- Use the clutch, but don't ride the clutch.
- Don't take the transmission out of gear and coast to a light or stop sign.
- Don't run over a curb while turning.
- Don't forget to slow down on rough roads. (Bouncing the examiner will not help you score points.)
- Don't forget to maintain a safe following distance.

6 General Knowledge Questions

To help you prepare for the CDL General Knowledge Test, a number of review questions have been created for your use. The following questions are not the actual test questions, but they are similar to those you will see on the Knowledge Test. You may write the answers next to each question or you may opt to use an additional sheet of paper, putting the answers next to the number corresponding to the question. Then you can use these tests several times, if necessary.

The following statements are either true or false. Mark your answer in the blank provided. Then, check your answers using the key at the end of the chapter.

_____ 1. Your vehicle and cargo weight cannot be regulated by state laws.

_____ 2. It is okay to load tires beyond their rating.

_____ 3. An empty vehicle is likely to go into a rear-wheel skid.

_____ 4. A vehicle that is overloaded to the rear is likely to cause a rear-wheel skid.

_____ 5. A vehicle is likely to tip over if it has a high center of gravity.

_____ 6. You are required to keep a log of your time.

_____ 7. Once you receive your CDL from one state, you do not have to report any traffic violations you are convicted of in a different state.

_____ 8. A driver will lose his or her CDL for a year if he or she is convicted of driving under the influence (DUI), driving while intoxicated (DWI), or driving while on drugs.

_____ 9. If a driver uses a commercial motor vehicle to commit a felony involving controlled substances, then the driver will lose his or her CDL for life.

_____10. Drivers who operate commercial motor vehicles in an unsafe manner cannot earn a CDL.

_____11. To obtain a CDL, drivers must take the General Knowledge Test.

_____12. You do not have to list all the names and addresses of all employers who ever hired you to apply for a job driving a commercial motor vehicle.

_____13. Drivers may still drive a commercial motor vehicle even if they are disqualified.

_____14. Serious driving violations in a commercial motor vehicle include excessive speeding, reckless driving, or any traffic offense that causes a fatality.

_____15. If you refuse to take a drug test from any employer, it is the same as if you tested positive.

_____16. Once a driver passes an employer's road test, he or she does not have to pass the CDL Skills Test.

_____17. Unless a vehicle is placarded for hazardous materials, it does not have to carry a fire extinguisher.

_____18. The CDL Skills Test can be taken in any vehicle.

_____19. A driver must know the CDL laws and meet the requirements in FMCSR Part 391.

____20. After a serious illness or injury that affects your driving ability, you must renew all medical certificates.

____21. Carriers do not have to test drivers for drugs before they hire them.

____22. Brakes that lock up are usually the result of the driver panicking, not faulty equipment.

____23. Tires that are flat or have leaks may be used on a commercial motor vehicle only with caution.

____24. Drivers of a commercial motor vehicle must signal 50 feet before making a turn.

____25. When stopped on the highway, drivers must put on the four-way flashers and keep them on until returning to the road.

____26. Commercial motor vehicles require service brakes, emergency brakes, and parking brakes.

____27. All of the warning lights on the dash should come on when you first start your vehicle.

____28. The battery box on a commercial motor vehicle must have a secure cover.

____29. A few beers have about the same effect as a couple of shots of hard liquor like scotch.

____30. The best cure for fatigue is caffeine.

____31. Rust around the wheel nuts often indicates that the nuts are loose.

____32. Upshifting at a higher rpm as you reach higher gears is called progressive shifting.

____33. Turn signals facing forward can be either white or amber.

____34. Use a special coolant tester to check your antifreeze during winter weather.

____35. Ice on the radiator shutters will melt after the engine warms up.

____36. The normal oil pressure while idling is 5 to 15 psi.

____37. Vehicles marked "Dangerous" are classified as carrying hazardous materials.

____38. Drivers should turn vehicle lights on one half-hour after sunset until one half-hour before sunrise.

____39. After opening the circuit breaker, you must replace it.

____40. Vacuum pressure creates the braking force in the braking system.

____41. Check the tire pressure when the tire is cold.

____42. Total stopping distance is the vehicle length plus reaction time distance plus braking distance.

____43. Driving down the highway alongside other vehicles makes it difficult to change lanes and can cause you to get trapped.

____44. When headlights become dirty, visibility can be reduced by 50 percent.

____45. When an oncoming vehicle has its high beams on, you should flash your high beams at the driver.

____46. When a driver is using drugs or alcohol, he or she will drive too fast, too slow, or change speed for no reason.

____47. To avoid steering into a crash, apply the brake while turning.

____48. During hot weather, tire pressure can become higher than normal, so you should let air out of your tires when the pressure exceeds 105 psi.

____49. During hot weather, roads can become slippery and dangerous because of bleeding tar on the road.

____50. Be careful when downshifting while going down a steep incline, because you might get stuck in neutral.

____51. An emergency vehicle is marked with lights and a siren.

____52. Bridge laws control traffic on a bridge.

____53. Tire load means the maximum weight that a tire can safely carry.

____54. Even if your load is sealed, you are still responsible for exceeding gross weight or axle limits.

____55. The lighter your load, the shorter your stopping time and distance will be.

____56. Slam on the brakes to avoid a front-wheel skid.

____57. Releasing the brake is the first step to correcting a drive-wheel braking skid.

____58. If you have to leave the road to avoid another vehicle, make sure to turn widely.

____59. The most common type of skid occurs when the rear wheels lose traction due to over-braking or acceleration.

____60. To determine the best engine speed for shifting, you should use the information in the vehicle's owner's manual.

____61. Turn the retarders off whenever road conditions are hazardous, like when roads are wet, icy, or covered with snow.

____62. You should exceed the posted speed limit to make lane changes, turns, merges, and tight maneuvers.

____63. As a courtesy, you should signal other drivers to let them know when it is safe to pass.

____64. It is illegal to drive your vehicle in a way that would cause an accident or cause it to break down.

____65. Blocking, which is secured to the cargo compartment floor, is used to prevent cargo from moving or shifting.

____66. To protect your cargo and others on the road, you should use a tarp.

____67. After starting a trip, you should check your cargo after traveling 50 miles.

____68. It is important to perform a post-trip inspection after every run on every vehicle you operate.

____69. You should check your cargo securement devices whenever you stop during a trip.

____70. The lighter your load, the less traction your vehicle will have.

____71. Just because size and weight distributions are legal does not mean that they will ensure safe operation in bad weather.

____72. To secure cargo, use as few tiedowns as possible.

____73. The drive tires of your vehicle must have 1/4 inch of tread.

____74. Steering axle tires must have at least 1/4 inch of tread.

____75. Poisonous fumes entering the cab are a dangerous hazard of exhaust system leaks.

____76. A bent tie rod is a steering system defect.

____77. All mud flaps should touch the ground.

____78. Dry bulk tanks are stable in curves and turns.

____79. A state official has the authority to put your vehicle "out of service" if he or she conducts a roadside inspection and finds your vehicle to be unsafe.

____80. Normal clutch travel distance is more than two inches.

____81. During a pre-trip inspection, check the brake lights by pulling the red knob.

____82. After you have completed the seven-step inspection, regardless of your vehicle, you are ready to roll.

____83. In some states, you may be required to have snow chains mounted during winter months.

____84. A few seconds after starting the engine, the oil pressure should come up to normal.

____85. The average engine temperature ranges from about 180 to 250 degrees Fahrenheit.

The following statements are multiple choice. Mark your answer in the blank provided. Then, check your answers with the key at the end of the chapter.

____ 1. In a pre-trip inspection, what should your tires look like?
   (A) Tires should not be mismatched in size and ply, nor worn or damaged.
   (B) Tread depth should be less than 4/32 of an inch on the front tires, and 2/32 of an inch on all other tires.
   (C) Dual tires should be touching.
   (D) All of the above.

____ 2. In a pre-trip inspection, what should you check for in your wheels and rims?
   (A) Look for rust around wheel nuts, which indicates looseness.
   (B) Cracked or damaged wheels or rims.
   (C) Mismatched or bent lock rims.
   (D) All of the above.

____ 3. During a pre-trip inspection, check your brakes and suspension system for:
   (A) Brake shoes and pads with fluid in them.
   (B) Shoes worn thinner than 1/4 inch.
   (C) Cracked, missing, or broken parts.
   (D) All of the above.

____ 4. Federal and state laws prohibit driving an unsafe vehicle, so you should make sure that you fix which of the following problems?
   (A) A small leak of power steering fluid.
   (B) Steering wheel play of more than 10 degrees (two inches on a 20-inch wheel).
   (C) A leak in the exhaust system.
   (D) All of the above.

____ 5. You should always have which of the following emergency equipment in your vehicle?
   (A) At least one fire extinguisher.
   (B) Warning triangles.
   (C) Spare electrical fuses.
   (D) All of the above.

____ 6. During a pre-trip inspection, don't inspect which of the following in your engine compartment?
   (A) Valve clearance.
   (B) Electrical wire insulation.
   (C) Engine oil level.
   (D) Hose condition.

___ 7. Before the trip and while traveling, what should you check for?
(A) Cargo securement.
(B) Vehicle gauges.
(C) Tires.
(D) All of the above.

___ 8. During an en-route inspection, what should you check?
(A) Brakes and tires.
(B) Coupling devices.
(C) Cargo.
(D) All of the above.

___ 9. How do you start your vehicle on an uphill grade?
(A) Let the vehicle roll backwards and then engage the clutch.
(B) Use the parking brake to keep the vehicle from rolling backwards and then engage the clutch.
(C) Slip the clutch slowly while accelerating.
(D) Take your foot off the brake and shift quickly.

___10. How should you accelerate?
(A) Accelerate until you feel a jerking motion.
(B) Accelerate smoothly so you won't cause coupling damage.
(C) Accelerate quickly when traction is poor.
(D) All of the above.

___11. When you start after stopping and your drive wheels begin to spin, what should you do?
(A) Apply the brakes.
(B) Take your foot off the accelerator.
(C) Turn your engine off.
(D) All of the above.

___12. How should you hold the steering wheel?
(A) You can put your hands anywhere on the steering wheel.
(B) With both hands close to the bottom of the wheel.
(C) With your hands on 3 o'clock and 9 o'clock, respectively.
(D) With your hands on 12 o'clock and 6 o'clock, respectively.

___13. How should you adjust your speed when it is raining or snowing?
(A) On packed snow, keep your speed constant.
(B) On a wet road, use caution.
(C) Allow extra time for stopping, because it takes longer and it will be harder to turn without skidding.
(D) All of the above.

___14. Hydroplaning:
(A) Occurs when water or slush forms a film between the tires and the road.
(B) Can occur at any speed.
(C) Is more likely to occur when tire pressure is low.
(D) All of the above.

___15. At night you should always:
(A) Watch the vehicles that are approaching.
(B) Make sure that your stopping distance is within your sight distance.
(C) Drive faster with low beams than high beams.
(D) All of the above.

——16. What can cause you to skid?
   (A) Over accelerating.
   (B) Turning too slowly.
   (C) Not using your brakes.
   (D) All of the above.

——17. To correct a tractor drive-wheel acceleration skid, you should:
   (A) Countersteer.
   (B) Apply more power to the wheel.
   (C) Apply the brakes.
   (D) Stop accelerating and push in the clutch.

——18. How do you correct a tractor rear-wheel braking skid?
   (A) Turn into the skid.
   (B) Don't brake, turn quickly, and countersteer.
   (C) Slide sideways and stop.
   (D) Slide sideways and spin out.

——19. Retarders:
   (A) Provide emergency braking.
   (B) Apply extra braking power to the non–drive axles.
   (C) Help slow the vehicle and reduce brake wear.
   (D) Prevent skidding.

——20. When using retarders, what is a major concern?
   (A) They cause extra brake wear.
   (B) They may cause the drive wheels to skid when the traction is poor.
   (C) Their use may be illegal on some highways.
   (D) They can cause the steering axle brakes to quit.

——21. While driving, you should look ahead:
   (A) 1 to 3 seconds.
   (B) 6 to 9 seconds.
   (C) 12 to 15 seconds.
   (D) 20 to 25 seconds.

——22. When traveling at highway speed, you should look ahead:
   (A) 1/8 of a mile.
   (B) 1/32 of a mile.
   (C) 1/4 of a mile.
   (D) 1/10 of a mile.

——23. You should check the mirrors to see:
   (A) The location of the rear of your vehicle in a turn.
   (B) The condition of some of your tires.
   (C) Traffic gaps when merging.
   (D) All of the above.

——24. What is important to remember about using mirrors?
   (A) Even when using mirrors, there may be "blind spots."
   (B) You should check your mirrors twice before making a lane change.
   (C) Convex mirrors make things look closer.
   (D) Look in the mirror for several seconds each time.

——25. Which of the following is true when using your turn signal?
   (A) When turning, turn your signal off as you turn.
   (B) When turning, signal early.
   (C) Use your turn signal only when changing lanes in heavy traffic.
   (D) All the above.

___26. Which of the following is true about using your vehicle lights?
   (A) During the day, use headlights when it's raining or snowing.
   (B) Flash your brake lights to warn those behind you that you are stopping.
   (C) Turn on your lights when you are parked on the side of the road.
   (D) All of the above.

___27. Which of the following is true about how to mark a stopped vehicle?
   (A) If you are stopped longer than ten minutes, put out reflective triangles at spaces of 10, 100, and 200 feet from the vehicle.
   (B) Keep the vehicle taillights on.
   (C) Place a triangle back beyond a hill that prevents oncoming traffic from seeing your vehicle within 250 feet.
   (D) Don't use the four-way flashers in daylight.

___28. Avoid using your horn because:
   (A) It does not do a good job of letting people know where you are.
   (B) It may startle other drivers.
   (C) It takes air pressure away from the air brakes.
   (D) All of the above.

___29. Speed and weight have what type of effect on stopping distance?
   (A) Empty trucks have a shorter stopping distance.
   (B) When you double your speed, it will take three times the distance to stop.
   (C) The heavier the vehicle, the more the brakes have to stop.
   (D) All of the above.

___30. Who is responsible for making sure that cargo is not overloaded?
   (A) The driver.
   (B) State and federal agents.
   (C) The shipper.
   (D) All of the above.

___31. Why should you cover the cargo?
   (A) Federal and state laws require it.
   (B) To protect the cargo and keep it from spilling.
   (C) Because of Department of Transportation specifications.
   (D) All of the above.

___32. What is important to know about loading cargo?
   (A) Make sure that the cargo is low and even.
   (B) Put lighter cargos toward the back.
   (C) The higher the center of gravity, the safer the cargo is.
   (D) All of the above.

___33. On the freeway during rush hour where most cars are going 35 miles per hour, the safest speed for your vehicle is:
   (A) 20 miles per hour.
   (B) 25 miles per hour.
   (C) 35 miles per hour.
   (D) 45 miles per hour.

___34. Whenever you are being tailgated, you should:
   (A) Increase the space in front of you.
   (B) Go faster.
   (C) Slow down.
   (D) Flash your taillights.

_____35. During hot weather, your tires:
- (A) Can be cooled by driving if they overheat.
- (B) Decrease in air pressure as the weather gets warmer.
- (C) Should be inspected every 150 miles or every three hours.
- (D) All of the above.

_____36. If your engine begins to overheat, what should you do?
- (A) Stop the vehicle and remove the radiator cap.
- (B) Finish your trip, and then check your engine.
- (C) Stop as soon as possible and shut off your engine.
- (D) Keep your engine running.

_____37. When traveling down a steep hill, how should you use your brakes?
- (A) Pump the brakes lightly.
- (B) Pump the brakes using lots of pressure.
- (C) Use strong pressure that increases as you move downward.
- (D) Light, even, and steady pressure.

_____38. What is the meaning of the red triangles with an orange center on the back of a vehicle?
- (A) This vehicle is an emergency vehicle.
- (B) The vehicle is slow moving.
- (C) The driver is a student.
- (D) The cargo of the vehicle is hazardous.

_____39. To avoid a crash, you should:
- (A) Steer with one hand and downshift with the other.
- (B) Apply the brakes as you steer and turn.
- (C) Don't turn any more than needed to avoid a crash.
- (D) Avoid countersteering.

_____40. Countersteering is:
- (A) Turning the wheel counterclockwise.
- (B) Steering back and forth several times.
- (C) Turning the wheel more than needed.
- (D) Turning the wheel back in the other direction once you've passed something in your path.

_____41. If an oncoming vehicle drifts into your lane on a two-lane road, what should you do?
- (A) Steer away from the vehicle to the left, trading places.
- (B) Maintain your position until you're seen.
- (C) Brake hard.
- (D) Steer to the right to avoid the vehicle.

_____42. When can you use your brakes if you must leave the road in an emergency?
- (A) Only when you feel the vehicle start to tip over.
- (B) When your speed drops to about 20 miles per hour.
- (C) As soon as possible.
- (D) When one wheel is still on the pavement.

_____43. If you are on the right shoulder going 55 miles per hour, what is the safest way to get onto the road?
- (A) Stay on the shoulder if it is clear and come to a stop, then return to the road when it's safe.
- (B) Brake hard and steer sharply onto the road.
- (C) Maintain your speed and steer gently onto the road.
- (D) Countersteer.

____44. What is controlled braking?
    (A) Gently tapping on the brakes.
    (B) Locking the brakes for a short time.
    (C) Keeping the vehicle in a straight line when braking.
    (D) All of the above.

____45. If your hydraulic brakes go out, what should you do?
    (A) Try pumping the brakes to generate pressure.
    (B) Downshift.
    (C) Use the parking brake.
    (D) All of the above.

____46. Sign(s) of tire failure is(are):
    (A) A loud bang.
    (B) Heavy steering.
    (C) Vibration.
    (D) All of the above.

____47. If you have a blowout in your front tire on a level highway at 50 miles per hour, what should you do first?
    (A) Quickly drive to the shoulder.
    (B) Countersteer.
    (C) Stay off the brake until the vehicle slows.
    (D) Press hard on the brakes.

____48. Which of the following is true about backing?
    (A) Helpers should be used.
    (B) Back toward the driver side of the vehicle when you have a choice.
    (C) Avoid backing whenever you can.
    (D) All of the above.

____49. Which of the following is true about double-clutching and shifting?
    (A) Use your tachometer and road speed to tell you when to shift.
    (B) Double-clutch only on slippery roads.
    (C) If you miss a gear when upshifting, bring your vehicle to a stop.
    (D) Double-clutch only with a heavy load.

____50. What is important about downshifting?
    (A) Downshift after you go down a hill.
    (B) Downshift before you enter a curve.
    (C) When you double-clutch, let the engine rpm decrease while the shift lever is in neutral and the clutch is released.
    (D) All of the above.

____51. During a front-wheel skid, what will the vehicle do?
    (A) Continue to go straight, even when you steer.
    (B) Start spinning.
    (C) Go into a spin if you apply the brakes.
    (D) Go into a spin if you steer.

____52. What can cause a truck fire?
    (A) Tires with low air pressure.
    (B) An electrical short circuit.
    (C) Flammable cargo.
    (D) All of the above.

____53. Use the B:C fire extinguishers on:
(A) Burning liquids and electrical fires.
(B) Wood and paper fires.
(C) Cloth fires.
(D) All of the above.

____54. Use the A:B:C fire extinguishers on:
(A) Burning liquids and electrical fires.
(B) Wood and paper fires.
(C) Cloth fires.
(D) All of the above.

____55. You can use water on what type of fires:
(A) Electrical fires.
(B) Gasoline fires.
(C) Tire fires.
(D) All of the above.

Check Yourself—General Knowledge Review Questions Answer Key

True/False

1. F; 2. F; 3. T; 4. F; 5. T; 6. T; 7. F; 8. T; 9. T; 10. F; 11. T; 12. T; 13. F; 14. T; 15. T; 16. F; 17. F; 18. F; 19. T; 20. T; 21. F; 22. T; 23. F; 24. F; 25. T; 26. T; 27. T; 28. T; 29. T; 30. F; 31. T; 32. F; 33. F; 34. T; 35. F; 36. T; 37. T; 38. F; 39. F; 40. F; 41. T; 42. F; 43. T; 44. T; 45. F; 46. T; 47. T; 48. F; 49. T; 50. T; 51. F; 52. F; 53. T; 54. T; 55. F; 56. F; 57. T; 58. F; 59. T; 60. T; 61. T; 62. F; 63. F; 64. T; 65. T; 66. T; 67. T; 68. T; 69. T; 70. T; 71. T; 72. F; 73. F; 74. F; 75. T; 76. T; 77. F; 78. F; 79. T; 80. F; 81. F; 82. F; 83. T; 84. T; 85. F.

Multiple Choice

1. A; 2. D; 3. D; 4. D; 5. D; 6. A; 7. D; 8. D; 9. B; 10. B; 11. B; 12. C; 13. C; 14. D; 15. B; 16. A; 17. D; 18. B; 19. C; 20. B; 21. C; 22. C; 23. D; 24. A; 25. B; 26. D; 27. A; 28. B; 29. C; 30. A; 31. B; 32. A; 33. C; 34. A; 35. C; 36. C; 37. D; 38. B; 39. C; 40. D; 41. D; 42. B; 43. A; 44. C; 45. D; 46. D; 47. C; 48. D; 49. A; 50. B; 51. A; 52. D; 53. D; 54. D; 55. C.

7

A Review of Federal Motor Carriers Safety Regulations—Parts 383 and 391

The Commercial Driver's License involves specialized testing whereby professional drivers are certified to drive commercial vehicles. Studying is required for the tests administered by the Department of Motor Vehicles in your state. These tests are offered in most cities where the Department of Motor Vehicles has an office.

The CDL indicates that its holder has proved himself capable of handling the responsibilities that come with driving a commercial vehicle on public streets and highways (see Figure 7-1).

Passing the CDL also proves that you have knowledge of the law and observe certain regulations every time you climb into the cab of a truck or take the driver's seat in a van or a bus.

Professional drivers who operate commercial motor vehicles are covered by a series of regulations called the Federal Motor Carrier Safety Regulations (FMCSR), which are outlined in several sections.

In this chapter, we will examine two main parts of the FMCSR that should be familiar to professional drivers. Notice we said "should be familiar." Do not memorize this information just understand what these parts say and what they cover.

ROAD SENSE

These regulations are quite lengthy. We have condensed much of the material found in these parts, but this chapter still runs fairly long . . . so *pace yourself.* Don't try to read it all in one sitting.

Figure 7-1 With a Commercial Driver's License comes the responsibility of safely driving a commercial motor vehicle.

Before the Commercial Driver's License Program

It is widely recognized that driving commercial motor vehicles (CMVs) requires special skills and knowledge. Prior to implementation of the CDL program, any person licensed to drive an automobile could also legally drive a tractor-trailer or a bus in a number of states and in the District of Columbia. Even in many of the states that did have a classified licensing system, a person was not skills tested in a representative vehicle.

As a result, many drivers were operating motor vehicles that they may not have been qualified to drive. In addition, many drivers were able to obtain driver's licenses from more than one state and hide or spread convictions among several driving records and continue to drive.

The Commercial Motor Vehicle Safety Act of 1986

The Commercial Motor Vehicle Safety Act of 1986 was signed into law on October 27, 1986. The goal of the Act is to improve highway safety by ensuring that drivers of large trucks and buses are qualified to operate those vehicles and to remove unsafe and unqualified drivers from the highways. The Act retained the state's right to issue a driver's license, but established minimum national standards that states must meet when licensing CMV drivers.

The Act corrects the situation existing prior to 1986 by making it illegal to hold more than one license and by requiring states to adopt testing and licensing standards for truck and bus drivers to check a person's ability to operate the type of vehicle he plans to operate.

It is important to note that the Act does not require drivers to obtain a separate federal license; it merely requires states to upgrade their existing testing and licensing programs, if necessary, to conform with the minimum federal standards.

The CDL program places requirements on the CMV driver, the employing motor carrier, and the states.

The Driver

Drivers have been required to have a CDL in order to drive a CMV since April 1, 1992.

The Federal Highway Administration (FHWA) has developed and issued standards for testing and licensing CMV drivers. There is a new agency, the Federal Motor Carrier Safety Agency, which now has oversight responsibility for the CDL program. Among other things, the standards require states to issue CDLs to their CMV drivers only after the driver passes Knowledge and Skills tests administered by the state that are related to the type of vehicle to be operated. Drivers need CDLs if they are in interstate, intrastate, or foreign commerce and drive a vehicle that meets one of the following definitions of a CMV:

Classes of License

The federal standard requires that states issue a CDL to drivers according to the following license classifications:

- **Class A**—Any combination of vehicles with a GVWR of 26,001 or more pounds provided the GVWR of the vehicle(s) being towed is in excess of 10,000 pounds.

- **Class B**—Any single vehicle with a GVWR of 26,001 or more pounds, or any such vehicle towing a vehicle not in excess of 10,000 pounds GVWR.
- **Class C**—Any single vehicle, or combination of vehicles, that does not meet the definition of Class A or Class B, but is either designed to transport sixteen or more passengers, including the driver, or is placarded for hazardous materials.

Endorsements and Restrictions

Drivers who operate special types of CMVs also need to pass additional tests to obtain any of the following endorsements on their CDL:

T—Double/Triple Trailers (Knowledge Test only)
P—Passenger (Knowledge and Skills Tests)
N—Tank Vehicle (Knowledge Test only)
H—Hazardous Materials (Knowledge Test only)
X—Combination of Tank Vehicle and Hazardous Materials (Knowledge Test only)
S—School Bus (Knowledge and Skills Tests) (Required by the Motor Carrier Safety Improvement Act of 1999)

If a driver either fails the air brake component of the General Knowledge Test or performs the Skills Test in a vehicle not equipped with air brakes, the driver is issued an air brakes restriction, thus preventing the driver from operating a CMV equipped with air brakes.

Knowledge and Skills Tests

States develop their own tests which must be at least as stringent as the federal standards. Model driver and examiner manuals and tests have been prepared and distributed to the states to use, if they wish.

- The General Knowledge Test must contain at least 50 questions.
- To pass the Knowledge Tests (General and Endorsement), applicants must correctly answer at least 80 percent of the questions.
- To pass the Skills Test, applicants must successfully perform all the required skills (listed in 49 CFR 383.113). The Skills Test must be taken in a vehicle representative of the type of vehicle that the applicant operates or expects to operate.

Third-Party Skills Testing

Other states, employers, training facilities, governmental departments and agencies, and private institutions can serve as third-party skills testers for the state.

- Tests must be the same as those given by the state.
- Examiners must meet the same qualifications as state examiners.
- States must conduct an on-site inspection at least once a year.
- At least annually, State employees must evaluate the programs by taking third-party tests as if they were test applicants, or by testing a sample of drivers tested by the third party and then comparing pass/fail rates.

- The state's agreement with the third-party skills tester must allow the FMCSA and the state to conduct random examinations, inspections, and audits without prior notice.

Grandfathering Provision

States have the option to "grandfather" drivers with good driving records from the Skills Test according to the following criteria:

- Driver has a current license at time of application; and driver has a good driving record and previously passed an acceptable skills test; or driver has a good driving record in combination with certain driving experience.

"A Good Driving Record"

"A good driving record" means that a driver can certify that, during the two-year period immediately prior to applying for a CDL he:

- Has not had more than one license;
- Has not had any license suspended, revoked, or canceled;
- Has not had any convictions in any type of motor vehicle for major disqualifying offenses;
- Has not had more than one conviction for any type of motor vehicle for serious traffic violations;
- Has not had any violation of state or local law relating to motor vehicle traffic control arising in connection with any traffic accident, and has no record of an accident in which he was at fault.

"Driving Experience"

"Driving experience" means that a driver can certify and provide evidence that:

- He is regularly employed in a job requiring the operation of a CMV, and that either:
  - He has previously taken a behind-the-wheel Skills Test in a representative vehicle; or
  - He has operated a representative vehicle for at least two years immediately preceding his application for a CDL.

A Commercial Driver's License Document

A state determines the license fee, the license renewal cycle, most renewal procedures, and continues to decide the age, medical, and other driver qualifications of its intrastate commercial drivers. Interstate drivers must meet the longstanding federal driver qualifications (49 CFR 391).

All CDLs must contain the following information:

- The words "Commercial Driver's License" or "CDL"
- The driver's full name, signature, and address
- The driver's date of birth, sex, and height

- A color photograph or digitized image of the driver
- The driver's state license number
- The name of the issuing state
- The date of issuance and the date of the expiration of the license
- The class(es) of vehicle that the driver is authorized to driver
- A notation of the "air brake" restriction, if issued
- The endorsement(s) for which the driver has qualified

States may issue learner's permits for purposes of behind-the-wheel training on public highways as long as learner's permit holders are required to be accompanied by someone with a valid CDL appropriate for that vehicle, and the learner's permits are issued for limited-time periods.

Waiver Provisions

All active duty military drivers were waived from the CDL requirements by the Federal Highway Administrator. A state, at its discretion, may waive firefighters, emergency response vehicle drivers, and farmers and drivers removing snow and ice in small communities from the CDL requirements, subject to certain conditions.

In addition, a state may also waive the CDL knowledge and skills testing requirements for seasonal drivers in farm-related service industries and waive certain knowledge and skills testing requirements for drivers in remote areas of Alaska. The drivers are issued restricted CDLs. A state can also waive the CDL hazardous materials endorsement test requirements for part-time drivers working for the pyrotechnics industry, subject to certain conditions.

Other Requirements

There are a variety of other requirements related to this legislation which affect the commercial drivers, their employing motor carriers, and the states.

Penalties

The federal penalty to a driver who violates CDL requirements is a civil penalty of up to $2,500 or, in aggravated cases, criminal penalties of up to $5,000 in fines, and/or up to 90 days in prison. An employer is also subject to a penalty of up to $10,000 if he or she knowingly uses a driver to operate a CMV without a valid CDL.

CDLIS Clearinghouse

States must be connected to the Commercial Driver's License Information System (CDLIS) and the National Driver Register (NDR) in order to exchange information about CMV drivers, traffic convictions, and disqualifications. A state must use both the CDLIS and NDR to check a driver's record, and the CDLIS to make certain that the applicant does not already have a CDL. *Members of the enforcement community seeking access to CDLIS data should visit the FMCSA Technical Support web site. Carriers needing CDLIS data should seek a commercial company that provides a clearinghouse service for this information, or contact the driver's state of licensure.*

BAC Standards

The FHWA has also established 0.04 percent as the blood alcohol concentration (BAC) level at or above which a CMV driver is deemed to be driving under the influence of alcohol and subject to the disqualification sanctions in the Act. States maintain a BAC level between 0.08 percent and 0.10 percent for non-CMV drivers.

Employer Notifications

Within 30 days of a conviction for any traffic violation, except parking, a driver must notify his employer, regardless of the nature of the violation or the type of vehicle which was driven at the time.

If a driver's license is suspended, revoked, canceled, or if the driver is disqualified from driving, his employer must be notified. The notification must be made by the end of the next business day following receipt of the notice of the suspension, revocation, cancellation, lost privilege, or disqualification.

Employers may not knowingly use a driver who has more than one license or whose license is suspended, revoked, or canceled, or who is disqualified from driving. Violation of this requirement may result in civil or criminal penalties.

Disqualifications

For a conviction while driving a CMV, drivers will be disqualified and lose their privilege to drive for 60 to 120 days:

- If they have two or more serious traffic violations within a three-year period. These include excessive speeding, reckless driving, improper or erratic lane changes, following the vehicle ahead too closely, and traffic offenses in connection with fatal traffic accidents.
- If they have one or more violations of an out-of-service order within a ten-year period.

Drivers will be disqualified and lose their privilege to drive for one year if they are convicted of:

- Driving under the influence of a controlled substance or alcohol; or
- Leaving the scene of an accident; or
- Using a CMV to commit a felony.

Drivers will be disqualified and lose their privilege to drive for three years if they are convicted of:

- Any of the one-year offenses while operating a CMV that is placarded for hazardous materials.

Drivers will be disqualified and lose their privilege to drive for life if they are convicted of:

- A second offense of any of the one-year or three-year offenses; or
- Having used a CMV to commit a felony involving manufacturing, distributing, or dispensing controlled substances.

States have the option to reduce certain lifetime disqualifications to a minimum disqualification period of ten years if the driver voluntarily completes a driver rehabilitation program approved by the state.

If a CDL holder is disqualified from operating a CMV, the state may issue him a license to operate non-CMVs. Drivers who are disqualified from operating a CMV can not be issued a "conditional" or "hardship" CDL or any other type of limited driving privileges to continue driving a CMV.

For disqualification purposes, convictions for out-of-state violations will be treated the same as convictions for violations that are committed in the home state. The CDLIS will ensure that convictions a driver receives outside his or her home state are transmitted to the home state so that the disqualifications can be applied.

FMCSR Part 383—The Commercial Driver's License

Subpart A—General

§383.1 Purpose and Scope

The purpose of this part is to help reduce or prevent truck and bus accidents, fatalities, and injuries by requiring drivers to have a single commercial motor vehicle driver's license and by disqualifying those drivers who operate commercial motor vehicles in an unsafe manner.

This part:

1. Prohibits a commercial motor vehicle driver from having more than one commercial motor vehicle driver's license.
2. Requires a driver to notify the driver's current employer and the driver's state of residence of certain convictions.
3. Requires that a driver provide previous employment information when applying for employment as an operator of a commercial motor vehicle.
4. Prohibits an employer from allowing a person with a suspended license to operate a commercial motor vehicle.
5. Establishes periods of disqualification and penalties for those persons convicted of certain criminal and other offenses and serious traffic violations, or those persons subject to any suspensions, revocations, or cancellations of certain driving privileges.
6. Establishes testing and licensing requirements for commercial motor vehicle operators.
7. Requires states to give knowledge and skills tests that meet federal standards to all qualified applicants for Commercial Driver's Licenses.
8. Sets commercial motor vehicle groups and endorsements.
9. Sets the knowledge and skills test requirements for the motor vehicle groups and endorsements.
10. Sets the federal standards for procedures, methods, and minimum passing scores for states and others to use in testing and licensing commercial motor vehicle operators.
11. Establishes requirements for the state-issued commercial license documentation.

FMCSR Part 391–Qualifications for CMV Drivers

The rules in this part establish minimum qualifications for persons who drive commercial motor vehicles as, for, or on behalf of, motor carriers. These rules also establish minimum duties of motor carriers with respect to the qualifications of their drivers.

Subpart A—General

§391.1 Scope of the Rules in this Part; Additional Qualifications; Duties of Carrier Drivers

These rules establish minimum qualifications for persons who drive commercial motor vehicles. These rules also establish minimum duties for motor carriers regarding the qualifications of their drivers.

§391.2 General Exemptions

(a) **Farm Custom Operation.** The rules do not apply to a driver who drives a commercial motor vehicle engaged in custom-harvesting operations, if the commercial motor vehicle is used to transport farm machinery, supplies, or both, or to transport custom-harvested crops to storage or market.

(b) **Apiarian Industries.** The rules in this part do not apply to a driver or beekeeper who is engaged in the seasonal transportation of bees.

Subpart B—Qualification and Disqualification of Drivers

§391.11 General Qualifications of Drivers

A person shall not drive a commercial motor vehicle unless he is qualified. A person is only qualified to drive a motor vehicle if he:

- Is at least 21 years old.
- Can read and speak the English language sufficiently to converse with the general public, to understand highway traffic signs and signals in the English language, to respond to official inquiries, and to make entries on reports and records.
- Can, because of experience, training, or both, safely operate the type of commercial motor vehicle he drives.
- Is physically qualified to drive a commercial motor vehicle.
- Has a currently valid commercial motor vehicle operator's license issued only by one state.
- Has prepared and furnished the motor carrier that employs him with the list of violations or the certificate as required by FMCSR Part 391.27.
- Is not disqualified to drive a commercial motor vehicle under the rules in Part 391.15.
- Has successfully completed a driver's road test and has been issued a certificate of driver's road test or has presented an operator's license or a certificate of road test which the motor carrier that employs him has accepted as equivalent to a road test.

§391.13 Responsibilities of Drivers

A motor carrier shall not require or permit a person to drive a commercial motor vehicle unless the person, because of experience, training, or both, determines whether the cargo he transports (including baggage in a passenger-carrying commercial motor vehicle) has been properly located, distributed, and secured in or on the commercial motor vehicle he drives.

The driver must also be familiar with methods and procedures for securing cargo in or on the commercial motor vehicle he drives.

§391.15 Disqualification of Drivers

General. A driver who is disqualified shall not drive a commercial motor vehicle. A motor carrier shall not require or permit a driver who is disqualified to drive a commercial motor vehicle.

Disqualification for Loss of Driving Privileges. A driver is disqualified for the duration of the driver's loss of his privilege to operate a commercial motor vehicle on public highways, either temporarily or permanently, by reason of the revocation, suspension, withdrawal, or denial of an operator's license, permit, or privilege. This disqualification continues until that operator's license, permit, or privilege is restored by the authority that revoked, suspended, withdrew, or denied it.

A driver who receives a notice that his license to operate a CMV has been revoked, suspended, or withdrawn shall notify the motor carrier that employs him of the notice before the end of the business day following the day the driver received it.

Disqualification for Criminal and Other Offenses

General Rule. A driver who is convicted of (or forfeits bond or collateral upon a charge of) a disqualifying offense is disqualified for the period of time specified if:

- The offense was committed during on-duty time and . . .
- The driver is employed by a motor carrier or is engaged in interstate, intrastate, or foreign commerce.

Disqualifying Offenses. The following offenses are disqualifying offenses:

- Driving a commercial motor vehicle while under the influence of alcohol.
- Driving a commercial motor vehicle while the person's alcohol concentration is 0.04 percent or more.
- Driving under the influence of alcohol, as prescribed by state law; or
- Refusal to undergo testing for presence of alcohol.
- Driving a commercial motor vehicle under the influence of an identified controlled substance, an amphetamine, a narcotic drug, a formulation of an amphetamine or a derivative of a narcotic drug.
- Transportation, possession, or unlawful use of an identified controlled substance, amphetamines, narcotic drugs, formulations of an amphetamine, or derivatives of narcotic drugs while the driver is on duty.
- Leaving the scene of an accident while operating a commercial motor vehicle.
- Committing a felony involving the use of a commercial motor vehicle.

Duration of Disqualification

First Offenders

A driver is disqualified for one year after the date of conviction or forfeiture of bond or collateral if, during the three years preceding that date, the driver was not convicted of, or did not forfeit bond or collateral upon a charge of an offense that would disqualify the driver under the rules of this section.

Exemption. The period of disqualification is six months if the conviction or forfeiture of bond or collateral solely concerned the transportation or possession of illegal or controlled substances.

Subsequent Offenders

A driver is disqualified for three years after the date of his conviction if, during the three years preceding that date, he was convicted of an offense that would disqualify him under the rules in this section.

Disqualification for Violation of Out-of-Service Orders

General Rule. A driver who is convicted of violating an out-of-service order is disqualified for the period of time as follows:

Duration of Disqualification for Violation of Out-of-Service Orders

First Violation

- A driver is disqualified for not less than 90 days nor more than one year if he is convicted of a first violation of an out-of-service order.

Second Violation

- A driver is disqualified for not less than one year nor more than five years if, during any ten-year period, the driver is convicted of two violations of out-of-service orders in separate incidents.

Third or Subsequent Violation

- A driver is disqualified for not less than three years nor more than five years if, during any ten-year period, he is convicted of three or more violations of out-of-service orders in separate incidents.

Special Rule for Hazardous Materials and Passenger Offenses

- A driver is disqualified for not less than 180 days nor more than two years if he is convicted of a first violation of an out-of-service order while transporting hazardous materials required to be placarded under the Hazardous Materials Transportation Act.

- A driver is also disqualified for not less than 180 days nor more than two years while operating commercial motor vehicles designed to transport more than fifteen passengers, including the driver.
- A driver is disqualified for a period of not less than three years nor more than five years if, during any ten-year period, the driver is convicted of any subsequent violations of out-of-service orders, in separate incidents, while transporting hazardous materials required to be placarded under the Hazardous Materials Transportation Act, or while operating commercial motor vehicles designed to transport more than fifteen passengers, including the driver.

Disqualification for Major Offenses. Table 7-1 contains a list of the offenses and periods for which a driver must be disqualified, depending upon the type of vehicle the driver is operating at the time of the violation, as follows:

Disqualification for Serious Traffic Violations. Table 7-2 contains a list of the offenses and the periods for which a driver must be disqualified, depending upon the type of vehicle the driver is operating at the time of the violation, as follows:

Disqualification for Railroad-Highway Grade Crossing Offenses. Table 7-3 contains a list of the offenses and the periods for which a driver must be disqualified, when the driver is operating a CMV at the time of the violation, as follows:

Disqualification for Violating Out-of-Service Orders. Table 7-4 contains a list of the offenses and periods for which a driver must be disqualified when the driver is operating a CMV at the time of the violation, as follows:

Subpart C—Background and Character

§391.21 Application for Employment

A person shall not drive a commercial motor vehicle unless he has completed and furnished the motor carrier that employs him with an application for employment.

This application for employment shall be made on a form furnished by the motor carrier. Each application form must be completed by the applicant, must be signed by him, and must contain the following information:

- The name and address of the employing motor carrier
- The applicant's name, address, date of birth, and Social Security number
- The addresses at which the applicant has resided during the three years preceding the date on which the application is submitted
- The date on which the application is submitted
- The issuing state, number, and expiration date of each unexpired commercial motor vehicle operator's license or permit that has been issued to the applicant
- The nature and extent of the applicant's experience in the operation of motor vehicles, including the type of equipment he has operated
- A list of all motor vehicle accidents in which the applicant was involved during the three years preceding the date the application is submitted, specifying the date and nature of each accident and any fatalities or personal injuries it caused

Table 7-1

List of Major Offenses and Periods of Driver Disqualification

If a driver operates a motor vehicle and is convicted of:	For a first conviction or refusal to be tested while operating a CMV, a person required to have a CDL and a CDL holder must be disqualified from operating a CMV for:	For a first conviction or refusal to be tested while operating a non-CMV, a CDL holder must be disqualified from operating a CMV for:
(1) Being under the influence of alcohol as prescribed by state law.	One year	One year
(2) Being under the influence of a controlled substance.	One year	One year
(3) Having an alcohol concentration of 0.04 percent or greater while operating a CMV.		
(4) Refusing to take an alcohol test as required by a state or jurisdiction under its implied consent laws or regulations as defined in §383.72 of this part.	One year	Not applicable
(5) Leaving the scene of an accident.	One year	One year
(6) Using the vehicle to commit a felony other than a felony described in paragraph (b)(9) of this table.	One year	One year
(7) Driving a CMV when, as a result of prior violations committed operating a CMV, the driver's CDL is revoked, suspended, or canceled, or the driver is disqualified from operating a CMV.	One year	Not applicable
(8) Causing a fatality through the negligent operation of a CMV, including but not limited to the crimes of motor vehicle manslaughter, homicide by motor vehicle, and negligent homicide.	One year	Not applicable
(9) Using the vehicle in the commission of a felony involving manufacturing, distributing, or dispensing a controlled substance.	Life—not eligible for ten-year reinstatement	Life—not eligible for ten-year reinstatement

Table 7-1
(continued)

For a first conviction or refusal to be tested while operating a CMV transporting hazardous materials required to be placarded under the Hazardous Materials Regulations (49 CFR part 172, subpart F), a person required to have a CDL and CDL holder must be disqualified from operating a CMV for:	For a second conviction or refusal to be tested in a separate incident of any combination of offenses in this table while operating a CMV, a person required to have a CDL and a CDL holder must be disqualified from operating a CMV for:	For a second conviction or refusal to be tested in a separate incident of any combination of offenses in this table while operating a non-CMV, a CDL holder must be disqualified from operating a CMV for:
Three years	Life	Life
Three years	Life	Life
Three years	Life	Not applicable
Three years	Life	Life
Three years	Life	Life
Three years	Life	Life
Three years	Life	Not applicable
Three years	Life	Not applicable
Life—not eligible for ten-year reinstatement	Life—not eligible for ten-year reinstatement	Life—not eligible for ten-year reinstatement

Table 7-2
List of Serious Traffic Violations and Periods of Driver Disqualification

If a driver operates a motor vehicle and is convicted of:	For a second conviction of any combination of offenses in this table in a separate incident within a three-year period while operating a CMV, a person required to have a CDL and a CDL holder must be disqualified from operating a CMV for:	For a second conviction of any combination of offenses in this table in a separate incident within a three-year period while operating a non-CMV, a CDL holder must be disqualified from operating a CMV, if the conviction results in the revocation, cancellation, or suspension of the CDL holder's license or non-CMV driving privileges for:
(1) Speeding excessively, involving any speed of 24.1 kmph (15 mph) or more above the posted speed limit.	60 days	60 days
(2) Driving recklessly, as defined by state or local law or regulation, including but not limited to, offenses of driving a motor vehicle in willful or wanton disregard for the safety of persons or property.	60 days	60 days
(3) Making improper or erratic traffic lane changes.	60 days	60 days
(4) Following the vehicle ahead too closely.	60 days	60 days
(5) Violating state or local law relating to motor vehicle traffic control (other than a parking violation) arising in connection with a fatal accident.	60 days	60 days
(6) Driving a CMV without obtaining a CDL.	60 days	60 days
(7) Driving a CMV without a CDL in the driver's possession.[1]	60 days	Not applicable
(8) Driving a CMV without the proper class of CDL and/or endorsements for the specific vehicle group being operated or for the passengers or type of cargo being transported.	60 days	Not applicable

[1]Any individual who provides proof to the enforcement authority that issued the citation, by the date the individual must appear in court or pay any fine for such a violation, that the individual held a valid CDL on the date the citation was issued, shall not be guilty of this offense.

Table 7-2
(continued)

For a third or subsequent conviction of any combination of offenses in this table in a separate incident within a three-year period while operating a CMV, a person required to have a CDL and a CDL holder must be disqualified from operating a CMV for:	For a third or subsequent conviction of any combination of offenses in this table in a separate incident within a three-year period while operating a non-CMV, a CDL holder must be disqualified from operating a CMV, if the conviction results in the revocation, cancellation, or suspension of the CDL holder's license or non-CMV driving privileges for:
120 days	120 days
120 days	120 days
120 days	120 days
120 days	120 days
120 days	120 days
120 days	Not applicable
120 days	Not applicable
120 days	Not applicable

Table 7-3
List of Railroad-Highway Offenses and Periods of Driver Disqualification

If a driver is convicted of operating a CMV in violation of a federal, state, or local law because:	For a first conviction, a person required to have a CDL and a CDL holder must be disqualified from operating a CMV for:	For a second conviction of any combination of offenses in this table in a separate incident within a three-year period a person required to have a CDL and a CDL holder must be disqualified from operating a CMV for:	For a third or subsequent conviction of any combination of offenses in this table in a separate incident within a three-year period a person required to have a CDL and a CDL holder must be disqualified from operating a CMV for:
(1) The driver is not required to always stop, but fails to slow down and check that tracks are clear of an approaching train.	No less than 60 days	No less than 120 days	No less than one year
(2) The driver is not required to always stop, but fails to stop before reaching the crossing, if the tracks are not clear.	No less than 60 days	No less than 120 days	No less than one year
(3) The driver is always required to stop, but fails to stop before driving onto the crossing.	No less than 60 days	No less than 120 days	No less than one year
(4) The driver fails to have sufficient space to drive completely through the crossing without stopping.	No less than 60 days	No less than 120 days	No less than one year
(5) The driver fails to obey a traffic control device or the directions of an enforcement official at the crossing.	No less than 60 days	No less than 120 days	No less than one year
(6) The driver fails to negotiate a crossing because of insufficient undercarriage clearance.	No less than 60 days	No less than 120 days	No less than one year

- A list of all violations of motor vehicle laws or ordinances (other than violations involving only parking) of which the applicant was convicted during the three years preceding the date the application is submitted
- A statement detailing the facts and circumstances of any denial, revocation, or suspension of any license, permit, or privilege to operate a motor vehicle that has been issued to the applicant, or a statement that no such denial, revocation, or suspension has occurred

Table 7-4
List of Out-of-Service Order Violations and Periods of Driver Disqualification

If a driver operates a CMV and is convicted of:	For a first conviction while operating a CMV, a person required to have a CDL and a CDL holder must be disqualified from operating a CMV for:	For a second conviction in a separate incident within a ten-year period while operating a CMV, a person required to have a CDL and a CDL holder must be disqualified from operating a CMV for:	For a third or subsequent conviction in a separate incident within a ten-year period while operating a CMV, a person required to have a CDL and a CDL holder must be disqualified from operating a CMV for:
(1) Violating a driver or vehicle out-of-service order while transporting nonhazardous materials.	No less than 90 days or more than one year	No less than one year or more than five years	No less than three years or more than five years
(2) Violating a driver or vehicle out-of-service order while transporting hazardous materials required to be placarded under part 172, subpart F of this title, or while operating a vehicle designed to transport 16 or more passengers, including the driver.	No less than 180 days or more than two years	No less than three years or more than five years	No less than three years or more than five years

- A list of the names and addresses of the applicant's employers during the three years preceding the date the application is submitted and the dates he was employed by those employers
- The reason for leaving the employ of that employer
- For those drivers applying to operate a commercial motor vehicle, a list of the names and addresses of the applicant's employers during the seven-year period preceding the three years for which the applicant was an operator of a commercial motor vehicle, together with the dates of employment and the reasons for leaving such employment

The following certification and signature line must appear at the end of the application form and be signed by the applicant: This certifies that this application was completed by me, and that all entries on it and information in it are true and complete to the best of my knowledge.

_____   _____

(Date)   (Applicant's signature)

Before an application is submitted, the motor carrier must inform the applicant that the information he has provided may be used, and that the applicant's previous employers will be contacted, for the purpose of investigating the applicant's safety performance history information. The prospective employer must also notify the driver in writing of his due process rights of denial and appeal regarding information received as a result of these investigations.

§391.23 Investigation and Inquiries

Each motor carrier shall make the following investigations and inquiries with respect to each driver it employs:

- An inquiry into the driver's driving record during the preceding three years to the appropriate agency of every state in which the driver held a motor vehicle operator's license or permit during those three years
- An investigation of the driver's safety performance history with Department of Transportation (DOT)–regulated employers during the preceding three years

A copy of the driver record(s) obtained in response to the inquiry or inquiries to each state driver record agency must be placed in the driver qualification file within 30 days of the date the driver's employment begins and be retained.

If no driving record exists from the state or states, the motor carrier must document a good-faith effort to obtain such information and certify that no record exists for that driver in that state. The inquiry to the state driver record agencies must be made in the form and manner each agency prescribes.

Replies to the investigations of the driver's safety performance history or documentation of good-faith efforts to obtain the investigation data must be placed in the driver investigation history file within 30 days of the date the driver's employment begins.

Any period of time required to exercise the driver's due process rights to review the information received, request a previous employer to correct or include a rebuttal, is separate and apart from this 30-day requirement to document investigation of the driver safety performance history data.

This investigation may consist of personal interviews, telephone interviews, letters, or any other method for investigating that the carrier deems appropriate. Each motor carrier must make a written record of each previous employer contacted, or good-faith efforts to do so.

The record must include the previous employer's name and address, the date the previous employer was contacted, or the attempts made, and the information received about the driver from the previous employer. Failures to contact a previous employer, or of them to provide the required safety performance history information, must be documented.

Prospective employers should report the failures of previous employers to respond to an investigation to the FMCSA and keep a copy of such reports in the driver investigation file as part of documenting a good-faith effort to obtain the required information.

Exception. For drivers with no previous employment experience working for a DOT-regulated employer during the preceding three years, documentation that no investigation was possible must be placed in the driver history investigation file within the required 30 days of the date the driver's employment begins.

The prospective motor carrier must investigate, at a minimum, the information listed in this paragraph from all previous employers of the applicant that employed the driver to operate a CMV within the previous three years. The investigation request must contain specific contact information on where the previous motor carrier employers should send the information requested. This information must include:

- General driver identification and employment verification information
- Information about accidents involving the driver that occurred in the three-year period preceding the date of the employment application
- Any accidents the previous employer may wish to provide

In addition to the investigations required, the prospective motor carrier employer must investigate the information from all previous DOT-regulated employers that employed the driver (within the previous three years from the date of the employment application) in a safety-sensitive function that required alcohol and controlled substance testing, including:

- Whether, within the previous three years, the driver had violated the alcohol and controlled substances prohibitions.
- Whether the driver failed to undertake or complete a rehabilitation program prescribed by a substance abuse professional (SAP). If the previous employer does not know this information (for example, an employer that terminated an employee who tested positive on a drug test), the prospective motor carrier must obtain documentation of the driver's successful completion of the SAP's referral directly from the driver.
- For a driver who had successfully completed a SAP's rehabilitation referral, and remained in the employ of the referring employer, information on whether the driver had any testing violations subsequent to completion of the rehab program.

A prospective motor carrier employer must provide to the previous employer the driver's written consent for the release of information. If the driver refuses to provide this written consent, the prospective motor carrier employer must not permit the driver to operate a commercial motor vehicle for that motor carrier.

Previous employers must also:

- Respond to each request for the DOT-defined information within 30 days of receiving the request. If there is no safety performance history information to report for that driver, previous motor carrier employers are nonetheless required to send a response confirming the nonexistence of any such data, including the driver identification information and dates of employment.
- Take all precautions reasonably necessary to ensure the accuracy of the records.
- Provide specific contact information in case a driver chooses to contact the previous employer regarding correction or rebuttal of the data.
- Keep a record of each request and the response for one year, including the date, the party to whom it was released, and a summary identifying what was provided.

The release of information under this section may take any form that reasonably ensures confidentiality, including letter, facsimile, or e-mail. The previous employer and its agents and insurers must take all precautions reasonably necessary to protect the driver safety performance history records from disclosure to any person not directly involved in forwarding the records, except the previous employer's insurer; however, the previous employer may not provide any alcohol or controlled substances information to the previous employer's insurer.

The prospective employer must notify drivers with DOT-regulated employment during the preceding three years that he has the following rights regarding the investigative information that will be provided to the prospective employer:

- The right to review information provided by previous employers.
- The right to have errors in the information corrected by the previous employer and for that previous employer to resend the corrected information to the prospective employer.
- The right to have a rebuttal statement attached to the alleged erroneous information, if the previous employer and the driver cannot agree on the accuracy of the information.

Drivers who have a previous DOT-regulated employment history in the preceding three years, and wish to review previous employer-provided investigative information must submit a written request to the prospective employer, which may be done at any time, including when applying, or as late as 30 days after being employed or being notified of denial of employment.

The prospective employer must provide this information to the applicant within five business days of receiving the written request. If the prospective employer has not yet received the requested information from the previous employer(s), then the five-business-days deadline will begin when the prospective employer receives the requested safety performance history information.

If the driver has not arranged to pick up or receive the requested records within 30 days of the prospective employer making them available, the prospective motor carrier may consider the driver to have waived his request to review the records.

Drivers wishing to request the correction of erroneous information in records received must send the request for the correction to the previous employer that provided the records to the prospective employer.

The previous employer must either correct and forward the information to the prospective motor carrier employer, or notify the driver within 15 days of receiving a driver's request to correct the data that it does not agree to correct the data.

If the previous employer corrects and forwards the data as requested, that employer must also retain the corrected information as part of the driver's safety performance history record and provide it to subsequent prospective employers when requests for this information are received. If the previous employer corrects the data and forwards it to the prospective motor carrier employer, there is no need to notify the driver.

- Drivers wishing to rebut information in records received must send the rebuttal to the previous employer with instructions to include the rebuttal in that driver's safety performance history.
- Within five business days of receiving a rebuttal from a driver, the previous employer must:
  - Forward a copy of the rebuttal to the prospective motor carrier employer.
  - Append the rebuttal to the driver's information in the carrier's appropriate file, to be included as part of the response for any subsequent investigating

prospective employers for the duration of the three-year data retention requirement.

The driver may submit a rebuttal initially without a request for correction, or subsequent to a request for correction.

The driver may report to the FMCSA the failures of previous employers to correct information or include the driver's rebuttal as part of the safety performance information.

The prospective motor carrier employer must use this information only as part of deciding whether to hire the driver. The employer must take all precautions reasonably necessary to protect the records from disclosure to any person not directly involved in deciding whether to hire the driver. The prospective motor carrier employer may not provide any alcohol or controlled substances information to the prospective motor carrier employer's insurer.

§391.25 Annual Inquiry and Review of Driving Record

Each motor carrier shall, at least once every 12 months, make an inquiry into the driving record of each driver it employs, covering at least the preceding 12 months, to the appropriate agency of every state in which the driver held a commercial motor vehicle operator's license or permit during the time period.

At least once every 12 months, motor carriers should review the driving record of each driver it employs to determine whether that driver meets the minimum requirements for safe driving or is disqualified to drive a commercial motor vehicle. In this review, the employer must consider any evidence that the driver has violated any applicable Federal Motor Carrier Safety Regulations or Hazardous Materials Regulations.

The motor carrier must consider the driver's accident record and any evidence that the driver has violated laws governing the operation of motor vehicles, and must give great weight to violations, such as speeding, reckless driving, and operating while under the influence of alcohol or drugs, that indicate that the driver has exhibited a disregard for the safety of the public.

§391.27 Record of Violations

Each motor carrier shall, at least once every 12 months, require each driver it employs to prepare and furnish it with a list of all violations of motor vehicle traffic laws and ordinances (other than violations involving only parking) of which the driver has been convicted or on account of which he has forfeited bond or collateral during the preceding 12 months.

- Each driver shall furnish the list required. If the driver has not been convicted of, or forfeited bond or collateral on account of, any violation which must be listed he shall so certify.
- The form of the driver's list or certification shall be prescribed by the motor carrier. The following form may be used to comply with this section.

§391.27 Record of Violations

Driver's Certification

I certify that the following is a true and complete list of traffic violations (other than parking violations) for which I have been convicted or forfeited bond or collateral during the past 12 months.	
Date of conviction	Offense
Location	Type of motor vehicle operated
If no violations are listed above, I certify that I have not been convicted or forfeited bond or collateral on account of any violation required to be listed during the past 12 months.	
(Date of certification)	(Drivers signature)
(Motor carrier's name)	
(Motor carrier's address)	
(Reviewed by: Signature)	(Title)

The motor carrier shall retain the list or certificate or a copy of it, in its files as part of the driver's qualification file.

Drivers who have provided information need not repeat that information in the annual list of violations required by this section.

Subpart D—Tests

§391.31 Road Test

A person shall not drive a commercial motor vehicle unless he has first successfully completed a road test and has been issued a certificate of driver's road test.

The road test shall be given by the motor carrier or a person designated by it. However, a driver who is a motor carrier must be given the test by a person other than himself.

The test shall be given by a person who is competent to evaluate and determine whether the person who takes the test demonstrates that he is capable of operating the commercial motor vehicle and any associated equipment the motor carrier intends to assign him.

As a minimum, the person who takes the road test must be tested on his skill at performing each of the following operations:

- The pre-trip inspection
- The coupling and uncoupling of combination units if the equipment he may drive includes combination units
- Placing the commercial motor vehicle in operation
- Use of the commercial motor vehicle's controls and emergency equipment
- Operating the commercial motor vehicle in traffic and while passing other motor vehicles
- Turning the commercial motor vehicle
- Braking, and slowing the commercial motor vehicle by means other than braking
- Backing up and parking the commercial vehicle

The motor carrier shall provide a road test form on which the person who gives the test shall rate the performance of the person who takes it at each operation or activity which is a part of the test. After he completes the form, the person who gave the test shall sign it.

If the road test is successfully completed, the person who gave it shall complete a certificate of the driver's road test. The form for the certificate of the driver's road test is essentially as follows:

Certification of Road Test

Driver's name

Social Security No.

Operator's or Chauffeur's License No.

State

Type of power unit   Type of trailer(s)

If passenger carrier, type of bus

This is to certify that the above-named driver was given a road test under my supervision on _____, 20_____, consisting of approximately _____ miles of driving.

It is considered my opinion that this driver possesses sufficient driving skills to operate safely the type of commercial motor vehicle listed above.

(Signature of examiner)

(Title)

(Organization and address of examiner)

A copy of the certificate shall be given to the person who was examined. The motor carrier shall retain the certificate in the driver qualification file of the person who was examined.

§391.33 Equivalent of Road Test

In place of, and as equivalent to, the road test required, a person who seeks to drive a commercial motor vehicle may present, and a motor carrier may accept:

- A valid Commercial Driver's License, which has been issued to him to operate specific categories of commercial motor vehicles and which, under the laws of that state, licenses him after the successful completion of a road test in a commercial motor vehicle of the type the motor carrier intends to assign to him; or
- A copy of a valid certificate of a driver's road test issued to him within the preceding three years.
- If a driver presents, and a motor carrier accepts, a license or certificate as equivalent to the road test, the motor carrier shall retain a legible copy of the license or certificate in its files as part of the driver's qualification file.

A motor carrier may require any person who presents a license or certificate as equivalent to the road test to take a road test or any other test of his/her driving skill as a condition to his employment as a driver.

Subpart E—Physical Qualifications and Examinations

§391.41 Physical Qualifications for Drivers

A person shall not drive a commercial motor vehicle unless he is physically qualified to do so and has on his person the original, or a photographic copy, of a medical examiner's certificate that he is physically qualified to drive a commercial motor vehicle.

The United States and Canada entered into a Reciprocity Agreement, effective March 30, 1999, recognizing that a Canadian commercial driver's license is proof of medical fitness to drive. Therefore, Canadian commercial motor vehicle (CMV) drivers are no longer required to have in their possession a medical examiner's certificate if the driver has been issued, and possesses, a valid Commercial Driver's License issued by a Canadian Province or Territory.

However, Canadian drivers who are insulin-using diabetics, who have epilepsy, or who are hearing impaired are not qualified to drive CMVs in the United States. Furthermore, Canadian drivers who do not meet the medical fitness provisions of the Canadian National Safety Code for Motor Carriers but who have been issued a waiver by one of the Canadian Provinces or Territories are not qualified to drive CMVs in the United States.

A person is physically qualified to drive a CMV if that person:

- Has no loss of a foot, a leg, a hand, or an arm, or has been granted a skill performance evaluation certificate
- Has no impairment of:
  - A hand or finger that interferes with prehension or power grasping
  - An arm, foot, or leg that interferes with the ability to perform normal tasks associated with operating a CMV, any other significant limb defect or limitation that interferes with the ability to perform normal tasks associated with operating a CMV or has been granted a skill performance evaluation certificate

- Has no established medical history or clinical diagnosis of diabetes mellitus currently requiring insulin for control
- Has no current clinical diagnosis of heart attack, recurring chest pain, coronary insufficiency, recurrent blood clots, or any other cardiovascular disease of a variety known to be accompanied by syncope, dyspnea, collapse, or congestive cardiac failure
- Has no established medical history or clinical diagnosis of a respiratory dysfunction likely to interfere with his ability to control and drive a CMV safely
- Has no current clinical diagnosis of high blood pressure likely to interfere with his ability to operate a CMV safely
- Has no established medical history or clinical diagnosis of rheumatic, arthritic, orthopedic, muscular, neuromuscular, or vascular disease which interferes with his ability to control and operate a CMV safely
- Has no established medical history or clinical diagnosis of epilepsy or any other condition which is likely to cause loss of consciousness or any loss of ability to control a CMV
- Has no mental, nervous, organic, or functional disease or psychiatric disorder likely to interfere with his ability to drive a commercial motor vehicle safely
- Has distant visual acuity of at least 20/40 (Snellen) in each eye without corrective lenses or visual acuity separately corrected to 20/40 (Snellen) or better with corrective lenses, distant binocular acuity of at least 20/40 (Snellen) in both eyes with or without corrective lenses, a field of vision of at least 70 degrees in the horizontal meridian in each eye, and the ability to recognize the colors of traffic signals and devices showing standard red, green, and amber
- First perceives a forced whispered voice in the better ear at not less than five feet with or without the use of a hearing aid or, if tested by use of an audiometric device, does not have an average hearing loss in the better ear greater than 40 decibels at 500Hz, 1,000Hz, and 2,000Hz with or without a hearing aid when the audiometric device is calibrated to American National Standard (formerly ASA Standard) Z24.5-1951
- Does not use a controlled substance, an amphetamine, a narcotic, or any other habit-forming drug

Exception. A driver may use a particular substance or drug, if the substance or drug is prescribed by a licensed medical practitioner who:

- Is familiar with the driver's medical history and assigned duties
- Has advised the driver that the prescribed substance or drug will not adversely affect the driver's ability to safely operate a commercial motor vehicle
- Has no current clinical diagnosis of alcoholism

§391.45 Persons Who Must Be Medically Examined and Certified

The following persons must be medically examined and certified as physically qualified to operate a commercial motor vehicle:

- Any person who has not been medically examined and certified as physically qualified to operate a commercial motor vehicle.

- Any driver who has not been medically examined and certified as qualified to operate a commercial motor vehicle during the preceding 24 months.
- Any driver authorized to operate a commercial motor vehicle only with an exempt intracity zone or only if the driver has not been medically examined and certified as qualified to drive in such a zone during the preceding 12 months.
- Any driver whose ability to perform his normal duties has been impaired by a physical or mental injury or disease.

§391.47 Resolution of Conflicts of Medical Evaluation

Applications

Applications for determination of a driver's medical qualifications under standards in this part will only be accepted if they conform to the requirements of this section.

Content

Applications will be accepted for consideration only if the following conditions are met:

1. The application must contain the name and address of the driver, motor carrier, and all physicians involved in the proceeding.
2. The applicant must submit proof that there is a disagreement between the physician for the driver and the physician for the motor carrier concerning the driver's qualifications.
3. The applicant must submit a copy of an opinion and report including results of all tests by an impartial medical specialist in the field in which the medical conflict arose. The specialist should be one agreed to by the motor carrier and the driver.

   A. When the driver refuses to agree on a specialist, and the applicant is the motor carrier, the applicant must submit a statement of his agreement to submit the matter to an impartial medical specialist in the field, proof that he has requested the driver to submit to the medical specialist, and the response, if any, of the driver to his request.

   B. If the motor carrier refuses to agree on a medical specialist, the driver must submit the opinion and test results of an impartial medical specialist, proof that he has requested the motor carrier to agree to submit the matter to the medical specialist, and the response, if any, of the motor carrier to his request.

4. The applicant must include a statement explaining in detail why the decision of the medical specialist is unacceptable.
5. The applicant must submit proof that the medical specialist was provided, prior to his determination, the medical history of the driver and an agreed upon statement of the work the driver performs.
6. The applicant must submit the medical history and statement of work provided to the medical specialist.
7. The applicant must submit all medical records and statements of the physicians who have given opinions on the driver's qualifications.

8. The applicant must submit a description and a copy of all written and documentary evidence upon which the party making application relies in the specified form.
9. The application must be accompanied by a statement of the driver that he intends to drive in interstate commerce not subject to the commercial zone exemption or a statement of the carrier that he has used or intends to use the driver for such work.
10. The applicant must submit three copies of the application and all records.

Information

The Director, Office of Bus and Truck Standards and Operations (MC-PSD), may request further information from the applicant if he determines that a decision cannot be made on the evidence submitted. If the applicant fails to submit the information requested, the Director of the Office of Bus and Truck Standards and Operations may refuse to issue a determination.

Action

Upon receiving a satisfactory application, the Director, Office of Bus and Truck Standards and Operations (MC-PSD), shall notify the parties (the driver, motor carrier, or any other interested party) that the application has been accepted and that a determination will be made. A copy of all evidence received shall be attached to the notice.

Reply

Any party may submit a reply to the notification within 15 days after service. Such reply must be accompanied by all evidence the party wants the Director, Office of Bus and Truck Standards and Operations (MC-PSD), to consider in making his determination. Evidence submitted should include all medical records and test results upon which the party relies.

Parties

A "party" is defined as the motor carrier and the driver, or anyone else submitting an application.

Petitions to Review, Burden of Proof

The driver or motor carrier may petition to review the Director's determination. Such petition must be submitted in accordance with the directions of this chapter, and the burden of proof in such a proceeding is on the petitioner.

Status of Driver

Once an application is submitted to the Director, Office of Bus and Truck Standards and Operations (MC-PSD), the driver shall be deemed disqualified until such time as the Director, Office of Bus and Truck Standards and Operations (MC-PSD), makes a determination, or until the Director, Office of Bus and Truck Standards and Operations (MC-PSD), orders otherwise.

§391.49 Alternative Physical Qualification Standards for the Loss or Impairment of Limbs

A person who is not physically qualified to drive and who is otherwise qualified to drive a commercial motor vehicle, may drive a commercial motor vehicle, if the Division Administrator, FMCSA, has granted a Skill Performance Evaluation (SPE) Certificate to that person.

SPE Certificate

Application. A letter of application for an SPE certificate may be submitted jointly by the person (driver applicant) who seeks an SPE certificate and by the motor carrier that will employ the driver applicant, if the application is accepted.

Application Address. The application must be addressed to the applicable field service center, FMCSA, for the state in which the co-applicant motor carrier's principal place of business is located.

Exception. A letter of application for an SPE certificate may be submitted unilaterally by a driver applicant. The application must be addressed to the field service center, FMCSA, for the state in which the driver has legal residence. The driver applicant must comply with all the requirements. The driver applicant shall respond to the requirements if the information is known.

A Letter of Application for an SPE Certificate

A letter of application for an SPE certificate should contain:

1. The identification of the applicant(s):
   * The name and complete address of the motor carrier coapplicant
   * The name and complete address of the driver applicant
   * The U.S. DOT Motor Carrier Identification Number, if known
   * A description of the driver applicant's limb impairment for which an SPE certificate is requested

2. A description of the type of operation the driver will be employed to perform:
   * State(s) in which the driver will operate for the motor carrier coapplicant (if more than ten states, designate general geographic area only)
   * Average period of time the driver will be driving and/or on duty, per day
   * Type of commodities or cargo to be transported
   * Type of driver operation (such as sleeper team, relay, owner operator, and so on)
   * Number of years experience operating the type of commercial motor vehicle(s) requested in the letter of application and the total years of experience operating all types of commercial motor vehicles

3. Description of the commercial motor vehicle(s) the driver applicant intends to drive:
   * Truck, truck tractor, or bus make, model, and year (if known)
   * Drive train
   * Transmission type (automatic or manual—if manual, designate the number of forward speeds)

- Auxiliary transmission (if any) and number of forward speeds
- Rear axle (designate single speed, two-speed, or three-speed)
- Type of brake system
- Steering—manual or power assisted
- Description of the type of trailer(s) (such as van, flatbed, cargo tank, drop frame, lowboy, or pole)
- Number of semitrailers or full trailers to be towed at one time
- For commercial motor vehicles designed to transport passengers, indicate the seating capacity of the commercial motor vehicle
- Description of any modification(s) made to the commercial motor vehicle for the driver applicant; attach photograph(s) where applicable

4. How the driver applicant is otherwise qualified:

- The coapplicant motor carrier must certify that the driver applicant is otherwise qualified under the current regulations.
- In the case of a unilateral application, the driver applicant must certify that he is otherwise qualified under the regulations.

5. Signature of applicant(s):

- The driver applicant's signature and the date signed
- Motor carrier official's signature (if application has a coapplicant), the title, and date signed
- Depending upon the motor carrier's organizational structure (corporation, partnership, or proprietorship), the signer of the application shall be an officer, partner, or the proprietor

The letter of application for an SPE certificate shall be accompanied by:

1. A copy of the results of the medical examination

2. A copy of the medical certificate

3. A medical evaluation summary completed by either a board-qualified or board-certified psychiatrist (doctor of physical medicine) or orthopedic surgeon. The coapplicant motor carrier or the driver applicant shall provide the psychiatrist or orthopedic surgeon with a description of the job-related tasks the driver applicant will be required to perform

The medical evaluation summary for a disqualified driver applicant should include:

1. An assessment of the functional capabilities of the driver as they relate to the driver's ability to perform normal tasks associated with operating a commercial motor vehicle

2. A statement by the examiner that the applicant is capable of demonstrating precision knowledge and operational ability, such as manipulating knobs and switches, prehension, and power grasp (for example, holding and maneuvering the steering wheel) with each upper limb separately. This requirement does not apply to an individual who was granted a waiver, absent a prosthetic device, prior to the publication of this amendment

8 FMCSR—Parts 392, 393, 395, and 396

The Federal Motor Carrier Safety Administration has developed rules that govern every professional driver of commercial motor vehicles. These rules can be found in their entirety at http://fmcsa.dot.gov on the Internet.

These rules are presented for your review and understanding.

FMCSR Part 392—Driving Motor Vehicles

Subpart A—General

§392.1 Scope of the Rules in this Part

Every motor carrier and its employees responsible for the management, maintenance, operation, or driving of commercial motor vehicles, or the hiring, supervising, training, assigning, or dispatching of drivers, shall be instructed in, and comply with, these rules.

§392.2 Applicable Operating Rules

Every commercial motor vehicle must be operated in accordance with the laws, ordinances, and regulations of the state in which it is being operated. However, if a regulation of the Federal Motor Carrier Safety Administration imposes a higher standard than the state law, the Federal Motor Carrier Safety Administration regulation must be complied with.

§392.3 Ill or Fatigued Operator

No driver shall operate a motor vehicle, and a commercial motor carrier shall not require or permit a driver to operate a commercial motor vehicle, while the driver's ability or alertness is impaired through fatigue, illness, or any other cause, as to make it unsafe for her to operate the commercial motor vehicle.

OTR SAFETY
In a case of a grave emergency where the hazard to occupants of the commercial motor vehicle or other users of the highway would be increased by compliance with this section, the driver may continue to operate the commercial motor vehicle to the nearest place at which that hazard is removed.

§392.4 Drugs and Other Substances

No driver shall be on duty and possess, be under the influence of, or use, any of the following drugs or other substances:

- Any 21 CFR 1308.11 Schedule I substance
- An amphetamine or any formulation thereof (including, but not limited, to "pep pills," and "bennies")
- A narcotic drug or any derivative thereof
- Any other substance which renders the driver incapable of safely operating a motor vehicle

No motor carrier shall require or permit a driver to violate these rules. The exception is the driver who has a prescription to take these from a licensed medical practitioner, and may do so as long as it does not affect the driver's ability to safely operate a motor vehicle.

§392.5 Alcohol Prohibition

No driver shall:

- Use alcohol, or be under the influence of alcohol, within four hours of going on duty or operating, or having physical control of, a commercial motor vehicle.
- Use alcohol, be under the influence of alcohol, or have any measured alcohol concentration or detected presence of alcohol, while on duty, or operating, or in physical control of a commercial motor vehicle.
- Be on duty or operate a commercial motor vehicle while the driver possesses wine, beer, and distilled spirits. However, this does not apply to the possession of wine, beer, or distilled spirits which are:
  - Manifested and transported as part of a shipment
  - Possessed or used by bus passengers

No motor carrier shall require or permit a driver to:

- Violate any provision of this section, or
- Be on duty or operate a commercial motor vehicle if, by the driver's general appearance or conduct or by other substantiating evidence, the driver appears to have used alcohol within the preceding four hours

Any driver who is found to be in violation of the provisions of this section shall be placed out-of-service immediately for a period of 24 hours.

- The 24-hour out-of-service period will commence upon issuance of an out-of-service order.
- No driver shall violate the terms of an out-of-service order issued under this section.

Any driver who is issued an out-of-service order under this section shall:

- Report such issuance to her employer within 24 hours, and
- Report such issuance to a state official, designated by the state that issued her driver's license, within 30 days unless the driver chooses to request a review of the order. In this case, the driver shall report the order to the state official within 30 days of an affirmation of the order by either the Division

Administrator or State Director for the geographical area for the region or the Administrator.

Any driver who is subject to an out-of-service order under this section may petition for review of that order by submitting a petition for review in writing within ten days of the issuance of the order to the Division Administrator or State Director for the region in which the order was issued. The Division Administrator or State Director may affirm or reverse the order. Any driver adversely affected by such order of the Division Administrator or State Director may petition the Administrator for review.

§392.6 Schedules to Conform with Speed Limits

No motor carrier shall schedule nor require the operation of any commercial motor vehicle between points in such a period of time as would necessitate the commercial motor vehicle being operated at speeds greater than those prescribed by the jurisdictions in or through which the commercial motor vehicle is being operated.

§392.7 Equipment—Inspection and Use

No commercial motor vehicle shall be driven unless the driver is satisfied that the following parts and accessories are in good working order. Nor shall any driver fail to use or make use of such parts and accessories when and as needed:

- Service brakes, including trailer brake connections
- Parking (hand) brake
- Steering mechanism
- Lighting devices and reflectors
- Tires
- Horn
- Windshield wiper or wipers
- Rear-vision mirror or mirrors
- Coupling devices

§392.8 Emergency Equipment—Inspection and Use

No commercial motor vehicle shall be driven unless the driver thereof is satisfied that the required emergency equipment is in place and ready for use. Nor shall any driver fail to use or make use of such equipment when and as needed (see Figure 8-1).

§392.9 Inspection of Cargo, Cargo Securement Devices, and Systems

General. A driver may not operate a commercial motor vehicle, and a motor carrier may not require or permit a driver to operate a commercial motor vehicle unless:

- The commercial motor vehicle's cargo is properly distributed and adequately secured as specified by the rulings in 393.100 through 393.142 of this subchapter.

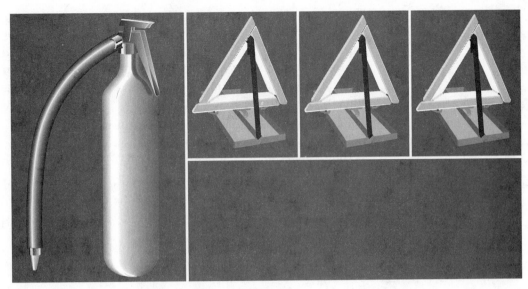

Figure 8-1   Emergency and safety equipment.

- The commercial motor vehicle's tailgate, tailboard, doors, tarpaulins, spare tire, and other equipment used in its operation, and the means of fastening the commercial motor vehicle's cargo, are secured.
- The commercial motor vehicle's cargo or any other object does not obscure the driver's view ahead or to the right or left sides, does not interfere with the free movement of her arms or legs, prevents her free and ready access to accessories required for emergencies, or prevents the free and ready exit of any person from the commercial motor vehicle's cab or driver's compartment.

Drivers of Trucks and Truck Tractors. The driver of a truck or truck tractor must:

- Assure herself that the cargo is properly distributed and secured before she drives that commercial motor vehicle.
- Inspect the cargo and the devices used to secure the cargo within the first 50 miles after beginning a trip, and cause any adjustments to be made to the cargo or load securement devices as necessary, including adding more securement devices, to ensure that cargo cannot shift on or within, or fall from, the commercial motor vehicle (see Figure 8-2).

Figure 8-2   Cargo should have at least one tiedown for each 10 feet of cargo. The driver should reexamine cargo, and make adjustments to it, en route.

- Reexamine the commercial motor vehicle's cargo and its load securement devices during the course of transportation and make any necessary adjustment to the cargo or load securement devices, including adding more securement devices, to ensure that cargo cannot shift on or within, or fall from, the commercial motor vehicle. Reexamination and any necessary adjustments must be made whenever:
  - The driver makes a change of her duty status.
  - The commercial motor vehicle has been driven for three hours or 150 miles, whichever occurs first.

These rules do not apply to the driver of a sealed commercial motor vehicle who has been ordered not to open it to inspect its cargo, or to the driver of a commercial motor vehicle that has been loaded in a way that makes inspection of its cargo impracticable.

§392.9a Operating Authority

Registration Required. A motor vehicle providing transportation that requires registration under 49 U.S.C. 13902 may not be operated without the required registration or operated beyond the scope of its registration.

Penalties. Every motor vehicle providing transportation requiring registration under 49 U.S.C. 13902 shall be ordered out-of-service if determined to be operating without registration or beyond the scope of its registration. In addition, the motor carrier may be subject to penalties.

Administrative Review. Upon the issuance of the out-of-service order, the driver shall comply immediately with such order. Opportunity for review shall be provided not later than ten days after the issuance of such order.

Subpart B—Driving of Vehicles

§392.10 Railroad Grade Crossings; Stopping Required

The driver of a commercial motor vehicle shall not cross a railroad track or tracks at grade unless she first:

- Stops the commercial motor vehicle within 50 feet of, and not closer than 15 feet to, the tracks (see Figure 8-3)
- Listens and looks in each direction along the tracks for an approaching train
- Determines that no train is approaching

When it is safe to do so, the driver may drive the commercial motor vehicle across the tracks in a gear that permits the commercial motor vehicle to complete the crossing without a change of gears. The driver must not shift gears while crossing the tracks.

These rules apply to every bus transporting passengers, commercial motor vehicle transporting any quantity of a Division 2.3 chlorine, and every commercial motor vehicle which, in accordance with the regulations of the Department of Transportation, is required to be marked or placarded with a Hazardous Materials classification.

Figure 8-3   Stop within 50 feet of all railroad crossings.

To practice safety while driving, you should always stop at a rail crossing. However, FMCSR permit that similar stop-look-and-listen stops need not be made at:

- A streetcar crossing, or railroad tracks used exclusively for industrial switching purposes, within a business district.
- A railroad grade crossing when a police officer or crossing flagman directs traffic to proceed.
- A railroad grade crossing controlled by a functioning highway traffic signal transmitting a green indication which, under local law, permits the commercial motor vehicle to proceed across the railroad tracks without slowing or stopping.
- An abandoned railroad grade crossing which is marked with a sign indicating that the rail line is abandoned.
- An industrial or spur line railroad grade crossing marked with a sign reading "Exempt." Such "Exempt" signs shall be erected only by, or with, the consent of the appropriate state or local authority.

§392.11 Railroad Grade Crossings; Slowing Down Required

Every commercial motor vehicle shall, upon approaching a railroad grade crossing, be driven at a rate of speed which will permit said commercial motor vehicle to be stopped before reaching the nearest rail of such crossing and shall not be driven upon or over such crossing until due caution has been taken to ascertain that the course is clear.

§392.14 Hazardous Conditions; Extreme Caution

Extreme caution in the operation of a commercial motor vehicle shall be exercised when hazardous conditions, such as those caused by snow, ice, sleet, fog, mist, rain,

Figure 8-4 Professional drivers should reduce speed when driving in hazardous conditions.

dust, or smoke, adversely affect visibility or traction. Speed shall be reduced when such conditions exist (see Figure 8-4).

If conditions become sufficiently dangerous, the operation of the commercial motor vehicle shall be discontinued and shall not be resumed until the commercial motor vehicle can be safely operated. Whenever compliance with the foregoing provisions of this rule increases hazard to passengers, the commercial motor vehicle may be operated to the nearest point at which the safety of passengers is assured.

§392.16 Use of Seat Belts

A commercial motor vehicle which has a seat belt assembly installed at the driver's seat shall not be driven unless the driver has properly restrained herself with the seat belt assembly. If your vehicle does not have a seatbelt, it is unsafe to drive.

Subpart C—Stopped Vehicles

§392.22 Emergency Signals; Stopped Commercial Motor Vehicles

Four-Way Flashers. Whenever a commercial motor vehicle is stopped upon the traveled portion of a highway or the shoulder of a highway for any cause other than necessary traffic stops, the driver shall immediately activate the vehicular hazard warning signal flashers and continue the flashing until the required warning devices are in place. The flashing signals shall be used during the time the warning devices are picked up for storage before movement of the commercial motor vehicle. The flashing lights may be used at other times while a commercial motor vehicle is stopped in addition to, but not in lieu of, the required warning devices.

Placement of Warning Devices

General Rule—Whenever a commercial motor vehicle is stopped upon the traveled portion or the shoulder of a highway for any cause other than necessary traffic stops, the driver shall, as soon as possible, but in any event within ten minutes, place the required warning devices in the following manner:

1. One on the traffic side of, and four paces (approximately 3 meters or 10 feet) from, the stopped commercial motor vehicle in the direction of approaching traffic.
2. One at 40 paces (approximately 30 meters or 100 feet) from the stopped commercial motor vehicle in the center of the traffic lane or shoulder occupied by the commercial motor vehicle and in the direction of approaching traffic.
3. One at 40 paces (approximately 30 meters or 100 feet) from the stopped commercial motor vehicle in the center of the traffic lane or shoulder occupied by the commercial motor vehicle and in the direction away from approaching traffic. (See Figure 8-5.)

Special Rules

Daylight Hours. During the period lighted lamps are not required, three bidirectional reflective triangles, or three lighted fusees or liquid-burning flares shall be placed as specified within a time of ten minutes. In the event the driver elects to use only fusees or liquid-burning flares in lieu of bidirectional reflective triangles or red flags, the driver must ensure that at least one fusee or liquid-burning flare remains lighted at each of the prescribed locations as long as the commercial motor vehicle is stopped or parked.

Business or Residential Districts. The placement of warning devices is not required within the business or residential district of a municipality, except during the time

Figure 8-5   Properly placed reflective triangles will warn other drivers of the disabled vehicle.

lighted lamps are required and when street or highway lighting is insufficient to make a commercial motor vehicle clearly discernable at a distance of 500 feet to persons on the highway.

Hills, Curves, and Obstructions. If a commercial motor vehicle is stopped within 500 feet of a curve, crest of a hill, or other obstruction to view, the driver shall place the warning signal required in the direction of the obstruction to view a distance of 100 feet to 500 feet from the stopped commercial motor vehicle so as to afford ample warning to other users of the highway.

Divided or One-Way Roads. If a commercial motor vehicle is stopped upon the traveled portion or the shoulder of a divided or one-way highway, the driver shall place the warning devices required, one warning device at a distance of 200 feet and one warning device at a distance of 100 feet in a direction toward approaching traffic in the center of the lane or shoulder occupied by the commercial motor vehicle. She shall place one warning device at the traffic side of the commercial motor vehicle within 10 feet of the rear of the commercial motor vehicle.

Leaking, Flammable Material. If gasoline or any other flammable liquid, or any combustible liquid or gas, seeps or leaks from a fuel container or a commercial motor vehicle stopped upon a highway, no emergency warning signal producing a flame shall be lighted or placed except at such a distance from any such liquid or gas as will assure the prevention of a fire or explosion.

§392.24 Emergency Signals; Flame Producing

No driver shall attach or permit any person to attach a lighted fusee or other flame-producing emergency signal to any part of a commercial motor vehicle.

§392.25 Flame-Producing Devices

No driver shall use or permit the use of any flame-producing emergency signal for protecting any commercial motor vehicle transporting Division 1.1, Division 1.2, or Division 1.3 explosives; any cargo tank motor vehicle used for the transportation of any Class 3 or Division 2.1, whether loaded or empty; or any commercial motor vehicle using compressed gas as a motor fuel. In lieu thereof, emergency reflective triangles, red electric lanterns, or red emergency reflectors shall be used.

Subpart D—Use of Lighted Lamps and Reflectors

§392.33 Obscured Lamps or Reflective Devices/Material

No commercial motor vehicle shall be driven when any of the required lamps or reflective devices/material are obscured by the tailboard, or by any part of the load or its covering, by dirt, or other added vehicle or work equipment or otherwise.

Subpart F—Fueling Precautions

§392.50 Ignition of Fuel; Prevention

No driver or any employee of a motor carrier shall:

- Fuel a commercial motor vehicle with the engine running, except when it is necessary to run the engine to fuel the commercial motor vehicle;
- Smoke or expose any open flame in the vicinity of a commercial motor vehicle being fueled;
- Fuel a commercial motor vehicle unless the nozzle of the fuel hose is continuously in contact with the intake pipe of the fuel tank;
- Permit, insofar as practicable, any other person to engage in such activities as would be likely to result in fire or explosion.

Subpart G—Prohibited Practices

§392.60 Unauthorized Persons Not to Be Transported

Unless specifically authorized in writing by the motor carrier under whose authority the commercial motor vehicle is being operated, no driver shall transport any person or permit any person to be transported on any commercial motor vehicle other than a bus. When such authorization is issued, it shall state the name of the person to be transported, the points where the transportation is to begin and end, and the date upon which such authority expires. No written authorization, however, shall be necessary for the transportation of:

- Employees or other persons assigned to a commercial motor vehicle by a motor carrier;
- Any person transported when aid is being rendered in case of an accident or other emergency;
- An attendant delegated to care for livestock.

ROAD SENSE

This section shall not apply to the operation of commercial motor vehicles controlled and operated by any farmer and used in the transportation of agricultural commodities or products from her farm or in the transportation of supplies to her farm.

§392.62 Safe Operation, Buses

No person shall drive a bus, and a motor carrier shall not require or permit a person to drive a bus unless:

- All standees on the bus are rearward of the standee line.
- All aisle seats in the bus conform to the requirements.

- Baggage or freight on the bus is stowed and secured in a manner which assures:
  - Unrestricted freedom of movement to the driver and his proper operation of the bus.
  - Unobstructed access to all exits by any occupant of the bus.
  - Protection of occupants of the bus against injury resulting from the falling or displacement of articles transported in the bus.

§392.63 Towing or Pushing Loaded Buses

No disabled bus with passengers aboard shall be towed or pushed; nor shall any person use, or permit to be used, a bus with passengers aboard for the purpose of towing or pushing any disabled motor vehicle, except in such circumstances where the hazard to passengers would be increased by observance of the foregoing provisions of this section, and then only in traveling to the nearest point where the safety of the passengers is assured.

§392.64 Riding Within Closed Commercial Motor Vehicles Without Proper Exits

No person shall ride within the closed body of any commercial motor vehicle unless there are means on the inside thereof of obtaining exit. Said means shall be in such condition as to permit ready operation by the occupant.

§392.66 Carbon Monoxide; Use of Commercial Motor Vehicle When Detected

No person shall dispatch or drive any commercial motor vehicle, or permit any passengers thereon, when the following conditions are known to exist, until such conditions have been remedied or repaired:

- Where an occupant has been affected by carbon monoxide
- Where carbon monoxide has been detected in the interior of the commercial motor vehicle
- When a mechanical condition of the commercial motor vehicle is discovered which would be likely to produce a hazard to the occupants by reason of carbon monoxide

§392.67 Heater, Flame-Producing; on Commercial Vehicle in Motion

No open flame heater used in the loading or unloading of the commodity transported shall be in operation while the commercial motor vehicle is in motion.

§392.71 Radar Detectors—Use and/or Possession

No driver shall use a radar detector in a commercial motor vehicle, or operate a commercial motor vehicle that is equipped with, or contains any, radar detector. Further, no motor carrier shall require or permit a driver to use a radar detector.

FMCSR Part 395—Hours of Service of Drivers

This section of the Federal Motor Carriers Safety Regulations defines "Hours of Service" and requires all drivers to keep a Record of Duty Status. Included in this section are descriptions of adverse driving conditions, emergency conditions, and relief from regulations. It also covers drivers who have been taken "out of service." These regulations apply to all motor carriers and drivers, with few exceptions.

Unlike most other professions, driving has its own schedule. The workday does not end at 5 PM. Oftentimes, you won't start working at 8 AM.

Professional drivers are governed by what is known as "hours of service," and FMCSR Part 395 sets the limits of these hours.

The number of hours and the kind of work you perform during this time depends on the hours you worked the day before.

Every hour and every type of duty you do is recorded in a logbook, the "record of duty status." This record helps drivers stay within the legal limits.

If a driver encounters adverse driving conditions and cannot safely complete the run within the ten-hour maximum driving time permitted, the driver is permitted or required to drive a commercial motor vehicle for not more than two additional hours in order to complete that run or to reach a place offering safety for the occupants of the commercial motor vehicle, and security for that vehicle and its cargo.

Definitions to Remember

Adverse driving conditions are snow, sleet, fog, other adverse weather conditions, a highway covered with snow or ice, or unusual road and traffic conditions, none of which were apparent based on information known to the person dispatching the run at the time it was begun.

Automatic onboard recording device is an electric, electronic, electromechanical, or mechanical device capable of recording a driver's duty status information accurately and automatically. The device must be integrally synchronized with specific operations of the commercial motor vehicle in which it is installed. At minimum, the device must record engine use, road speed, miles driven, date, and time of day.

Driver salesperson is any employee who is employed solely as such by a private carrier of property by commercial motor vehicle, who is engaged both in selling goods, services, or the use of goods, and in delivering by commercial motor vehicle the goods sold or provided, or upon which the services are performed, who does so entirely within a radius of 100 miles of the point at which she reports for duty, and who devotes not more than 50 percent of her hours on duty to driving time.

Selling goods, for purposes of this section, shall include all cases of solicitation or the obtaining of reorders or new accounts, and may also include other selling or merchandising activities designed to retain the customer or to increase the sale of goods or services, in addition to solicitation or the obtaining of reorders or new accounts.

Driving time is all time spent at the driving controls of a commercial motor vehicle.

Eight consecutive days means the period of eight consecutive days beginning on any day at the time designated by the motor carrier for a 24-hour period.

Multiple stops means that all stops made in any one village, town, or city may be computed as one.

On-duty time means all time from the time a driver begins to work or is required to be in readiness to work until the time the driver is relieved from work. On-duty time includes:

- All time at a plant, terminal, facility, or other property of a motor carrier or shipper, or on any public property, waiting to be dispatched, unless the driver has been relieved from duty by the motor carrier.
- All time inspecting, servicing, or conditioning any commercial motor vehicle at any time.
- All driving time.
- All time, other than driving time, in or upon any commercial motor vehicle, except time spent resting in a sleeper berth.
- All time loading or unloading a commercial motor vehicle, supervising (or assisting in the loading or unloading), attending a commercial motor vehicle being loaded or unloaded, remaining in readiness to operate the commercial motor vehicle, or in giving or receiving receipts for shipments loaded or unloaded.
- All time repairing, obtaining assistance, or remaining in attendance upon a disabled commercial motor vehicle.
- All time spent providing a breath sample or urine specimen, including travel time to and from the collection site, in order to comply with the random, reasonable suspicion, post-accident, or follow-up testing required by a motor carrier.
- Performing any other work in the capacity, employ, or service of a motor carrier and performing any compensated work for a person who is not a motor carrier.

Seven consecutive days means the period of seven consecutive days beginning on any day at the time designated by the motor carrier for a 24-hour period.

Sleeper berth is a berth conforming to the requirements of FMCSR §393.76.

Transportation of construction materials and equipment means the transportation of construction and pavement materials, construction equipment, and construction maintenance vehicles by a driver to or from an active construction site (a construction site between the mobilization of equipment and materials to the site to the final completion of the construction project) within a 50 air-mile radius of the normal work reporting location of the driver.

Twenty-four-hour period means any 24 consecutive-hour period beginning at the time designated by the motor carrier at the terminal from which the driver is normally dispatched.

Utility service vehicle is any commercial motor vehicle used or designed to facilitate the work or transportation of utility workers.

§395.1 Scope of Rules in this Part

General

- The rules in this part apply to all motor carriers and drivers.
- The exceptions from federal requirements do not preempt state laws and regulations governing the safe operation of commercial motor vehicles.

Adverse Driving Conditions—a driver who encounters adverse driving conditions and cannot, because of those conditions, safely complete the run within the maximum driving time permitted:

- May drive and be permitted or required to drive a commercial motor vehicle for not more than two additional hours in order to complete that run or to reach a place offering safety for the occupants of the commercial motor vehicle, and security for the commercial motor vehicle and its cargo. However, that driver may not drive or be permitted to drive:
  - For more than 13 hours in the aggregate following 10 consecutive hours off duty for drivers of property-carrying commercial motor vehicles.
  - After the end of the 14th hour since coming on duty following 10 consecutive hours off duty for drivers of property-carrying commercial motor vehicles.
  - For more than 12 hours in the aggregate following eight consecutive hours off duty for drivers of passenger-carrying commercial motor vehicles.
  - After she has been on duty 15 hours following 8 consecutive hours off duty for drivers of passenger-carrying commercial motor vehicles.

Emergency Conditions—in case of any emergency, a driver may complete her run without being in violation of the provisions of the regulations in this part, if such a run reasonably could have been completed absent the emergency.

In the case of specially trained drivers of commercial motor vehicles that are specially constructed to service oil wells, on-duty time shall not include waiting time at a natural gas or oil well site—*provided* that all such time shall be fully and accurately accounted for in records maintained by the motor carrier. Such records shall be made available upon request of the Federal Motor Carrier Safety Administration.

A passenger-carrying commercial motor vehicle driver does not exceed ten hours maximum driving time following eight consecutive hours off duty.

The motor carrier that employs the driver maintains and retains for a period of six months accurate and true time records showing:

(A) The time the driver reports for duty each day.
(B) The total number of hours the driver is on duty each day.
(C) The time the driver is released from duty each day.
(D) The total time for the preceding seven days for drivers used for the first time or intermittently.

Operators of Property-Carrying Commercial Motor Vehicles Not Requiring a Commercial Driver's License

Except as provided in this paragraph, a driver is exempt from the requirements if:

- The driver operates a property-carrying commercial motor vehicle for which a commercial driver's license is not required under part 383.
- The driver operates within a 150 air-mile radius of the location where the driver reports to and is released from work—that is, the normal work reporting location.
- The driver returns to the normal work reporting location at the end of each duty tour.
- The driver has at least 10 consecutive hours off duty separating each on-duty period.
- The driver does not drive more than 11 hours following at least ten consecutive hours off duty.

Sleeper Berths—(1) Property-Carrying Commercial Motor Vehicle

In General. A driver who operates a property-carrying commercial motor vehicle equipped with a sleeper berth, must, before driving, accumulate:

1. At least ten consecutive hours off duty;
2. At least ten consecutive hours of sleeper-berth time;
3. A combination of consecutive sleeper-berth and off-duty time amounting to at least ten hours; or

The driver should not drive more than 11 hours following one of the 10-hour off-duty periods and may not drive after the 14th hour after coming on duty following one of the 10-hour off-duty periods, and must exclude from the calculation of the 14-hour limit any sleeper berth period of at least 8, but less than 10, consecutive hours.

The State of Alaska

(1) Property-Carrying Commercial Motor Vehicle. A driver who is driving a property-carrying commercial motor vehicle in the state of Alaska must not drive or be required or permitted to drive:

- More than 15 hours following 10 consecutive hours off duty, or
- After being on duty for 20 hours or more following ten consecutive hours off duty
- After having been on duty for 70 hours in any period of seven consecutive days, if the motor carrier for which the driver drives does not operate every day in the week, or
- After having been on duty for 80 hours in any period of eight consecutive days, if the motor carrier for which the driver drives operates every day in the week

(2) Passenger-Carrying Commercial Motor Vehicle. A driver who is driving a passenger-carrying commercial motor vehicle in the state of Alaska must not drive or be required or permitted to drive:

- More than 15 hours following 8 consecutive hours off duty

- After being on duty for 20 hours or more following eight consecutive hours off duty
- After having been on duty for 70 hours in any period of seven consecutive days, if the motor carrier for which the driver drives does not operate every day in the week; or
- After having been on duty for 80 hours in any period of eight consecutive days, if the motor carrier for which the driver drives operates every day in the week

(3) A driver who is driving a commercial motor vehicle in the state of Alaska and who encounters adverse driving conditions may drive and be permitted or required to drive a commercial motor vehicle for the period of time needed to complete the run.

Hours of Service in a Nutshell

2003 Rule
Property-Carrying CMV Drivers
Compliance Through 09/30/05
2005 Rule
Property-Carrying CMV Drivers
Compliance On and After 10/01/05

May drive a maximum of 11 hours after ten consecutive hours off duty.

NO CHANGE

May not drive beyond the 14th hour after coming on duty, following ten consecutive hours off duty.

NO CHANGE

May not drive after 60/70 hours on duty in seven/eight consecutive days.

- A driver may restart a seven/eight consecutive day period after taking 34 or more consecutive hours off duty.

NO CHANGE

Commercial Motor Vehicle (CMV) drivers using a sleeper berth must take ten hours off duty, but may split sleeper-berth time into two periods provided neither is less than two hours. CMV drivers using the sleeper berth provision must take at least eight consecutive hours in the sleeper berth, plus two consecutive hours either in the sleeper berth, off duty, or any combination of the two.

Passenger-carrying carriers/drivers are not subject to the new hours-of-service rules. These operations must continue to comply with the hours-of-service limitations specified in 49 CFR 395.5.

Short-Haul Provision

Drivers of property-carrying CMVs, which do not require a CDL for operation and who operate within a 150 air-mile radius of their normal work reporting location:

- May drive a maximum of 11 hours after coming on duty following 10 or more consecutive hours off duty.

- Are not required to keep records-of-duty status (RODS).

- May not drive after the 14th hour after coming on duty five days a week or after the 16th hour after coming on duty two days a week.

Employer must:

- Maintain and retain accurate time records for a period of six months showing the time the duty period began, ended, and the total hours on duty each day in place of RODS.

Drivers who use the above-described short-haul provision are not eligible to use 100 air-mile provision 395.1(e) or the current 16-hour exception in 395.1 (o).

Figure 8-6 Hours-of-Service Guidelines.

FMCSR §395.8: Driver's Record of Duty Status

Every driver must keep a "record of duty status" or "log book," which is a record of how you spent your time during each 24-hour period. If you keep a handwritten log, you must make two copies and use a form—called a grid—that meets requirements of FMCSR Part 395. (See Figure 8-7.)

1. Every driver who operates a commercial motor vehicle shall record his or her duty status, in duplicate, for each 24-hour period. The duty status time shall be recorded on a specified grid. The grid may be combined with any company forms.

2. Every driver who operates a commercial motor vehicle shall record his or her duty status by using an automatic onboard recording device that meets the requirements.

   The duty status shall be recorded as follows: (a) "off duty" or "OFF," (b) "sleeper berth" or "SB" (only if a sleeper berth is used), (c) "driving" or "D," and (d) "on duty not driving" or "ON." For each change of duty status (for example, the place of reporting for work, starting to drive, on-duty not driving, and where released from work), the name of the city, town or village, with state abbreviation, shall be recorded.

Note: If a change of duty status occurs at a location other than a city, town, or village, show one of the following: (1) the highway number and nearest milepost, followed by the name of the nearest city, town, or village and the state abbreviation, (2) the highway number and the name of the service plaza followed by the name of the nearest city, town, or village, and the state abbreviation, or (3) the highway numbers of the nearest two intersecting roadways followed by the name of the nearest city, town, or village, and the state abbreviation.

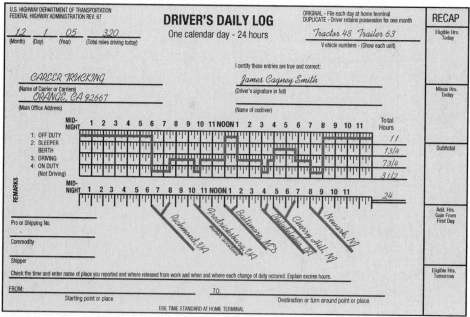

Figure 8-7   Daily log showing entries for a midnight-to-midnight run.

The following information must be included on the form in addition to the grid:

1. Date
2. Total miles driving today
3. Truck or tractor and trailer number
4. Name of carrier
5. Driver's signature/certification
6. 24-hour period starting time (for example, midnight, 9:00 AM, noon, 3:00 PM)
7. Main office address
8. Remarks
9. Name of co-driver
10. Total hours (far right edge of grid)
11. Shipping document number(s), or name of shipper and commodity

Failure to complete the record of duty activities, failure to preserve a record of such duty activities, or the making of false reports in connection with such duty activities shall render the driver and/or carrier liable to prosecution.

The driver's activities shall be recorded in accordance with the following provisions:

1. Entries should be current. Drivers shall keep their record of duty status current to the time shown for the last change of duty status.
2. Entries should be made by the driver only. All entries relating to the driver's duty status must be legible and in the driver's own handwriting.
3. Date. The month, day, and year for the beginning of each 24-hour period shall be shown on the form containing the driver's duty status record.
4. Total miles driven today. Total mileage driven during the 24-hour period shall be recorded on the form containing the driver's duty status record.
5. Commercial motor vehicle identification. The driver shall show the number assigned by the motor carrier or state and the license number of each commercial motor vehicle operated during each 24-hour period on his or her record of duty status. The driver of an articulated (combination) commercial motor vehicle shall show the number assigned by the motor carrier or the state, and the license number of each motor vehicle used in each commercial motor vehicle combination operated during that 24-hour period on her record of duty status.
6. The name of the motor carrier. The name(s) of the motor carrier(s) for which work is performed shall be shown on the form containing the driver's record of duty status. When work is performed for more than one motor carrier during the same 24-hour period, the beginning and finishing time, showing AM or PM, worked for each motor carrier shall be shown after each motor carrier's name. Drivers of leased commercial motor vehicles shall show the name of the motor carrier performing the transportation.
7. Signature/certification. The driver shall certify to the correctness of all entries by signing the form containing the driver's duty status record with his or her legal name or name of record. The driver's signature certifies that all entries required by this section made by the driver are true and correct.
8. Time base to be used. The driver's duty status record shall be prepared, maintained, and submitted using the time standard in effect at the driver's home terminal for a 24-hour period beginning with the time specified by the motor carrier for that driver's home terminal. The term "seven or eight

consecutive days" means the seven or eight consecutive 24-hour periods as designated by the carrier for the driver's home terminal.

9. The 24-hour period starting time must be identified on the driver's duty status record. One-hour increments must appear on the graph, be identified, and preprinted. The words "Midnight" and "Noon" must appear above or beside the appropriate one-hour increment.
10. The main office address. The motor carrier's main office address shall be shown on the form containing the driver's duty status record.
11. Recording days off duty. Two or more consecutive 24-hour periods off duty may be recorded on one duty status record.
12. Total hours. The total hours in each duty status: off duty other than in a sleeper berth, off duty in a sleeper berth, driving, and on duty not driving shall be entered to the right of the grid. The total of such entries shall equal 24 hours.
13. Shipping document number(s), or name of shipper and commodity, shall be shown on the driver's record of duty status.

Graph Grid. The graph grid must be incorporated into a motor carrier record-keeping system, which must also contain the information required (see Figure 8-8).

Graph Grid Preparation. The graph grid may be used horizontally or vertically and shall be completed as follows:

1. Off duty—Except for time spent resting in a sleeper berth, a continuous line shall be drawn between the appropriate time markers to record the period(s) of time when the driver is not on duty, is not required to be in readiness to work, or is not under any responsibility to perform work.
2. Sleeper berth—A continuous line shall be drawn between the appropriate time markers to record the period(s) of time off duty resting in a sleeper berth, as defined in §395.2. (If a non-sleeper berth operation, sleeper berth need not be shown on the grid.)
3. Driving—A continuous line shall be drawn between the appropriate time markers to record the period(s) of driving time.
4. On duty–not driving—A continuous line shall be drawn between the appropriate time markers to record the period(s) of time on duty not driving specified in §395.2.
5. Location–Remarks—The name of the city, town, or village, with the state abbreviation where each change of duty status occurs shall be recorded.

Note: If a change of duty status occurs at a location other than a city, town, or village, show one of the following: (1) the highway number and nearest milepost followed by the name of the nearest city, town, or village, and the state abbreviation, (2) the highway number and the name of the service plaza followed by the name of the nearest city, town, or village, and the state abbreviation, or (3) the highway numbers of the nearest two intersecting roadways followed by the name of the nearest city, town, or village, and the state abbreviation.

Filing Driver's Record of Duty Status. The driver shall submit or forward by mail the original driver's record of duty status to the regular employing motor carrier within 13 days following the completion of the form.

Drivers Used by More Than One Motor Carrier. (1) When the services of a driver are used by more than one motor carrier during any 24-hour period in effect at the

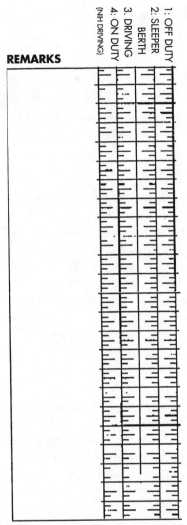

Figure 8-8　Groups grid.

driver's home terminal, the driver shall submit a copy of the record of duty status to each motor carrier.

The record shall include:

1. All duty time for the entire 24-hour period.
2. The name of each motor carrier served by the driver during that period, and the beginning and finishing time, including AM or PM, worked for each carrier.

     Motor carriers, when using a driver for the first time or intermittently, shall obtain from the driver a signed statement giving the total time on duty during the immediately preceding seven days and the time at which the driver was last relieved from duty prior to beginning work for the motor carrier.

Retention of Driver's Record of Duty Status. (1) Each motor carrier shall maintain records of duty status and all supporting documents for each driver it employs for a period of six months from the date of receipt.

The driver shall retain a copy of each record of duty status for the previous seven consecutive days which shall be in his or her possession and available for inspection while on duty.

§395.13 Drivers Declared Out of Service

Authority to Declare Drivers Out of Service

Every special agent of the Federal Motor Carrier Safety Administration (as defined in Appendix B to this subchapter) is authorized to declare a driver out of service and to notify the motor carrier of that declaration, upon finding at the time and place of examination that the driver has violated the out of service criteria.

Out-of-Service Criteria

1. No driver shall drive after being on duty in excess of the maximum periods permitted by this part.
2. No driver required to maintain a record of duty status shall fail to have a record of duty status current on the day of examination and for the prior seven consecutive days.
3. **Exception.** A driver failing only to have possession of a record of duty status current on the day of examination and the prior day, but who has completed records of duty status up to that time (the previous six days), will be given the opportunity to make the duty status record current.

Responsibilities of the Driver

- No driver who has been declared out of service shall operate a commercial motor vehicle until that driver may lawfully do so under the rules.
- No driver who has been declared out of service for failing to prepare a record of duty status shall operate a commercial motor vehicle until the driver has been off duty for the appropriate number of consecutive hours required by this part and is in compliance with this section.
- A driver to whom a form has been tendered declaring the driver out of service shall, within 24 hours thereafter, deliver or mail the copy to a person or place designated by the motor carrier to receive it.

§395.15 Automatic Onboard Recording Devices

Authority to Use Automatic Onboard Recording Device

- A motor carrier may require a driver to use an automatic onboard recording device to record the driver's hours of service in lieu of complying with the requirements of keeping a written daily log.
- Every driver required by a motor carrier to use an automatic onboard recording device shall use such a device to record the driver's hours of service.

Information Requirements

- Automatic onboard recording devices shall produce, upon demand, a driver's hours of service chart, an electronic display, or a printout showing the time and sequence of duty status changes including the driver's starting time at the beginning of each day.
- The device shall provide a means whereby authorized federal, state, or local officials can immediately check the status of a driver's hours of service. This

information may be used in conjunction with handwritten or printed records of duty status for the previous seven days.

- Support systems used in conjunction with onboard recorders at a driver's home terminal or the motor carrier's principal place of business must be capable of providing authorized federal, state, or local officials with summaries of an individual driver's hours of service records, including the required information. The support systems must also provide information concerning onboard system sensor failures and the identification of edited data.
- The driver shall have in her possession records of duty status for the previous seven consecutive days available for inspection while on duty. These records shall consist of information stored in, and retrievable from, the automatic onboard recording device, handwritten records, computer-generated records, or any combination thereof.
- All hard copies of the driver's record of duty status must be signed by the driver. The driver's signature certifies that the information contained thereon is true and correct.

Submission of a Driver's Record of Duty Status

- The driver shall submit, electronically or by mail, to the employing motor carrier, each record of the driver's duty status within 13 days following the completion of each record;
- The driver shall review and verify that all entries are accurate prior to submission to the employing motor carrier; and
- The submission of the record of duty status certifies that all entries made by the driver are true and correct.

Performance of Recorders—motor carriers that use automatic onboard recording devices for recording their drivers' records of duty status in lieu of the handwritten record shall ensure that:

- A certificate is obtained from the manufacturer certifying that the design of the automatic onboard recorder has been sufficiently tested to meet the requirements of this section and under the conditions it will be used.
- The automatic onboard recording device permits duty status to be updated only when the commercial motor vehicle is at rest, except when registering the time a commercial motor vehicle crosses a state boundary.
- The automatic onboard recording device and associated support systems are, to the maximum extent practicable, tamperproof and do not permit altering of the information collected concerning the driver's hours of service.
- The automatic onboard recording device warns the driver visually and/or audibly that the device has ceased to function.
- Automatic onboard recording devices with electronic displays shall have the capability of displaying the required information found in the driver's daily log.

PART II

Professional Driver Skills

9 Vehicle Inspections

One of the most important tasks you must master is vehicle inspection. It is your initial key to safe trips.

A vehicle inspection is the first step toward safe operations.

State and federal law requires that you, the driver, conduct a thorough vehicle inspection each time you take your vehicle onto the highway. FMCSR Part 383 states that professional drivers must be familiar with FMCSR Part 396—and this includes the vehicle inspection. Further, the FMCSR Part 392.7 states:

> *No motor vehicle shall be driven unless the driver thereof shall have satisfied himself or herself that the following parts and accessories are in good working order, nor shall any driver fail to use or make use of such parts and accessories when and as needed:*

- *Service brakes, including trailer brake connections*
- *Parking (hand) brake*
- *Steering mechanism*
- *Lighting devices and reflectors*
- *Tires*
- *Horn*
- *Windshield wiper or wipers*
- *Rear-vision mirror or mirrors*
- *Coupling devices*

These guidelines are used by most states on their CDL tests, and the guidelines also state that professional drivers must be able to demonstrate they can conduct a thorough vehicle inspection. Most examiners will request that you conduct an inspection as part of the CDL Skills Test.

In this segment of the Skills Test, you may be requested to describe the different systems and parts on your vehicle as you conduct your inspection. Or, the examiner may choose to stop your inspection periodically to ask questions about the equipment.

ROAD SENSE

One more hint for the inspection portion of the CDL Skills Test: Have an inspection routine developed ahead of time so you won't miss anything. With a routine, you won't forget or overlook something and you won't get confused. Get a routine and keep the same routine each time you inspect your vehicle.

Who Inspects?

Generally, the main inspection responsibility is assigned to the motor carrier. The carrier must also perform periodic inspections of their vehicles, called an "annual inspection." But, in most cases, it is the driver's responsibility to inspect the vehicle before and after each trip.

There is one other group that inspects a commercial vehicle—these are federal and state inspectors, and they can conduct an inspection at any time. It may be at a weigh station or it may be while you are driving down the road. For such inspections, you either (1) have to stop at an inspection point or (2) the inspector pulls you over to conduct a roadside inspection . . . anywhere in the country.

When these inspections occur, if the vehicle is found to be unsafe in any area, it can be put "out of service," which means you won't be going anywhere until the vehicle is repaired and is safe to put back on the highway.

When Are Inspections Conducted?

As the name tells you, pre-trip inspections are conducted *before* each trip. These inspections are so important that you should record them in your log book. During these inspections, you look for problems and damage to the vehicle that could cause a breakdown or an accident. Any damage you find must be repaired before the vehicle heads for the highway.

A post-trip inspection, as you would expect, is conducted at the *end* of the trip—or if the trip lasts several days, at the end of each day or at the end of each shift on that trip.

The post-trip inspection may include filling out a Vehicle Condition Report, and listing any damage or other problems you find. This helps the carrier know when something needs to be fixed on specific pieces of equipment.

But any veteran driver will also tell you that you ensure your personal safety and the safety of others by inspecting your vehicle *during* the trip, watching gauges for trouble and using your senses—sight, hearing, smell, and touch—to check for any problems that may occur when you're on the road.

While driving, you should plan to stop every 150 miles or every three hours for an "en-route" inspection (see Figure 9-1). Loads do shift and bindings do loosen, so it is important to make sure your cargo is still safe.

OTR SAFETY
Remember to do a complete walkaround every time you stop the vehicle.

A veteran driver will also encourage you to check critical systems every time you stop. The systems found on almost every vehicle that ensure its safe operation are:

- Lights and wiring
- Brakes
- Windows
- Fuel and fuel system
- Coupling devices (on combinations)
- Tires
- Windshield wipers and defrosters
- Rear-view mirrors

Figure 9-1   Enroute inspections save time and lives.

- Horn
- Speedometer
- Floor
- Rear bumper
- Flags on oversized or projecting loads
- Seatbelts
- Emergency equipment
- Cargo straps, webbing, and other devices used to secure the load
- Frame
- Cab
- Wheels, rims, and tires
- Steering
- Suspension

Some states may require vehicles to have more equipment than that listed here. This chapter will cover those items required by most states. Before taking the CDL, you should learn about the requirements in the state where your headquarters is located, as well that of any state you'll be driving in.

OTR SAFETY

It is possible to be put "out of service" in one state for a condition on your vehicle that is acceptable in the next three states.

Vehicle Inspection

Lights and Reflectors

1. Make sure all required lights and reflectors are in place.
2. Make sure they are all clean and in working order.

Electrical System

1. Check for wiring problems:

   A. Loose wires should be reattached.
   B. Broken and worn wires should be replaced.
   C. Corrosion around attachments should be cleaned with a wire brush.

2. Check the fuses and replace any that have blown.
3. Inspect the battery:

   A. Check that each cell has a vent cap.
   B. Clean clogged vent caps.
   C. Check fluids in a wet-charged battery.
   D. Check the battery mount to make sure hold-down bars fit well.
   E. Check the battery box to make sure it is in place and free of cracks or leaks.
   F. Check the cables for wearing or fraying.
   G. Check connections to ensure they are tight.

4. In the cab:

   A. Check the voltmeter and ammeter to make sure readings are in the normal range.

Brake System (Excluding Air Brakes)

1. Inspect all four wheels by doing the following:

   A. At each wheel, check for cracks, and inspect the hubs for any leaking fluid.
   B. Check the brake drums for cracks.
   C. Check the brake shoes for fluid or fluid on pads—and for missing or broken shoes. Any problems? They should be replaced or repaired immediately!
   D. Check the brake lines for worn or weak spots.
   E. Make sure the lines aren't kinked or twisted.
   F. Check the hydraulic fluid level in the master cylinder (when inspecting the engine area). Use a sight glass or visual—check the vehicle manual for the proper inspection method. Make sure the fluid level reaches the mark indicated. Leaks in this area mean trouble.

2. In the cab, check the hydraulic brake system. To do so:

   A. Turn the engine on (the transmission is in neutral).
   B. Pump the brake pedal three times.

C. Then, press firmly on brake pedal—no less than five seconds (some manufacturers specify longer). The pedal should not move.
D. If the pedal moves, or is not firm, there is air in the lines.
E. If the pedal sinks toward the floor, that's a sign of a leak, and it must be fixed.

3. Check vacuum brakes (if available). To do so:

A. Push on the brakes. If you have to push hard, there may be defects in the vacuum system.
B. If you experience brake fade, that is also a sign of a problem.

4. Check the parking brakes (see Figure 9-2). To do so:

A. Put your seatbelt on.
B. Put the vehicle in gear and let it move slowly forward.
C. Apply the parking brake. The vehicle should stop. If it doesn't, get the parking brake repaired before your trip.

5. Check the service brake. To do so:

A. Drive forward at about five miles per hour.
B. Push the pedal firmly. If the vehicle veers left or right, this could mean brake trouble.
C. If there is a pause before the brakes "catch," this could signal another problem.
D. If the brake pedal "feels" weird—takes too much time to catch or requires too much effort to push—have the brakes checked and repaired before going anywhere.

TO TEST THE PARKING BRAKES MOVE FORWARD SLOWLY

Figure 9-2   Careful inspection means safer operation.

Cab

1. The cab should be neat, orderly, and clean.

    A. Doors should open and close easily and securely.
    B. Check for loose, sagging, or broken parts.
    C. Make sure the hood is securely fastened.
        Tie Rod Steering Wheel Steering Shaft Power Steering Cylinder Steering Arm Spindle Steering Knuckle Drag Link Pitman Arm Gear Box Hydraulic Fluid Reservoir
    D. Be sure the seats are secured firmly in place.
    E. Required front bumpers should be secure.
    F. Rear bumpers are required for vehicles higher than 30 inches from the ground (empty). If the bumper is in place, check to see it is firmly in place.

Steering System

1. Make sure the steering column is securely mounted and steering wheel is secure, moves easily, and is free of cracked spokes.
2. "Steering wheel lash" or "free play" (the number of turns a steering wheel makes before wheels move) should be no more than 10 degrees or two-inches on the rim of a 20-inch steering wheel, according to FMCSR Part 393. If free play exceeds limits, the vehicle will be difficult to steer.
3. Check the U-joints for wear, slack, damage, or signs of welding repair (not acceptable for U-joint repair).
4. Check that the gearbox is free of damage, and that bolts and brackets are in place and secure.
5. Make sure the pitman arm is secure.

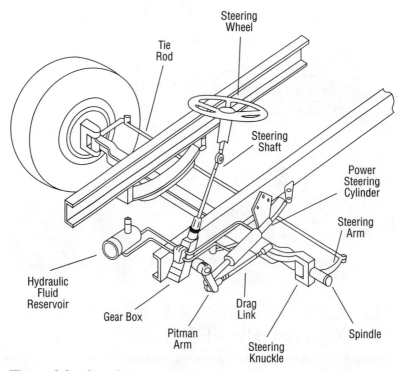

Figure 9-3   Steering system.

For Vehicles with Power Steering

1. Make sure all parts are free of damage and in good operating order.
2. Belts that are frayed, cracked, or slipping should be replaced or adjusted.
3. Look for leaks in the lines and tank and make sure the tank contains ample power-steering fluid.
4. If you see missing nuts, bolts, cotter keys, or other damaged parts, replace them immediately. The same goes for a damaged, loose, or broken steering column, gear box, or tie rod.

Windows and Glass

Check out all window glass and the windshield. The viewing area must be free of stickers and it must be clean—no dirt and no discolorations should be apparent. And remember, only factory tints to reduce glare are allowed! No cracks should be longer than one inch.

Wipers and Defrosters

All vehicles with windshields must have one or two windshield wiper blades and a windshield defroster.

1. Blades must be on each side of the centerline of the windshield.
2. Wipers must be automatic and in working condition.
3. Make sure rubber blades do the job. Loose rubber blades don't work.
4. Old blades—stiff, loose, or crumbling—must be replaced.
5. Turn the defroster on and off at every inspection, putting your hand over the vent to confirm the release of warm air.
6. Washers are optional—if you have them, test them and check fluid level. If they don't work, make sure the lines aren't kinked, broken, or leaking.

Rear-View and Side-View Mirrors

Rear-view mirrors on each side of the cab should be adjusted when you're in the driver's seat. You should be able to see down both sides to the rear of the vehicle. Mirrors should also be clean and free of damage.

Horn

Make sure the horn is working. All vehicles are required to have one.

OTR SAFETY

A note to the wise: Watch blowing or sounding your horn in a truck stop! Some drivers may be sleeping.

Seatbelts

Make sure your seatbelt is well-anchored and in good condition.

Floor

Floorboards should be clean and free of holes.

Frame

On every inspection, check for looseness, cracks, sagging, or damage over the frame. Check for missing or loose bolts.

Fuel System

Check your tank or tanks:

1. They should be securely mounted.
2. Check for damage or leaks.
3. The fuel crossover line should be secure and high enough off the roadway to be free of possible damage. Your truck may or may not have crossover lines.
4. Fuel caps should be in place.
5. Make sure neoprene gaskets are in place.

Exhaust System

A malfunctioning exhaust system could cost you your life.

1. Check for broken, loose, or missing exhaust pipes, mufflers, tailpipes, or stacks.

Coupling Devices

Portions of the coupling device include saddle mounts, tow bars, and pintle hooks, as well as safety chains used in tow-away situations.

1. Visually check—for bends or warping—all parts used to couple vehicles.
2. Safety chains should not have broken or twisted links.
3. Check to be sure that the lights, reflectors, steering, and brakes work on all vehicles—both the towed vehicle and the towing vehicle.

Tires

1. Look for worn treads, and body ply or belts showing through the tread.
2. Look for separation of the tread or sidewall.
3. Look for deep cuts or cracks that reveal ply or belt beneath them.
4. Look for damaged or cracked valve stems—or missing stems and valve caps.

5. If tire is low or flat—or has any damage like that mentioned earlier—get it repaired.
6. Listen for air leaks—and look for bulges (it could mean a blowout later).
7. Check the inflation pressure with a tire gauge.
8. Check for wear—should have no less than 4/32-inch of tread depth in every major groove on the front and 2/32-inch of tread depth on other wheels (Figure 9-4).
9. Dual tires—make sure they're not touching each other or another part of the vehicle.
10. All tires should be the same size—and the same type. Radial and bias-ply tires should not be used on the same axle—this is forbidden in most states.
11. No regrooved tires should be placed on the front of the tractor or tractors with an 8,000-plus pounds front-axle rating.

Figure 9-4   Checking tire tread depth.

OTR SAFETY
When checking your tires, remember the acronym ICD: inflation, condition, depth.

Wheels and Rims

Check for cracks or damaged wheels or rims:

1. Look for missing spacers, studs, lugs, and clamps.
2. Look for damaged or mismatched lock rings.
3. If welding has been used to repair wheels or rims, note as a defect.
4. If you see rust around wheel nuts, use a wrench to check for looseness.
5. Out-of-round (oval or egg-shaped) stud or bolt holes on rims indicate problems.
6. Check the hub oil supply—and make sure there are no leaks.

Mud Flaps or Splash Guards

A common state requirement is that mud flaps must be as wide, or wider, than the tires.

- Mud flaps should be no more than six inches from the ground with the vehicle fully loaded.

Tire Chains

Another state-by-state requirement concerns driving in snow and ice: include tire chains in your equipment. Be able to mount and remove them if asked to by the CDL examiner. Check home state regulations and regulations in every state in which you'll be operating. Tire chains are usually required in the mountain regions.

Suspension System

Don't drive a rig with suspension problems, such as broken or cracked parts. (See Figure 9-5.)

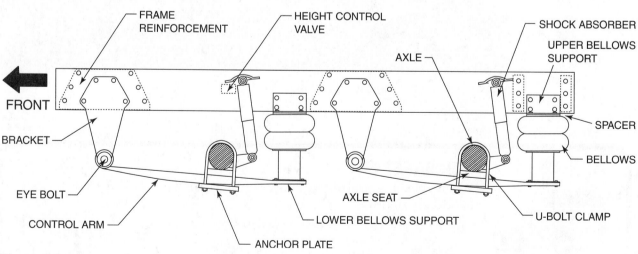

Figure 9-5   Suspension system.

Emergency Equipment

1. A fire extinguisher must be securely mounted with easy access. It should be checked as part of the inspection. Most vehicles require that the extinguisher have a 10 B_C rating from Underwriters Laboratory (UL) located near the UL certification. Is the nozzle clear? Is the tip of the ring pin in place? Check the pressure gauge to ensure the needle is in the green area.
2. Three reflective emergency triangles should be onboard (see FMCSR Part 393.95 for a full description and options).
3. Make sure you have spare fuses and know how to install them—unless your vehicle has circuit breakers.
4. Accident notification kit (Tip: Keep a disposable camera in the accident kit to visually record damages).
5. Emergency phone numbers.

Cargo Securement

Safely loaded cargo (no room for shifting or falling) should be inspected and the following should be in good working condition:

1. Tailgate
2. Doors
3. The cab guard or header board (headache rack) should be free of damage and securely in place
4. Stakes/sideboards—if necessary—should be in good condition
5. Tarps—must be tied down and tight
6. Spare tire
7. Binders
8. Chains
9. Winches
10. Braces and support
11. Curbside doors—must be secured and locked
12. Cargo—should be loaded without blocking the view or impeding the driver's arms and legs
13. Hauling sealed loads? Security seals must be placed on doors
14. Hauling hazardous materials? You need placards, proper paperwork—and the HazMat Endorsement on your CDL

OTR SAFETY
Anything you find during the pre-trip inspection that is broken or functioning improperly must be repaired before you take the vehicle on the road. Federal and state laws forbid operating an unsafe vehicle.

Your Inspection Routine

Every driver should create an inspection routine, a way of checking all necessary items on straight trucks or vehicle combinations. Thus, the driver should inspect the truck the same way every time when making an inspection. Learn this routine well—and perform it perfectly.

ROAD SENSE

For the CDL test, check with the examiner to find out if you will be permitted to use a checklist for your inspection. Then, as you perform the inspection, tell the examiner what you're inspecting and tell about the problems and/or defects that are most common at each site.

Remember that you may be asked by the examiner to begin your inspection at any position on the vehicle. But the standard routine is:

1. Approach the vehicle.
2. Look underneath for leaking fluids.
3. Look around for any obstacles.
4. Raise the hood or tilt the cab to check the engine compartment. If you tilt the cab, make sure everything in it is secured inside the cab.
5. Start the engine and inspect inside the cab.
6. Check the lights and reflectors.
7. Walk around the vehicle, inspecting each section.
8. Check the signal lights.
9. Check the brakes.

The seven-step pre-trip inspection is, by far, the most commonly used routine. Here is what you look at during each step of the routine:

Vehicle Overview

Begin your inspection by approaching the vehicle and noting the general condition.

1. Look for damage, whether the vehicle is leaning (flat tire, shifted cargo, or overloaded—or a suspension problem).
2. Look down on the ground. Is there any fresh leakage of coolant, fuel, grease, or oil?
3. Check the area for people and hazards (low wires, low limbs, and so on).
4. Look at the most recent inspection reports, both pre-trip and post-trip. If items listed affect safety, check to ensure that the mechanic's certification indicates repairs were made, or that no repair was needed.
5. Inspect these areas yourself to find out what was done about problems noted on the last inspection.

Engine Compartment

1. Parking brakes should be on and/or wheels should be chocked.
2. Raise the hood, open the engine compartment door, or tilt the cab (after stowing any loose items in the cab).

3. Check the engine oil level.
4. Check the coolant level—should be above the "Low" mark.
5. Check radiator shutters (if you still have them)—remove any ice and check to ensure the winter front isn't closed. Inspect the fan—make sure blades are undamaged and hoses and wires are out of the way.
6. Power steering? Check the fluid level with a dipstick in the oil tank. Check the condition of the hoses.
7. Is the battery in this compartment? Perform the check now.
8. Automatic transmission? Check the fluid level (you may do this with the engine running).
9. Check the drive belts for damage, wear, and tightness. If belts slide easily over a pulley, it's too loose or worn.
10. Look over the engine compartment for any leaks—fuel, oil, power-steering fluid, battery fluid, hydraulic fluid, and coolant. (See Figure 9-6.)
11. Check the wiring for any wear, breaks, or other problems.
12. Lower and/or latch the hood or cab or the engine compartment door.
13. Check and clear debris or obstacles from any handholds, steps, or deck plates leading to the cab.

Inside the Cab

As you get into the cab, look around and inspect the cab's inside. Put your seatbelt on. Make sure the parking brake is on and that the vehicle is in neutral or park, then:

1. Start the engine and listen for a few seconds for any unusual noises.
2. Check the gauges—the oil pressure should go to normal within seconds.
3. The ammeter and voltmeter—normal readings.

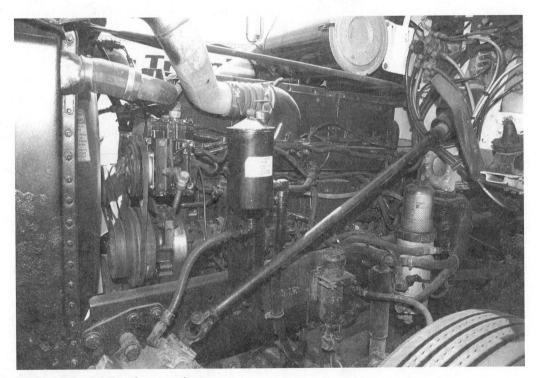

Figure 9-6 View of an engine.

4. The coolant temperature—should start "Cold" and gradually rise to normal.
5. The engine oil temp should slowly rise to normal.
6. The oil, coolant, and charging circuit warning lights come on and should go off almost immediately.
7. All controls should be in working order. Check loose or sticking controls, or any damage or improper readings or settings to the following:

   A. Steering wheel
   B. Accelerator
   C. Foot brake
   D. Parking brake
   E. Retarder controls (if available)
   F. Transmission controls
   G. Interaxle differential lock (if available)
   H. Horn
   I. Windshield wipers/washers (if available)
   J. Headlights
   K. Dimmer switch
   L. Turn signals
   M. Four-way flashers
   N. Clearance, identification, and marker light switch(es)

8. If there's a clutch, test it by pushing it in until there's slight resistance.

If it takes more than one or two inches to find resistance, there's a problem. If there is no free play before getting to any resistance, have the clutch adjusted immediately.

1. Check the mirrors and windshield for defects or problems.
2. Check to confirm you have required emergency equipment in good working order.
3. Check both optionals and items required by state laws, such as mud flaps and tire chains.

Turn Off the Engine and Check the Lights

1. Make sure the engine is off (take the key with you—very important) and the parking brake is set.
2. Turn on the headlights (low beams) and four-way flashers. Go to the front of the vehicle to check that all are working.
3. Get back into the cab. Turn on the high beams. Check to see that they work.
4. Turn off headlights and four-way flashers.
5. Turn on parking, clearance, side-marker, and identification lights.
6. Turn on right turn signal—then get out of cab and begin your walkaround.
7. The key may need to be in the ignition and in the on position to check the turn indicators.

Walkaround Inspection

Start with the driver's side of the cab—cover the front and then work down the opposite side. Go over the rear of the vehicle and back to the driver's side of the cab.

1. General—Walk around, inspecting as you go.

   A. Clean all lights, reflectors, and glass as you walk around.

2. Check the left front—The driver's door glass should be clean.

   A. Locks should be in working order.
   B. Check the condition of wheels, rims, and tires—there should be no missing, bent, or broken studs, clamps, or lugs.

      a. Tires must be properly inflated, and the valve stem and cap in place. There should be no serious cuts, slashes, bulges, or signs of tread wear.
      b. Test lug nuts for looseness (rust streaks coming from the lug nuts also indicate looseness).
      c. The hub oil level should be good with no leaks.

   C. Left front suspension—Make cure the springs, spring hangers, shackles, U-bolts, and shock absorbers are in good condition.
   D. The left front brake drum and hoses must be in good condition.
   E. Check the brake chambers and slack adjusters.

3. Check the front.

   A. Check the front axle for cracks or other problems.
   B. Check for loose, worn, bent, damaged, or missing parts of the steering system and test for looseness.
   C. The windshield should be free of damage and clean. The wipers should be in good working order—check for proper spring tension in the wiper arm.
   D. Check blades for stiff rubber and ensure that they are secure.
   E. Parking, clearance, and identification lights should be clean, operational, and of the proper color—amber in front.
   F. The right turn signal light must be clean, operating, and of the proper color—amber or white.

4. Check the right front.

   A. Check all items on the right front just as for the left front.
   B. If it's a cab-over-engine model, all primary and safety locks must be engaged and working.
   C. The right fuel tank should be securely mounted, with no leaks. Fuel crossover lines must be secure, there must be adequate fuel in the tank for the trip, and caps and gaskets must be on and secure.
   D. The condition of visible parts—The rear of the engine must have no leaks, transmission should not be leaking, the exhaust system must be secure and not leaking or touching wires or lines. There should be no cracks or bends in the frame and cross members.
   E. Airlines and electrical wiring—no snagging, rubbing, or wearing.
   F. The spare tire carrier must not be damaged and the spare tire/wheel must be the right size at the proper inflation.
   G. Cargo must be secure—the cargo should be blocked, braced, tied, and chained. The header board should be secure, and sideboards and stakes must be free of damage and properly placed. The canvas or tarp must be secured to prevent tearing, billowing, or blocking mirrors.
   H. Oversized loads must have the required signs properly mounted and all required permits in the driver's pouch.
   I. Curbside cargo compartment doors must be closed and latched with all required security seals in place.

5. Check the right rear—Inspect the condition of the wheels, rims, and tires. There should be no missing, bent, or broken spacers, studs, clamps, or lugs. Tires should be evenly matched, must be of the same type (no mixing of radial and bias types), and should be properly inflated with valve stems and caps in place. No cuts, bulges, or tread wear should be evident. Make sure tires are not rubbing and are clear of debris.

   A. Wheel bearing/seals should not be leaking.
   B. Suspension—the condition of springs, spring hangers, shackles, and U-bolts must be good, the axle must be secure, and the drive axle(s) should not be leaking gear oil.
   C. Check the condition of the torque rod arms and bushings.
   D. Check the condition of the shock absorber(s).
   E. If the vehicle has a retractable axle, check the lift mechanism. If air-powered, check for leaks.
   F. Brakes—the brake drums must be in good condition, and the hoses must be checked for wear, rubbing, and so on.
   G. Check the brake chambers and slack adjusters.
   H. Lights and reflectors. The side-marker lights must be clean, operating, and red at the rear—others must be amber. Same for the side markers.

6. Check the rear—Rear clearance and identification lights should be clean, operating, and red at the rear. Reflectors must be clean and red at the rear. Taillights must be clean, operating, and red at the rear. The right turn signal must be operating and of the proper color—red, yellow, or amber at the rear.

   A. License plates must be present, clean, and secure.
   B. Splash guards must be properly fastened, undamaged, and not dragging or rubbing tires.
   C. The cargo must be secure, properly blocked and braced, tied, and chained. Tailboards must be up and secure. The end gates must be free of damage and secured in stake sockets.
   D. The canvas or tarp must be secured to avoid billowing, tearing, blocking the rear-view mirror, or covering the rear lights.
   E. For over-length or over-width loads, have all signs and additional flags and lights in the proper position and have all required permits.
   F. Rear doors should be closed and locked.

7. Check the left side. Check everything you checked on the right side, as well as:—Batteries (if not located in the engine compartment) and the battery box (should be securely attached and the cover should also be secure).

   A. Batteries should not be damaged or leaking, and there should be no movement.
   B. Check battery fluid levels—except maintenance-free types.
   C. Confirm cell caps and vents are in place, free of debris, and secure.

Check the Signal Lights

1. Get in and turn off all the lights.
2. Turn on the stop lights (apply the trailer hand brake).
3. Turn on left turn signals.

Get out and check the lights.

1. The left front turn signal—make sure the light is clean, operating, and is the proper amber or white color on signals facing the front.
2. The left rear turn signal and stoplights—Make sure the lights are clean, operating, and are the proper red, yellow, or amber color.

Start the Engine and Check the Brake System

1. Before starting the engine and performing a brake system check, fasten your seatbelt!
2. Get in and turn off the lights. They're not needed for driving.
3. Check all required papers, trip manifests, permits, and so on.
4. Secure all loose articles in the cab.
5. Start the engine.
6. Test for hydraulic leaks—If the vehicle has hydraulic brakes, pump them three times. Then apply pressure to the pedal and hold it for five seconds. The pedal should not move. If it does, there may be a leak or other problem. Fix it before beginning your trip.
7. Test the air brakes.
8. Test the parking brake—Fasten the seatbelt, allow the vehicle to move forward slowly, and then apply the parking brake. If it doesn't stop the vehicle, get it fixed.
9. Test the service brake stopping action—Drive the vehicle at about five miles per hour, and then push the brake pedal firmly. If the vehicle pulls to one side, this could mean possible brake trouble. Any unusual feel of the pedal or delayed stopping action could signal a problem.
10. Check the air brakes on doubles and triples like any other combination vehicle.

Let's Review

Read each question and all of the answers provided. Place the letter of the correct answer in the space provided. Once you have answered all the questions, check your answers against the answer key which follows.

_____ 1. When you're conducting a pre-trip inspection, your fuel tank should be:
    (A) Full and topped off.
    (B) At "add".
    (C) Almost full.
    (D) At "low".

_____ 2. When inspecting tires, a bulge means:
    (A) Tire pressure is at capacity.
    (B) Tires can go across rough terrain.
    (C) The tire could blow out.
    (D) All of the above.

_____ 3. To test your service brakes:
    (A) Go forward at five miles per hour and push the brake pedal firmly.
    (B) Pump brakes and pull the emergency brake lever.
    (C) Roll backward and push in the clutch.
    (D) None of the above.

    4. When you inspect your brakes, check:
       (A) Discs for ripples.
       (B) Hubcaps for lubrication.
       (C) Drums, shoes, and linings for leaks, cracks, or wear.
       (D) None of the above.

    5. When checking hydraulic brakes, the engine should be:
       (A) Off, and the transmission in reverse.
       (B) On, and the transmission in neutral.
       (C) Off, and the transmission in neutral.
       (D) None of the above.

    6. True or False. Federal law states that your vehicle must have mud flaps.

    7. When inspecting an air suspension system, leaking air means:
       (A) Too much air has been injected.
       (B) Not enough air is in the tank.
       (C) A defect has occurred.
       (D) All of the above.

    8. The best way to check tire inflation pressure is to:
       (A) Use a tire gauge.
       (B) Use a tire billy.
       (C) Kick the tire.
       (D) All of the above.

    9. Vehicle inspections should be done:
       (A) Before the trip.
       (B) After the trip.
       (C) On the road.
       (D) All of the above.

   10. When inspecting wiring and electrical systems, look for:
       (A) Broken or loose wires.
       (B) Worn insulation.
       (C) Bare wires making contact with each other.
       (D) All of the above.

Answers to Let's Review

1. C; 2. C; 3. A; 4. C; 5. B; 6. False; 7. C; 8. A; 9. D; 10. D.

10 Basic Vehicle Control

Basic Driving Skills

As a professional driver, you'll be spending most of your working hours operating a vehicle. As a professional driver, you also will be expected to have excellent skills in handling this vehicle in any number of situations.

Once again, it's your responsibility to read closely and carefully, take good notes, and review what you've learned before setting a time to take the tests leading to the CDL.

It also will be helpful to take a copy of the Federal Motor Carrier Safety Regulations (you can get one from the local Department of Motor Vehicles or look at the FMCSR web pages on the Internet). Look at Subpart G and you'll find a list of driving skills necessary to earn a CDL.

So, let's get started—you'll learn a lot in this chapter.

Be Prepared!

When you climb into that cab, you take on many new responsibilities, including your own well-being and the well-being of fellow motorists. But you also take on the responsibility for your vehicle, its safe operation, its maintenance, and its performance of the task it was built to do. When someone talks about operating a vehicle safely—much like your personal vehicle—several things come to mind. These may include:

- Steering on the highway
- Shifting gears to go up and down hills
- Accelerating when necessary
- Braking when necessary

As you swing up in the cab, you should be reviewing some of these basic driving skills so that you will be in complete command of the vehicle and its systems and controls. If you're driving this vehicle for the first time, take time to inspect it. A professional driver never starts an engine without first thoroughly going over a vehicle to make certain it will respond to his or her every command.

Before taking the driver's seat, look at the details of the cab—the handholds, the steps—and make sure they are free of greasy substances or dirt.

As you sit in the driver's seat of a new vehicle, adjust the seat as much as you can to fit your height and your comfort. But the most important thing about the height of the seat is whether or not you can *comfortably* reach the controls.

Check out the control panel . . . what do you see?

Become familiar with the panel and then check out the shift lever to determine the kind of transmission and the shifting pattern. Next, find all the controls and gauges you'll need to operate the vehicle safely.

FMCSR Part 383—Basic Vehicle Control

§383.111 Required Knowledge

All commercial motor vehicle operators must have knowledge of the following general areas:

Safe Operations Regulations. Driver-related elements of the regulations contained in 49 CFR Parts 382, 391, 392, 393, 395, 396, and 397, such as motor vehicle inspection, repair, and maintenance requirements; procedures for safe vehicle operations; the effects of fatigue, poor vision, hearing, and general health upon safe commercial motor vehicle operation; the types of motor vehicles and cargoes subject to the requirements; and the effects of alcohol and drug use upon safe commercial motor vehicle operations.

Commercial Motor Vehicle Safety Control Systems. Proper use of the motor vehicle's safety system, including lights, horns, side- and rear-view mirrors, proper mirror adjustments, fire extinguishers, symptoms of improper operation revealed through instruments, motor vehicle operation characteristics, and diagnosing malfunctions. Commercial motor vehicle drivers shall have knowledge on the correct procedures needed to use these safety systems in an emergency situation (for example, skids and loss of brakes).

Safe Vehicle Control. This consists of the following:

1. Control systems
2. Basic control
3. Shifting
4. Backing
5. Visual search
6. Communication
7. Speed management
8. Space management
9. Night operation
10. Extreme driving conditions
11. Hazard perceptions
12. Emergency maneuvers
13. Skid control and recovery

§383.113 Required Skills

The following are required skills all CDL applicants must possess and be able to demonstrate.

Basic Vehicle Control Skills. All applicants for a CDL must possess and demonstrate basic motor vehicle control skills for each vehicle group that the driver operates or expects to operate. These skills should include the ability to start, stop, and to move the vehicle forward and backward in a safe manner.

Safe Driving Skills. All applicants for a CDL must possess and demonstrate the safe driving skills for their vehicle group. These skills should include proper visual search methods, appropriate use of signals, speed control for weather and traffic conditions, and their ability to position the motor vehicle correctly when changing lanes or turning.

Air Brake Skills. All CDL applicants shall demonstrate the following skills with respect to inspection and operation of air brakes.

Pre-Trip Inspection Skills. Applicants shall demonstrate the skills necessary to conduct a pre-trip inspection, which includes the ability to:

- Locate and verbally identify air brake operating controls and monitoring devices.
- Determine the motor vehicle's brake system condition (if needing any proper adjustments) and to make sure air system connections between motor vehicles have been properly made and secured.
- Inspect the low-pressure warning device(s) to ensure that they will activate in emergency situations.
- Determine, with the engine running, that the system maintains an adequate supply of compressed air.
- Determine that the required minimum air pressure build-up time is within acceptable limits and that required alarms and emergency devices automatically deactivate at the proper pressure level.
- Operationally check the brake system for proper performance.

Driving Skills. Applicants shall successfully complete the required skills tests in a representative vehicle equipped with air brakes.

Test Area. Skills tests shall be conducted in on-street conditions or under a combination of on street and off-street conditions.

Simulation Technology. A state may utilize simulators to perform skills testing, but under no circumstances should they substitute for the required testing in on-street conditions.

Safe Vehicle Control

Control Systems

The purpose and function of the controls and instruments commonly found on commercial motor vehicles.

Basic Control

The proper procedures for performing various basic maneuvers.

Start Your Engines!

The proper procedures for performing basic maneuvers.

Ready to turn on the ignition? If you're running a gasoline engine, depress the gas pedal at least once, all the way to the floor, and then turn the ignition key. After the engine turns over, depress the accelerator to increase the revolutions per minute (rpm). This supplies gas to the engine.

If you're starting a diesel engine, don't depress the gas pedal. Fuel injectors will inject metered diesel fuel into the cylinders to get the engine started and keep it running, so just push the clutch to the floor and hold it while you turn the key.

By doing this, you'll cause electricity to flow from the batteries to the starter motor—this turns the flywheel and cranks the engine, and the air and fuel ignite in each cylinder. When this happens, the pistons are pushed down and that turns the crankshaft. As soon as a diesel engine fires, release the key.

Any questions? If so, read these few paragraphs again.

OTR SAFETY

When you start the gasoline engine, keep your clutch pedal down to the floor—this will assist you in starting the engine safely and it will also place less wear and tear on the engine.

Most mechanics will tell you that engines work more efficiently when they've had a chance to warm up. Gasoline engines need about five minutes. A diesel engine should warm up to about 120 degrees Fahrenheit before you engage the clutch. Normal operating temperature for a diesel is between 165 and 185 degrees Fahrenheit.

Warming up the engine heats most of the liquids needed to run the engine. But check the owner's manual to make sure you're doing the right thing for your vehicle.

OTR SAFETY

Don't allow the vehicle to roll back when it's being started and warmed up. You might hit somebody . . . or something. Start the truck with the parking brake on—and release it when you've got enough engine power to keep from rolling back.

Once you're in gear and ready to go, increase your speed gradually to keep from damaging the vehicle and the engine. Rough acceleration can also damage the coupling, especially in situations where there is poor traction, such as in rain or snow. Too much power too fast may cause the wheels to spin. If that happens, don't lose control. Take your foot off the accelerator.

Slowing the Vehicle

You can slow your vehicle by using the brakes or, in some situations, by downshifting. But there's another option—some vehicles have "retarders" that help slow the vehicle without using the brake. Thus, retarders reduce wear on your brakes.

This is called "jacking the trailer." Retarders come in several varieties—all can be turned on or off by the driver. Some retarders offer power adjustments. When the driver turns on the retarders, their braking power is applied to the drive wheel when you let up on the accelerator.

OTR SAFETY

When driving on wet, icy, or snowy roads, turn the retarders off. If left on, they could cause you to skid.

Shutting Down the Engine

The engine has been running for a few hours and now it's time to shut it down. Perform the following steps to do so:

1. Let it idle for about three minutes. Why? This keeps the lubricant flowing while the hot engine starts to cool.
2. When you stop the engine, be sure to take your foot off the accelerator.
3. Set the parking brake before leaving your vehicle.

Steering

Let's talk about steering. As with driving any other vehicle, the old-fashioned 10 o'-clock and 2 o'clock positions for the hands are best for controlling the steering wheel. Pretend the steering wheel is a clock face. Place your left hand at 10 o'clock and your right hand at 2 o'clock. Rest the thumbs on top of the wheel. When turning, don't cross your arms over the wheel.

Instead, pick up your hands, one at a time, and reposition them.

Shifting

The basic shifting rules and terms, as well as shift patterns and procedures for common transmissions.

For most new drivers, shifting gears on a truck is the biggest concern. In fact, in some companies who have programs where spouses can learn to drive so they can team with their significant others, women learn to drive with automatic transmissions so they won't have to deal with the fear of shifting.

For now though, let's look at gear-shifting step by step:

1. First of all, it's a good idea to read the owner's manual for the vehicle and then use your tachometer as a guide for shifting ranges.
2. The rpm where you shift becomes higher as you move up through the gears. Find out what's right for each vehicle you drive.
3. You can also use road speed—and what speeds each gear is good for. Then, by using the speedometer, you'll know when to shift up.
4. Experienced drivers can tell by the sound of the engine when it's time to shift.

Double-Clutching

If your vehicle has a manual transmission, changing gears will require double-clutching—a basic up-shifting method where you (1) release the accelerator and (2) push in the clutch and shift to neutral at the same time.

Now, release the clutch, let the engine slow down to the rpm required for the next gear, then simultaneously push in the clutch and shift to the higher gear. Release the clutch and press the accelerator at the same time.

OTR SAFETY

If you stay in neutral too long, it may be hard to get into the next gear. So, don't force it! Remain in neutral, increase your engine speed to match your road speed and try again.

Downshifting

To downshift:

1. Release the accelerator, push in the clutch, and shift to neutral simultaneously.
2. Release the clutch and press the accelerator. Increase the engine and gear speed to the rpm required for the next lowest gear.
3. Push in the clutch and shift to the lower gear.
4. Release the clutch and press on the accelerator at the same time.

OTR SAFETY

Hint: Watch the speedometer or tachometer and downshift at the correct rpm or road speed. When starting down a hill: Downshift before going down the hill. Slow down and shift down to a speed you can control without slamming on your brakes.

OTR SAFETY

Warning: If your brakes overheat, you may lose braking power just when you need it most. One rule of thumb—shift to a gear lower than one you'd use to climb this same hill.

Backing

The procedures and rules for various backing maneuvers.

OTR SAFETY

First, an interesting fact—Most backing accidents cause damage to the top of the vehicle. That's right! Low-hanging branches or wires can damage the top of the vehicle or tear off an exhaust stack, so before backing up, make sure the area is clear of wires, low branches, the eaves of a building, and so on.

The next most common damage occurs to the rear of the trailer, so check that area before you start backing up.

Most damage and most accidents occur on the right side of the vehicle, because the "blind spot" is there—from the rear axle to midway up the trailer, and from midway down the door to the ground.

Think your spotter mirror will help? Not always—it won't show you everything you need to see at once.

The following are some easy steps for straight-line backing (see Figure 10-1):

1. Turn off any distractions—your CB, your radio, your CD player—and focus totally on what you're doing.
2. Get out of the truck and check the area under the truck, at the rear, and the area around where you're backing up for low limbs, wires, or anything that would damage your rig.

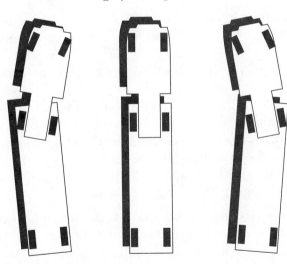

Turning Toward   Backing   Turning Toward
Right Mirror   Straight   Left Mirror
Corrects Right Drift   Corrects Left Drift

1. Position Vehicle Properly
2. Back as Slowly as Possible
3. Constantly Check Behind with Mirrors
4. Use Push-Pull Method of Steering
   • When the Trailer Gets Bigger in One Mirror,
     Turn the Steering Wheel Toward That Mirror to
     Correct the Drift

Figure 10-1 Steps in straight-line backing.

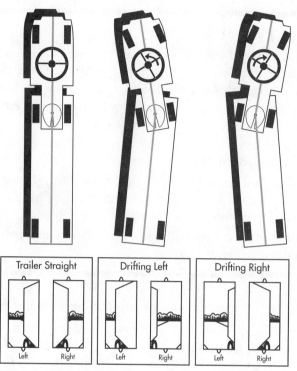

Figure 10-2   Watch both sides of the vehicle when backing.

3. Put on your flashers—never back up without them. They warn others about what you're doing so they'll take the necessary precautions and stay out of your way.
4. Using your mirrors, watch both sides but don't open your door and lean out. (See Figure 10-2.)
5. When backing up a trailer, turn the steering wheel in the opposite direction of where you want the trailer to go (see Figure 10-3). If you want it to go right, turn the steering wheel left. If you want it to go left, turn the wheel right. This is called "jacking the trailer."
6. Once the trailer starts to turn, turn the wheel the other way—to follow the trailer. This is called "following the trailer."

Okay let's review. To turn the trailer, turn the steering wheel in the opposite direction you want the trailer to go. Once the trailer has begun turning, "follow the trailer" by turning the wheel the other way.

Visual Search

The importance of proper visual search, and proper visual search methods.

This may sound basic, but to be a professional driver and keep a clean driving record, you need to train yourself to be aware of what's happening around your vehicle at all times. This means in front, to the sides, and behind.

If you are not aware—or visually alert at all times—you leave yourself open to accidents. How far ahead should you look when you're driving?

Remember that you are handling a vehicle three or four times the length of a four-wheeler, so your forward vision must be at least 12 to 15 seconds ahead of where the vehicle is on the highway.

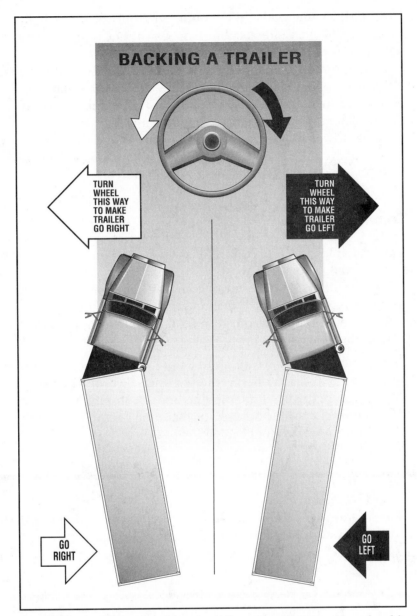

Figure 10-3   When backing a trailer, turn the steering wheel in the opposite direction of where you want to go. This is called "jacking the trailer."

It takes longer for a tractor-trailer rig to change lanes. It takes longer for the rig to stop. And it takes a little time for your brain to translate what you want to do and then send this signal to your hands and feet.

So, looking ahead a quarter mile is necessary. If you're driving city streets—and at lower speeds than highway driving—then you should look (and plan) ahead at least one block.

As you're looking a quarter-mile down the road, your eyes still need to take in what's going on around you. Much like checking both mirrors, shift your eyes from near to far vision and watch for:

- Vehicles coming into your lane
- Vehicles entering the highway
- Vehicle brake lights and slowing traffic

Also, check the road and its condition. Look for traffic lights and signs.

Approaching an intersection? Slow down. The same goes for stop signs or amber warning lights.

Driving down the highway, your main focus must be the road ahead, but quickly check each mirror from time to time to know what's happening around you. However, don't spend a lot of time doing so. Train yourself to glance quickly into each mirror. Then, focus on what's happening ahead of you.

Some drivers like using a curved mirror—these show a wider view than flat mirrors—but everything looks smaller and farther away. Make allowances if you want to use a "bug-eye" (or "fish-eye" or "spotter") mirror.

Communication

The principles and procedures for proper communications and the hazards of failure to signal properly.

Your rig offers several ways of communicating with other drivers. These include turn signals, brake lights, reflectors, and vehicle lights.

Remember to put on your turn signal well before you plan to turn.

Use your brake lights for the following situations:

1. Tap the brake a few times to let other drivers know you're slowing down.
2. Use the flashers when you're driving slowly or when you've stopped your rig.
3. If you're driving a van or a bus and are stopping to let passengers disembark, let other drivers know you're planning to stop by flashing your brake lights. Don't stop without giving notice.

OTR SAFETY

Several states have laws about when to use emergency flashers—be sure you know these before entering into a new state.

How else can you communicate with other drivers? Think about your personal experience driving on the highway or on city streets. Many times you have passed another automobile or a pedestrian or a bicyclist and they probably didn't know you were there.

There are some theories that say, "If you don't think that they know you are there, tap on the horn lightly so they won't suddenly move in front of you while you're passing them." But you also don't want to blast your horn to startle them and make them lose control. It is a fine line between warning and startling, so use caution.

At night, flashing your lights from low beam to high beam and back is a good way to let someone in front of you know you're coming ahead.

In hazy weather, your vehicle's lights make it easier to see. The same is true for rain or snow. Use your headlights on low beam and your identification lights. And if you need to pull off the road in any weather, your flashers will make you more visible and will let other drivers know you've stopped.

OTR SAFETY

If you plan to be stopped on the shoulder for more than ten minutes, regulations say you must put out your reflective triangles—on the traffic side within ten feet of the front and rear of your vehicle. You should also place triangles about 100 feet behind your vehicle and 100 feet ahead if you stop on a curve or a hill. (See Figure 10-4.)

If you have to stop your rig on a hill—place markers within 500 feet so oncoming traffic will be looking for you as they come up the hill.

On a one-way or divided highway—your markers should be placed at 10, 100, and 200 feet toward approaching traffic (see Figure 10-6.). The whole point is to *make yourself visible if your vehicle is stopped anywhere on the roadway.*

Speed Management

The importance of understanding the effects of speed.

You've been on the highway as trucks zoomed past. It may have appeared that those drivers were breaking the speed limit—and some were.

How fast you should drive is your decision, but before you make it, you should understand the factors that go into deciding what speed you should travel.

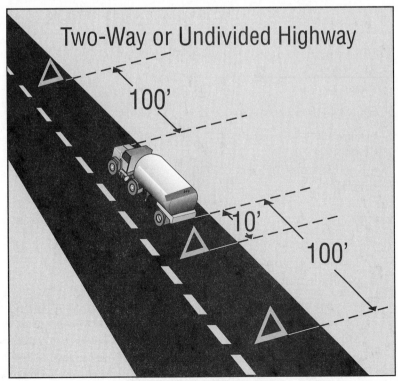

Figure 10-4 Place reflective triangles on the traffic side of your vehicle as shown.

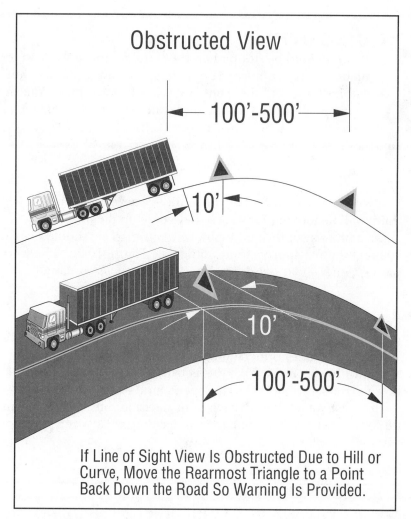

Figure 10-5 When stopped on a hill, place warning markers within 500 feet of your vehicle.

Some of those factors are.

- Weather
- Visibility
- Road conditions
- Traffic
- Hills
- Traction

Another question you need to consider when setting your speed: How much time will it take me to stop if I have to?

Stopping distance is calculated by:

- **Perception time**—how long it takes your brain to interpret what your eyes see as a hazard up ahead. If you are an alert driver, looking 3/4 of a mile up the road, it will take you about 3/4 of a second to see and interpret an upcoming hazard. In that time, if you're traveling 55 mph, your vehicle will travel 60 feet.
- **Reaction time**—how long it takes your brain to make your body react to the upcoming hazard. That involves your brain deciding what to do and your foot

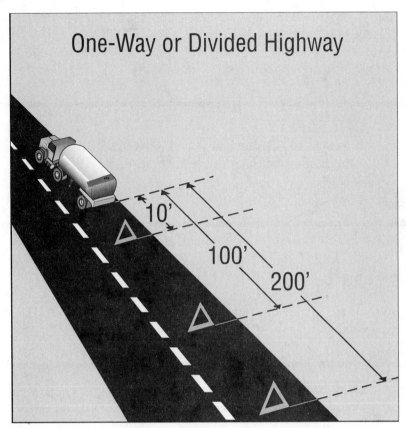

Figure 10-6   On a divided highway, place markers at 10,100, and 200 feet toward oncoming traffic.

easing off the accelerator and pushing the brake. The average reaction time for most drivers is 3/4 of a second—so add another 60 feet to your vehicle's stopping distance.

- **Braking time**—If you have good reaction time and good brakes, if you are traveling 55 mph on good roads and dry conditions, it will take a loaded rig about 170 feet—and four to five seconds—to stop.
- **Total stopping distance**—from the time you see the hazard until your rig has stopped—about the length of a football field. If you're traveling faster than 55 mph, the distance it takes to stop increases. Here's the equation: If you double your speed, it will take you four times the distance to stop.

The distance the vehicle travels once the brakes make contact with the drum. With good braking technique and perfectly adjusted brakes on good, dry, pavement the vehicle going 55 mph will travel 150 additional feet until it comes to a complete stop.

Don't forget about the weight factor. If your vehicle is fully loaded, it will require more braking power to stop, but an empty vehicle requires more distance to stop because it will have less traction and could cause you to go into a skid more easily.

Road Conditions—An Important Factor in Determining Speed

As you gain professional driving experience, you'll become familiar with the states that offer well-maintained highways and those that do not. Some states offer well-paved roads with roomy shoulders. Some states are notorious for roads full of chuckholes, no shoulders, and terrible upkeep.

It is common sense that the roads that are well-maintained are those where you can travel at higher—but safer—speeds.

OTR SAFETY

Remember: You cannot steer or brake your vehicle without traction. Traction is the friction between the vehicle's tires and the road.

Some road conditions make traction difficult, some make it easier. Slippery roads and roads with lots of curves reduce traction.

When a road is wet, icy, or snow-covered, traction is more difficult, so you must travel at slower speeds. It is more difficult to stop and easier to skid on these surfaces.

OTR SAFETY

One rule of thumb: When roads are wet, your stopping distance doubles. Most drivers recommend reducing your traveling speed by one-third when roads are wet, icy, or snowy. On packed snow, reduce speeds by one-half or more. An experienced driver will tell you, when snow is packed—*stop driving as soon as possible.*

Space Management

The procedures and techniques for controlling the space around the vehicle.

If you think about it, driving safely is simply a matter of allowing enough space around your vehicle—to move forward, to change lanes, and to make maneuvers necessary to drive safely. The following indicates how much space you need:

Ahead

Make sure you're not following the vehicle in front of you too closely. If you are, slow down and back off. A good rule of thumb: Keep one second of space between you and the vehicle in front of you for every 10 feet of vehicle length you have. So, if you've got a 40-foot vehicle and you're traveling 40 mph, you'll need four seconds between you and the vehicle in front of you. Add another second for bad weather or slippery road conditions and one more second for night driving. In the worst conditions—leave at least seven seconds of space between you and the next vehicle.

How do you calculate seconds? Watch the front vehicle pass a certain marker along-side the road—it may be a billboard or a mile marker. Then count—one-thousand-and-one, one-thousand-and-two—until you've counted at least four seconds before you pass that same marker. If you can't count four seconds between that vehicle and yours, slow down!

Behind

You have no control on how closely other vehicles follow you, but one rule to follow is always keep to the right. If you're heavily loaded and can't keep up with the speed of the rest of the traffic, stay to the right.

In bad weather, you'll see many other drivers tend to follow 18-wheelers because they rely on professional drivers to get them through a rough part of the driving. So, when other vehicles follow closely, avoid any quick changes, and if you have to reduce your speed, do so as gradually as possible. If you are making a turn, signal early.

OTR SAFETY
If you're being followed too closely, never speed up! If another driver is tailgating, it is much safer to do so at a slower speed!

Sides

The best way to keep safe distances on the sides of your vehicle is to never drive side-by-side with another vehicle. Also, be aware that you have certain "blindspots," so make certain you don't change lanes or turn without checking to make sure there's no obstruction here.

If you do have to travel next to another vehicle, make certain there is enough space for the two of you. And be aware of wind conditions—high winds can make it hard to stay in your lane and gusts do strange things, so it is important to have enough space around your vehicle.

Above

You've seen bridge markings that display the height of the bridge. These markings tell truckers how much clearance there is between the bridge and the top of the truck. But here's the kicker—sometimes these posted heights are not accurate due to a variety of reasons, perhaps because of road resurfacing that has caused the roadway to be higher, or because of packed snow or other situations.

OTR SAFETY
Remember that a loaded trailer rides lower than an empty trailer. If you're in doubt about whether you have enough clearance to pass safely under a bridge, go slowly. If you're not sure you can make it, take another route.

OTR SAFETY

Also remember—before backing, get out of your cab and check overhead clearance, watching for branches and wires.

Below

There are several obstacles to consider. First, when crossing a railroad track, don't get hung on the track if the dirt approach has worn away. Second, always check under your truck before backing up. Finally, if you see something on the roadway that may get hung up under your rig, try to avoid the obstacle, but don't make any sudden and unsafe maneuvers out of your lane.

Night Operation

Preparations and procedures for night driving.

What makes night driving more challenging? Is it because drivers can't see as far down the road at night as they can during the day? Is it because hazards can't be seen as readily, and reaction times must be rapid-fire?

Sometimes vision is less keen at night than during daylight hours—or it may be that the driver is tired and simply is not as alert as usual. All of these reasons make night driving more difficult.

The following are some suggestions to make night driving safer:

1. Clean headlights mean better night vision—your headlights become your main light source at night.
2. If headlights are out of adjustment, have this corrected before going on the road at night.
3. Make sure reflectors, marker lights, tail lights, clearance lights, and identification lights are all clean and in working order.
4. Clean windshields can also make a difference in your night vision—so make certain your windshield and mirrors are clean on the inside and outside before you start driving.
5. It goes without saying—avoid drugs that tend to take the edge off of your alertness or make you drowsy. The same goes for drinking—when you're driving at night (or any other time), there's no room for alcohol or other chemical use.
6. When driving at night, eat a light evening meal—a heavy meal will make you groggy and will compromise your alertness.
7. If you think coffee will keep you going a few more miles, think again! Coffee will only make you jittery and bug-eyed.
8. The only cure for sleepiness or fatigue is sleep.

Extreme Driving Conditions

The basic information on operating in extreme driving conditions and the hazards that are encountered in extreme conditions.

The following are some other things to consider:

- **Icy bridges**—in cold weather, roadways on bridges will freeze before the roads themselves ice over. Drive carefully when the temperature drops into the freezing range (32 degrees Fahrenheit or lower).
- **Wet ice**—when melting occurs, wet ice is more slippery than normal icy conditions.
- **Black ice**—a thin coating of ice that is usually invisible because you can see the roadway through it. Many drivers, thinking there is no ice on a road, have had problems—sometimes fatal—with black ice. Anytime temperatures are in the freezing range (32 degrees Fahrenheit or lower) and the road appears to be wet—be alert for black ice.
- **Ice checks**—to find out about the road conditions, roll down your window and check for ice on the mirror or mirror support. If you find ice on these, that's a sign there's probably ice on the highway.
- **Rain**—Whether it's pouring rain or only misting, those first few drops will mix with the oil on the road to make the road very slick. If it continues to rain for awhile, this mixture washes away, but be aware: *roads are more slippery at the beginning of a rainstorm.*

  To regain control of a hydroplaning vehicle, first, release the accelerator. Then, push in the clutch to slow your vehicle and let the wheels turn on their own. If you start to skid, don't use the brake to slow down. Instead, push in the clutch to let the wheels turn.

OTR SAFETY

About hydroplaning: If water or slush collects on the roadway, your vehicle could ride on top of the water—much like you do on water skis. If you're riding on top of the water instead of on top of the roadway, your vehicle will have no traction—and when there's no traction, you'll have problems steering and braking your vehicle.

Note: Even if you're traveling 30 mph, your vehicle could hydroplane. Watch for puddles as well—if water is deep enough, your vehicle can hydroplane here, too.

OTR SAFETY

Remember: hydroplaning is more likely to occur if tire pressure is low or if the treads are worn on the tires. If the treads aren't deep enough, they won't carry the water away from the tires.

- **Hot weather**—
  - Watch for bleeding tar—in very hot weather, tar bleeds to the surface and can be very slippery.

- Make certain you slow down enough to keep the engine and tires from overheating. Keep your vehicle as cool as possible—this lessens the chance for tire failure, fire, or engine failure.
- Driving in the desert? Make certain you have enough coolant and good tires before you start your day.
- Check the water gauge and temperature gauge in your coolant from time to time. If the gauge goes above normal, there may be a chance of engine failure and possibly fire—so stop driving and try to find out what's wrong.
- Check your engine belts—make sure they're not too loose or too worn.
- If the engine fan doesn't work properly, it won't keep your engine cool.
- Make sure your hoses can handle the heat. If they're worn or frayed, have them replaced.

- **Other road conditions**—When the road curves, adjust your speed downward. If you take a curve too fast, you can lose traction and your vehicle will continue forward in a straight line—that's not good.

  If you enter a curve too fast and the wheels maintain traction, you may have a rollover—and the same goes for the short curves of a freeway ramp. If you're driving a tanker or any vehicle with a high center of gravity, the chances for rollover are even greater, even traveling at the posted speed.

  To avoid rollovers—slow before you begin the curve. Slow enough so you don't have to use your brakes.

  Whatever the weather or the road conditions, you should always travel at a speed that allows you to stop within the distance you can see ahead. For example, driving in fog you cannot see as far down the highway as you normally could. Slow your speed so that you can stop within the distance you can see down the road.

  At night, of course, your visual field is also limited. Sometimes you can use your high beams, but when low beams are required, decrease your speed so you can stop within the area you can see with your low beams.

  Driving in traffic? The best speed is the speed of the vehicles around you—if it is safe and if it is the legal speed.

  When driving on a downgrade—a long, steep hill—the most important thing to remember about driving is to enter the hill at a speed slow enough to prevent hard braking. If you have to brake heavily, you risk making your brakes too hot to slow you down.

  Follow these steps for a downgrade:

  1. Check brakes before starting downhill.
  2. Downshift to the gear that's one gear lower than you would use to climb the hill.
  3. Use retarders if you have them.
  4. If you need to use your brakes, use a light, steady pressure.

OTR SAFETY
Never exceed the speed limit for the curve. Your speed needs to be much slower!

OTR SAFETY

Remember: Trying to save time by going faster is a bad idea. Maintaining a faster speed is fatiguing and only increases your chances of having an accident.

Hazard Perceptions

The basic information on hazard perception and the clues for recognizing hazards.

Mastering the Turning Maneuver

When driving your personal vehicle, you probably think nothing of making a right or left turn. In a larger vehicle, however, turning can be a complex maneuver—and you need ample space to make turns successfully.

Professional drivers will tell you that right turns are more difficult to make than left turns. Why? Because in a right turn, you can't always see what's happening on the right of your vehicle as well as you can see on the left side (see Figure 10-7).

TRACTOR-TRAILER TRACKING CHARACTERISTICS

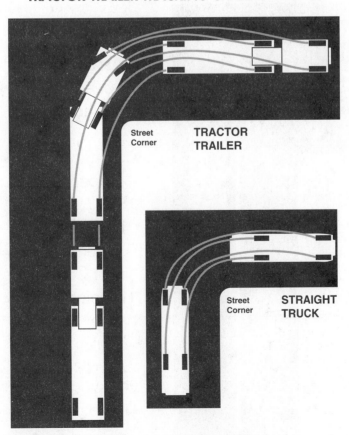

Figure 10-7 Making a successful right turn.

It takes practice to make a successful right turn, but following these steps will help:

1. Turn the vehicle slowly and surely to give yourself time to avoid problems.
2. If there's no room to turn wide at the beginning of the maneuver, swing wide as you complete the turn.
3. Don't go into the oncoming lane to turn widely as you start the turn. Why? Because people behind you may think you're going to make a left turn.
4. Keep the rear of your vehicle close to the curb. This helps you turn and keeps others from trying to pass on the right.
5. If crossing over into the next lane is necessary, give oncoming vehicles ample time to stop or go by. Don't back up for them because you run the risk of hitting someone behind you.

To make a left turn:

1. Roll to the center of the intersection before starting your turn.
2. Remember off-tracking and don't start your turn too soon.
3. If there are two turn lanes, always start a left turn from the outer turn lane.
4. Don't start your turn in the inside lane because you may have to swing right to make the turn (see Figure 10-8).

MAKING A LEFT TURN

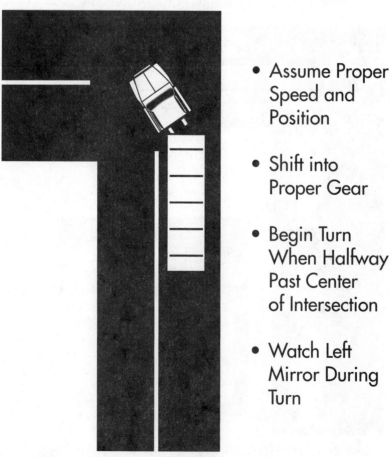

- Assume Proper Speed and Position

- Shift into Proper Gear

- Begin Turn When Halfway Past Center of Intersection

- Watch Left Mirror During Turn

Figure 10-8   Making a successful left turn.

Special Tactics for Road Hazards

There are a variety of road hazards—there always have been, and there always will be. So be prepared—train yourself about what to do. Being prepared reduces chances of accidents and of putting your life in danger.

The following are some of the various road hazards you will find, and the suggested tactics for overcoming these hazards:

- Work zones—some states are assigning heavy fines for dangerous driving around work zones. Be alert—drive at the recommended speed limit or below. Use your four-way flashers or brake lights to warn others behind you that you are taking this strip of the highway slowly and carefully.
- Sometimes when the road is being resurfaced, there may be narrower lanes and uneven road between lanes—so don't drive too near the edge. You'll also find it harder to steer in a drop-off area.
- Is there something in the road ahead—perhaps a box or a piece of tire? Do everything possible to miss it, but if you are unable to maneuver around it, go over it as slowly as possible.
- Are other drivers taking stupid risks? Give them plenty of room. And be suspicious of drivers who are weaving, leaving the road, stopping at the wrong time or waiting too long for a stop, driving with the windows down in cold weather, or speeding up and then slowing down suddenly.
- Be alert for sleepy drivers—especially in the early mornings.
- Watch rental trucks carefully—these drivers probably have little experience driving vans of this size.
- Remember: Anywhere vehicles are present, accidents are just waiting to happen. Keep your mind on your driving and your eyes on the road at all times.

Emergency Maneuvers

The basic information concerning when and how to make emergency maneuvers.

Anything can happen anytime in traffic. The professional driver is aware of this possibility and can, in most cases, avoid accidents. However, sometimes the driver can't control the situation.

The following are some tips for the professional driver when making emergency maneuvers:

- If you see an obstacle in your path, often the best maneuver is to steer around it—to turn to miss it. Stopping is not always the best option for these reasons:
  - You may not have enough room to stop, and
  - Sometimes a quick stop may cause the tractor-trailer rig to flip over.
- Countersteering—Once you've steered around the obstacle, you will turn the wheel back in the other direction. This is called "countersteering" and you must be prepared to steer in the opposite direction. A speedy reaction time is important in this maneuver.
- When turning to miss an obstacle, do it quickly and don't apply your brakes, because this could lock your brakes, causing you to skid out of control.
- In most situations, steering to the right will move you and your rig out of harm's way. If you are blocked on both sides, moving to the right is the best choice because you won't move into the oncoming traffic or cause anyone to move into the opposite lane.

- If you have to leave the paved roadway to avoid an accident, try to keep one set of wheels on the pavement for better traction.
- If your brakes fail, downshift to the lowest gear possible and try to pump the brakes. With hydraulic brakes, you can often build enough pressure to stop the vehicle. The emergency brake is another option—but be sure to press the release button or pull the release lever at the same time you pull the emergency brake. If nothing works, find an escape ramp or turn uphill. This will sometimes slow your vehicle.
- If your tires fail (if there's thumping, vibration, or steering feels tight), stop as soon as possible. To maintain control of your vehicle, hold the steering wheel firmly, and stay off the brake until the vehicle has slowed. Then pull off the road and stop.

Skid Control and Recovery

The information on the causes and major types of skids, as well as the procedures for recovering from skids.

Whenever your tires lose traction, a skid can result. The obvious move is to apply the brakes, but braking too hard may lock up your wheels.

Oversteering can also cause skidding, so don't turn the wheels more than the vehicle itself can turn.

Driving too fast is one of the most common reasons a vehicle goes into a skid. Manage your speed, matching it with road and weather conditions.

Other common reasons a rig will skid when the rear wheels lose traction—over-braking or over-accelerating. When the rear wheels skid, it is usually a result of over-braking and the wheels locking.

When you skid because of ice or snow on the road, simply take your foot off the accelerator and push in the clutch.

To correct a drive wheel braking skid, take your foot off the brake, allow the wheels on the rear to roll and—if you are on icy roads—push in the clutch to let the wheels turn freely. If the vehicle begins to slide sideways, steer in the direction you want the vehicle to go—and turn the wheel quickly. As a vehicle corrects its course, the tendency is to keep on turning, so unless you turn your wheel the other way quickly, you may start skidding again.

OTR SAFETY

A front-wheel skid usually occurs because you're driving too fast, the front tires are worn, or you're carrying too much weight on the front axle.

In a front-wheel skid, the best maneuver is to let the vehicle slow down. Stop turning or hard braking. Slow as quickly as possible without skidding.

Other Information for CMV Drivers

Relationship of Cargo to Vehicle Control

The principles and procedures for the proper handling of cargo.

Vehicle Inspections

The objectives and proper procedures for performing vehicle safety inspections, as follows:

- The importance of periodic inspection and repair to vehicle safety.
- The effect of undiscovered malfunctions upon safety.
- What safety-related parts to look for when inspecting vehicles.
- Pre-trip/en-route/post-trip inspection procedures.
- Reporting findings.

Hazardous Materials

What constitutes hazardous material requiring an endorsement to transport.

- Classes of hazardous materials.
- Labeling/placarding requirements.
- And the need for specialized training as a prerequisite to receiving the endorsement and transporting hazardous cargoes.

Air Brakes

- Air brake system nomenclature.
- The dangers of a contaminated air supply.
- Implications of severed or disconnected air lines between the power unit and the trailer(s).
- Implications of low air pressure readings.
- Procedures to conduct safe and accurate pre-trip inspections.
- Procedures for conducting en-route and post-trip inspections of air-actuated brake systems, including the ability to detect defects that may cause the system to fail.

Other Information for Operators of Combination Vehicles

Coupling and Uncoupling

The procedures for proper coupling and uncoupling a tractor to semi-trailer.

Vehicle Inspection

The objectives and proper procedures that are unique to performing vehicle safety inspections on combination vehicles.

11 Safety Control Systems

The subject of this chapter is just what you would expect, given its title: knowing the equipment included in your vehicle's safety control systems. After you finish reading it, you will understand where these systems are, how they work, and when to use them. We will be looking at all aspects of the system, letting you in on why they are there and how they can help.

Let's get started.

Control Systems

Lights

FMCSR Part 393 describes the types of lights and reflectors that must be used on commercial motor vehicles, as well as those needed in every situation—from road operations to tow-away procedures (see Figure 11-1).

The reasons for lights and reflectors are:

- To help others see you
- To help you see others
- To signal intentions, such as lane changes, slow-downs, or stops
- To communicate with other vehicles

Figure 11-1 Know the location and function of all of your vehicle's lights and reflectors.

Laws require that you have your lights on one half hour before sunset until one half hour after sunrise.

The following are those lights and reflectors required on commercial motor vehicles:

- **Headlights**—two white headlights, one to the right and one to the left, on the front of the tractor. Required on buses, trucks, and truck tractors. Headlights must have a high-beam and low-beam setting.
- **Fog lamps and other bad weather lights**—required in addition to, but not instead of, headlights.

The following are required for buses, trucks, semi-trailers, full trailers, and pole trailers:

- **A front side marker lamp**—two amber lights, one on each side of the front of buses and trucks, tractors, semi-trailers, and full trailers.
- **Side marker lamps**—two amber lights to each side or near the center between the front and rear side marker lamps. Required for buses, trucks, semi-trailers, full trailers, and pole trailers.
- **Front side reflectors**—two amber reflectors on each side toward the front of buses and trucks, tractors, semi-trailers, full trailers, and pole trailers.
- **Side reflectors**—two amber reflectors on each side or near the midpoint between the front- and rear-side reflectors of buses and trucks, large semi-trailers, large full trailers, and pole trailers.
- **Front turn signals**—two amber signals to the left and right front of the tractor.

The following signals can be above or below the headlights. They are required on buses, trucks, and truck tractors.

- **Front identification lamps**—three amber lights at the center of the vehicle or cab. Required on large buses, trucks, and truck tractors.
- **Front clearance lamps**—two amber lamps at each side of the front of large buses, trucks, truck tractors, large semi-trailers, full trailers, pole trailers, and projecting loads.
- **Rear side marker lamps**—one red light on each side of the lower-left and lower-right rear of the side of buses and trucks, semi-trailers and full trailers, and pole trailers.
- **Rear side reflectors**—red reflectors located just below the rear side marker lamps. Required on buses, trucks, semi-trailers, full trailers, and pole trailers.
- **Rear identification lamps**—three red lights centered in the top rear of large buses and trucks, large semi-trailers, full trailers, and pole trailers. Not required on smaller vehicles.
- **Rear clearance lamps**—two red lights at the top right and left of the rear of large trucks and buses, tractors, semi-trailers, full trailers, pole trailers, and projecting loads. These lamps outline the overall width. Not required on smaller vehicles.
- **Rear reflectors**—two red reflectors on the lower right and lower left of the rear of small and large buses and truck trailers, full trailers, and pole trailers.
- **Stop lamps**—two red lights, one at the lower right and one at lower left of the rear of the vehicle. All vehicles are required to have these. Not required on projecting loads.
- **The license plate lamp**—one white light at center rear on buses, trucks, tractors, semi-trailers, full trailers, and pole trailers.

- **The backup lamp**—one white light at the rear of buses, trucks, and truck tractors.
- **Rear turn signal lamps**—two amber or red lights, each located at lower right and lower left of the rear of trucks and buses, tractors, semi-trailers, full trailers, pole trailers, and converter dollies.
- **Parking lamps**—two amber or white lights located just below the headlights on small buses and trucks.
- **Four-way flashers**—two amber lights at the front and two amber lights or red lights at the rear of the vehicle. These are usually the front and rear turn signal lights, equipped to do double duty as warning lights. They can be set to flash simultaneously. Required on buses and trucks, tractors, semi-trailers, full trailers, pole trailers, and converter dollies.

The Horn

Every vehicle must have a horn and, like the lights, it is used to communicate with other motorists. The horn often distracts or alarms other drivers, so don't use it without a good reason. When you inspect your vehicle, make certain your horn works—if it doesn't, look for a blown fuse or faulty or broken wire.

Mirrors

Most commercial motor vehicles have rear-view mirrors on each side of the cab, while a few vehicles may have an outside mirror on the driver's side. A mirror inside the vehicle gives a view of the rear of the rig. In the large, flat mirror, you should be able to see traffic and the sides of your trailer. You should also be able to see the road behind you from mid-trailer on back.

OTR SAFETY

Adjust mirrors so you can see the ground, starting in front of the trailer wheels and including all of both lanes. In the small convex mirror, you should be able to see traffic. Convex mirrors also help you see the "blind spots" along the middle of your vehicle.

Fire Extinguishers

FMCSR Part 393 mandates carrying a fire extinguisher in your truck—*always*. You should also have the extinguisher inspected every two years.

When fighting fires, it is important to know that types of fires are grouped according to class.

- **Class A Fires**—involve wood, paper, cloth, trash and other ordinary material
- **Class B Fires**—fires fueled by gasoline, grease, oil, paint, or other flammable liquids
- **Class C Fires**—electrical fires

Most trucks carry a five-pound. fire extinguisher—it's the law. These can put out Class B and C fires.

If the vehicle is hauling hazardous materials that are placarded, you must have a ten-pound. B:C fire extinguisher filled with a dry chemical. When squeezing the handle on this kind of extinguisher, a needle punctures an air pressure cartridge inside the tank, releasing air pressure that forces the powder out of the tank. This powder travels through the hose, out the nozzle, and onto the fire. In this case, the fire is extinguished by smothering it.

How Do You Use the Extinguisher?

1. Aim it at the base of the fire. This is the real problem, not the flames.
2. When using the extinguisher, stay as far from the fire and flames as possible. Position yourself with your back to the wind.
3. Continue dousing the fire until whatever is burning has cooled—regardless of whether there is visible smoke or flames. Make sure the fire is completely out so it won't start again.

Vehicle Fires

All professional drivers have the responsibility of knowing how to put out a vehicle fire. The first priority in this situation is to protect your life and the lives of others. Following such measures, you should try to save the vehicle and its cargo. To accomplish this, you will need to know about fires and have a working fire extinguisher.

Q. What causes vehicle fires?
A. Fires can start after accidents, as a result of a fuel spill, or from the improper use of flares.

- There's also the possibility of a tire fire. Underinflated tires and dual tires that touch create enough friction to cause fires.
- On some trucks, there's a strong possibility of electrical fires, usually due to short circuits caused by damaged insulation or loose wires.
- Carelessness is a major cause of vehicle fires, including behaviors such as smoking around the fuel pump, improper fueling, and loose fuel connections.
- In addition, fires can be caused by flammable cargo or cargo that is improperly sealed, ventilated, or loaded.

All of these reasons make it very important to perform a complete pre-trip inspection of your vehicle's electrical, fuel, and exhaust systems, including the tires and cargo.

Q. Do I need to check all along the way?
A. It's always a good idea to check the tires, wheels, and truck body for signs of heat—whenever you stop during the trip.

Always fuel the vehicle safely and be careful with any part of the vehicle that usually creates heat or flame.

Check gauges and other instruments often while driving. Use mirrors to look for signs of smoke, and if any system is overheating, fix it before you have a bigger problem.

Q. What if there is a fire in or around my vehicle?

A. Keep in mind that caution is most important. Drivers who don't know what to do during a fire have made the situation worse. Don't be one of them! In case of a fire, follow these procedures:

- Get the vehicle off the road and stop. Park in an open area, away from buildings, trees, brush, and other vehicles. *Don't pull into a service station!*
- Use your CB or cell phone to notify police, highway patrol, or 911. Be sure to give them your location.
- Keep the fire from spreading. Before trying to put out the fire, do what you can to keep it from traveling elsewhere.
- For engine fires, turn off the engine. Don't open the hood if you don't have to. Aim the fire extinguisher through the radiator louvers or from beneath the vehicle.
- In case of a cargo fire, keep the doors shut! Opening the doors will feed the fire with air from outside.
- Use water on burning wood, paper, or cloth—but not electrical because you could receive an electrical shock. Don't use water on a gasoline fire. It will only feed and spread the flames.
- A burning tire should be cooled, so you will need to douse it with a lot of water.
- If no water is in the area, throw sand or dirt on the flames.
- Use the correct kind of fire extinguisher.

Instruments and Gauges

The instrumental panel of a truck is called "the dashboard" or "the dash." Some of the gauges you'll find on the dashboard monitor the operation of the engine. Others monitor different systems, reporting on their conditions at all times. (See Figure 11-2.)

The Ammeter

- Normal is zero.
- A continuous high charge (+) or discharge (−) means problems with the electrical system.

The ammeter, also located on the dashboard, is used to indicate the amount of charge or discharge the battery is receiving from the generator. It should read "zero" when the engine and the electrical system are off. Starting the engine will move the needle from zero to the charge side. Once the engine is on and warm, the needle should drop back to zero. It is also normal for it to read slightly on the charging side.

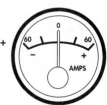

VOLTMETER

Starting
- Green — Well Charged Battery
- Yellow — Low Battery Charge
- Red — Very Low Charge

Operating
- Green — Okay
- Red — Voltage Output Too High!

AMMETER
- Normal is ZERO
- Continuous High Charge + or Discharge − Means Problems With the Electrical System

Figure 11-2 Gauges used to measure the electrical system.

The Voltmeter

Starting

- Green—Well-Charged Battery
- Yellow—Low Battery Charge
- Red—Very Low Charge

Operating

- Green—Okay
- Red—Voltage Output too High!

Besides gauges and warning lights, the dashboard also contains switches and controls that are used to operate the vehicle or its systems. A simple example is the air-conditioning. There's a switch and when you move it, it turns on the air conditioning system.

Starting at the far left on most dashboards you'll see the air-conditioning vent. Next to it are five gauges:

The Voltmeter Gauge

The voltmeter shows whether or not the battery is charging properly. This gauge can be identified by the word *Volts* on the lower portion of the gauge; a picture of the battery may also be included.

The gauge consists of three segments, each showing a different condition:

- The far left segment (red) shows undercharging.
- The middle (green) segment shows the normal battery condition.
- The far right-hand (red) segment indicates overcharge. A pointer shows the condition of the battery at the moment.

If the voltmeter shows a continuous undercharging or overcharging condition, there's a problem in the charging system.

The Engine Temperature Gauge

The engine temperature gauge is usually marked "Temp" or "Water Temp." This gauge indicates the temperature of the engine's cooling system in degrees. The typical gauge has a range from 100 to 250 degrees Fahrenheit.

Normal temperature is between 165 and 185 degrees Fahrenheit. If you are driving in hot weather, the temperature will read higher, so don't be alarmed.

The Oil Pressure Gauge

The oil pressure gauge indicates how the engine is being lubricated, which is measured in pounds per square inch (psi).

When the engine is running and the oil is cold, the gauge will show a high reading. When the engine has been running for awhile and the oil is warmer, the reading will go back to normal. When the engine is running at normal temperatures and the oil is hot, the normal idle pressure runs from 5 to 15 psi. In normal operation, pressure runs from 30 to 75 psi.

OTR SAFETY
Remember! Always check this instrument after starting the engine. If no pressure is indicated, stop the engine at once because you can damage the motor by running it with no oil pressure.
• Idling • Operating • Low, Dropping, Fluctuating: 5–20 psi, 35–75 psi

A low reading may mean that the oil level is low, there may be a leak, or the filter could be clogged.

If you have an oil temperature gauge, make sure the temperature is within the normal range while you are driving.

The Pyrometer

The pyrometer displays the engine exhaust temperature. The safe range will be indicated next to the gauge on the dashboard. High exhaust temperatures could be trouble, meaning a leak or clog in the air intake or the exhaust system. Or there could be problems with the fuel ignition. Or the vehicle could be in the wrong gear ratio for the load, grade, or altitude.

On most dashboards, below these instruments are gauges that indicate the temperature of various parts of the vehicle during operation. These are:

- The transmission temperature gauge—oil temperatures range from 180 to 250 degrees Fahrenheit. These are only guidelines.
- Rear axle and forward rear axle temperature gauges—the normal temperature range for axles is from 160 to 220 degrees Fahrenheit. These are only guidelines.

The range of some transmissions—like the Fuller Transmission—may be 180 to 225 degrees Fahrenheit.

OTR SAFETY
If the temperature gauge on this transmission reads 250 degrees Fahrenheit, you're almost to a critical range. Check the owner's manual to find out what's normal.

Like the engine temperature gauge previously described, these gauges display information in degrees. A high reading will tell you there are problems in that particular part of the vehicle. If the temperature is high, stop the vehicle before more damage occurs.

Warning Lights

The warning lights include:

- The left-hand turn signal (LH)
- The water level warning light (WATER)

- The oil level warning light (OIL)
- The high beam (HB)
- The low air light (AIR)
- The differential lock warning lights (DL)
- The right-hand turn signal (RH)
- The cab lock light (not on all trucks; only on tilt-up cabs)
- The Antilock Braking System (ABS) light

There may also be warning buzzers, depending on the vehicle's manufacturer. This cluster of lights is sometimes called the "telltale" panel because some will tell you if a control is working and some will tell you if a gauge or control is not working. Still others will tell you there is a big problem that demands your attention *now!*

Engine Starts

When starting the engine:

- The cluster lights should come on for a few moments to indicate that they are working properly.
- If a light doesn't come on, check to see whether it is broken or a problem exists.
- If a light stays on, that means you have a problem. Do not operate the vehicle until you determine what the problem is and have it repaired.

Important Questions and Answers

Q. Are turning indicators really important?

A. Turn signal warning lights come on whenever the right or left turn signal is used. If they don't come on, something is wrong. Either the warning light is defective or the signal is not working. Turn signals are a safety tool for all professional drivers because they let other motorists know what you plan to do. It is illegal to drive without them.

Q. What's happening when the water temperature, oil level, and low air lights come on?

A. It means something is wrong. If the water temperature in the coolant plant gets too high, the water temperature light will come on. If the oil pressure is too low, the oil pressure light will come on. And if the air pressure in the braking system drops below 60 psi, the low air lights will come on. Some of these warning lights are also equipped with buzzers when something goes wrong.

Q. What do the high beam and differential lock lights do?

A. The high beam light tells you your high beams are on. The differential lock light tells you the differential lock is in the locked position.

Q. What does the charging circuit warning light indicate?

A. This light is standard on some vehicles, but not on others. It comes on if your battery isn't charging. It's usually lit when the starter switch is turned on, telling you the light is working. It goes out as soon as the engine starts— unless there is a problem.

Q. What does the low vacuum warning light indicate?

A. When this light comes on, it means the vacuum in the brake booster is below safety limits and it may be that you are low on braking power. What do you do next? You don't drive the vehicle until the brake problem is checked out and repaired.

On some cabs, there is a cab lock warning light that tells you when the cab tilt lock isn't secure—not a good thing!

Behind the Steering Wheel

Behind the steering wheel are a number of components, including:

- **The tachometer**—usually called "the tach," this shows how many revolutions the engine crankshaft makes per minute (rpm), and tells you when it's time to shift gears. To read engine rpm, multiply the number on the tach by 100. So, if you see 15 on the tach and multiply by 100, you have the rpm—1500 (see Figure 11-3).

  - The average diesel engine horsepower goes to a maximum of 1800 rpm.
  - The engine's range may be from 500 rpm at idle to 2100 rpm.

- **The speedometer/odometer**—the speedometer shows the vehicle's road speed in miles per hour (mph). The odometer (located inside the speedometer) keeps track of the total miles the vehicle has traveled. Mileage is shown in one-tenth mile increments.

- **The throttle**—you may want to think of the throttle as the accelerator pedal on the dashboard. You pull it out to set engine speed and use it in cold climates to keep the engine warm during idle.

- **The ignition switch**—(or starter) supplies electricity to the engine and other systems. When the key is turned, it turns on the accessory circuits. As soon as the engine starts, release the key. If you have a "false start," let the engine cool for 30 seconds before giving it another try.

The next part of the dashboard contains the fuel gauge, fuel filter gauge, and the air brakes control.

- **The fuel gauge**—shows the fuel level in the fuel supply tanks.

Some vehicles have more than one tank—if your vehicle does, be sure to check the fuel level in all tanks before deciding you're out of fuel.

- **The fuel filter gauge**—has a colored band divided into two segments to indicate the condition of the fuel filter. It has numbered markings as well as a white segment on the left, and red segments for the middle and the right. If the needle reads "red," you have a clogged fuel filter.

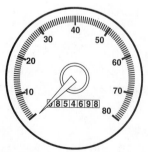

SPEEDOMETER

- Measures speed in MPH

TACHOMETER

- Measures engine speed in RPMs

- Tells you when to shift

Figure 11-3 The speedometer/odometer.

- **The air brakes control**—if your vehicle is equipped with air brakes. (Information about air brakes is covered in the "Air Brakes Endorsement.")

After this cluster of fuel gauges and indicators, you'll find the light switches. This panel controls all the lights, except the dimmer switch for the high beams (which is on the floor and is operated by your foot).

Some vehicles display their light switches on a stalk to the left of the steering wheel. You may find your switches here, including the dimmer switch, turn signals, and flashers.

Below the light switches, you'll find other controls:

- **The inter-axle differential controls**—for vehicles with dual rear axles that have inter-axle differentials. In the unlocked position, these controls allow each axle shaft to turn at different speeds. The control should be set at "Unlocked" or "Off" unless the road is slippery. For these conditions, set the control to "Locked" or "On" to supply power to all wheels.
- **The windshield wipers**—on tilt cabs, electric wipers have two controls—one for each wiper. Some air wiper systems use one control knob, located on the dash, for both wipers. The position of the knob controls wiper speed and there is a separate control for the windshield washers.
- **The air-conditioning controls**—air speed controls determine the temperature in the cab, usually with low, medium, and high settings. There are controls for heating, cooling, and defrosting—much like automobiles.
- **The cold start and warm-up switch**—this switch is used in cold weather when the engine is hard to start. The switch will light to tell you it is on—but check the operator's manual for the engine and starting aid on your vehicle.
- **The exhaust brake switch**—if your vehicle has one, turn the exhaust brake switch to "On." This provides extra slowing power, which comes in handy for steep downgrades or when you're pulling an extra-heavy load.

On the floor of the cab, you'll find:

- **The accelerator pedal**—located just under the steering wheel, you can operate this pedal with your right foot to control engine speed. When you push this pedal, the vehicle will speed up. As you let your foot off, the vehicle slows down.
- **The brake pedal**—this is just to the left of the accelerator and is also operated with your right foot. When you press down on the pedal, the brakes are applied and the vehicle slows down.
- **The clutch pedal**—located to the left of the brake pedal, the clutch pedal is operated with your left foot. You press the clutch pedal to disengage the clutch and when you release the pedal, you engage the clutch.
- **The dimmer switch**—located on the floor to the left of the brake pedal (if it isn't on the dashboard). This switch allows you to move headlights from low beams to high beams. Low beams are best when driving in traffic.

OTR SAFETY
High beams help on dark open roads where there is little traffic and no street lights.

- **The transmission control lever**—some vehicles have a power take-off lever (PTO), which is really two knobs. Pull up on the first knob—it connects the PTO to the transmission. Pull up on the second knob to use the PTO.
- **The trailer brake hand-control valve**—this is usually found on the steering column and allows you to apply the trailer's service brakes without employing the tractor's service brakes.

Troubleshooting

As a professional driver, it is your job to read the gauges on your instrument panel and know what should be done when a light comes on, indicating a problem. This is called "problem-solving" and much of your skill at troubleshooting will come with time and experience.

To give you a foundation for troubleshooting, it is important that you understand what the major systems do when the truck is running. This review will also help you get ready for the CDL tests.

> **Q. How do I show that I can "troubleshoot" when I take the CDL?**
> **A.** One of the first ways is when the examiner asks questions about vehicle parts and systems as you are doing the pre-trip inspection. You must know what makes each system work and show knowledge about repairing small problems, should they arise.
>
> The systems and parts you will cover over the next few pages are also listed in the FMCSR Part 393. To learn about systems and parts:
>
> - Read FMCSR Part 393.
> - Read the owner's manual for your truck.
> - If you have specific questions, ask the carrier's maintenance personnel.
> - You may also find books in the bookstore or at the library on diesel mechanics, electricity, hydraulics, motor vehicles, and other related topics.

Wiring and Electrical Systems

Your commercial motor vehicle gets its power from an engine, and that power is electrical power.

Without electricity, you couldn't start your engine, you couldn't run your lights, and your instruments and gauges wouldn't work—so electricity is important to understand because it serves many purposes.

The following are some of the basics:

- An electron is a tiny particle carrying a negative charge of electricity.
- Electrical flow produces electrical current—and some materials conduct electrical current more easily than others.
- A good electricity conductor is a material whose electrons can be easily moved. Copper wire is such a conductor and it is frequently used to move an electrical charge from its source to its point of use. Because rubber is not a good conductor of electrical current, copper wire is usually surrounded with rubber insulation.
- Insulated wires bring electrical current where electricity is needed.
- Terminals are the connecting devices between the electrical wires and the part where electricity is needed. Terminals connect wires to the components.
- There is also a main terminal where the wires start. This same main terminal contains the system circuit breakers and fuses.

Q. What is a "closed" or "continuous" circuit?

A. A circuit is a continuous path made up of a conductor (wire) and a source of power that moves the current around the circuit (batteries and alternator or generator).

The components that use electricity (the vehicle's starter and lights, for example) are a part of the path. This type of circuit is called a "complete" or "closed" circuit, because the current can flow only if all parts of the circuit are grounded.

There must be a wire (conductor) to bring the electrons back to where they started.

Two kinds of circuits exist where electricity will not flow:

- **Open circuit**—occurs when the normal flow of electrical current is stopped. One of the reasons for this stoppage could be corroded connections or broken wires.

- **Short circuit**—occurs when electrical current bypasses part of the normal circuit. So instead of going to the light bulb, for example, the current stops before it gets to the bulb and flows back to the source (the battery).

This happens because the insulation has come off a section of wire and it touches another wire, allowing the electrical current to take the shortest route back to the source of power.

The following conditions may cause a short circuit:

- The wires on an electrical coil lose their insulation and touch each other.

OTR SAFETY

You should always take a close look at the wiring for rubbing, fraying, or breaks each time you do a pre-trip inspection! Replace broken wires and any insulation that is worn.

Regulations require that wiring be installed and insulated so shorts won't occur.

- A wire rubs against the frame or other metal part of the vehicle until that bare wire touches another piece of metal.

Q. What does grounding mean?

A. A grounding circuit works for your safety:

- When electrical wires burn or break, the normal path or circuit is broken. But instead of stopping, the current looks for a way to complete the trip. If you saw the broken wires and picked them up with both hands, your body would complete the circuit, and that wouldn't be good.

- If wires had rubbed to the point that the insulation was worn off and a short circuit occurred, and the wire was touching the metal of the vehicle's frame, if you touched the frame, you would again become part of the circuit—and strong current could kill you.

A ground provides an alternate safe path for the current if the normal path is accidentally broken.

Batteries

These little black boxes convert chemical energy into electrical energy. Once this is done, they supply power to the rest of the vehicle's electrical system.

The parts of the battery include:

- **The case**—this neatly holds all the parts together.
- **The vent caps**—these are located on top of the battery. They allow gas build-up to escape. Remove the vent caps to check the battery—you may find them clogged and in need of cleaning from time to time.
- **Individual cells**—there are dry-charged, wet-charged, and maintenance-free batteries. A dry-charged battery has no fluids in it when it leaves the factory and the dealer adds water to the battery when it is sold. A wet-charged battery has fluid in it when it leaves the factory. These two types must be checked for fluid levels when you do a pre-trip inspection. Maintenance-free batteries require no additional liquid.
- **Cell connectors**—these transport the electricity from the cell to the power supply.
- **Two terminal posts**—these are located on top of the battery. One is a positive post (the larger one), and the other is a negative post.

OTR SAFETY

Electricity can be dangerous if you do not exercise extreme caution when working with it.

The following are some tips for working safely with batteries:

- Disconnect the battery ground strap before you begin any electrical or engine work.
- Connect the ground strap last when you install a new battery.
- Never lay metal tools or other objects on the battery.
- Never hook up the battery backwards—make sure to connect the positive cable to the positive terminal post. Connect the negative cable to the negative post. (The positive cable clamp and terminal usually are larger than the negative cable clamp and terminal.)
- Be careful when handling batteries. Battery acid is corrosive.
- Don't lean too closely to the battery when adding water—any splash could get into your eyes.
- Keep fires away from batteries. If you're a smoker, save your cigarette until after you've finished working under the hood.

Circuit Breakers and Fuses

To protect the circuit from short circuits and current overloads, circuit breakers and fuses act as built-in protection. The following are a few facts to be aware of:

- A current overload happens when a circuit gets more current than it can handle.

- Wires are rated according to how much load they can handle. If they become overloaded, they may burn.

A short circuit usually causes the overload. When you turn on the lights, the radio, and the starter, the flow of the electricity actually slows down. If there is a short circuit, these systems won't work. This means the current coming through the wire is more than the wire can handle, so it overheats and burns. Fuses and circuit breakers prevent this from happening.

Q. What do I do if a fuse blows?

A. You may think the answer is obvious, but some people don't know that the fuse must be replaced before the circuit can be completed again. But if an overload has occurred, you also need to find the cause of the overload, or you'll immediately blow another fuse.

Circuit breakers are also rated by their capacity to carry current. The circuit breaker used in a circuit must match the circuit's current capacity.

One More Important Electrical Part

The detachable electrical connection—working in combination between the tractor and the trailer—supplies power from the tractor's power plant to the trailer, where it powers the trailer's lights.

Straight trucks don't have detachable electrical connections.

The Electrical System

Most CMVs contain a basic 12-volt electrical system. And if you look closely, you'll see many of the same parts you would find in your personal vehicle. All depend on the battery for electrical power—to start the engine and for other functions.

Once the engine starts, the alternator or generator supplies the power that keeps the battery charged and runs the truck's systems. Older vehicles rely on generators, whereas newer vehicles rely on alternators.

A belt from the engine's crankshaft drives the generator when the engine is running.

That generator is then responsible for producing electricity to run all other electrical circuits—and at the same time, keep the battery charged.

When the engine is turned off, the stored energy in the battery provides the electrical "juice" to run the horn, lights, and other instruments.

The alternator does the same job that the generator is responsible for doing, but alternators are lighter, cheaper to build, and produce more current at low speeds.

Brakes

Even a novice mechanic knows the brakes stop the vehicle. The engine makes it go, the brakes make it stop, right?

Q. What makes the brakes work?

A. Friction. In drum brakes, the brake shoes move toward the brake drums.

The shoes have a lining or pad of coarse material, and when this is pushed into the drum, it creates friction—which stops the truck.

In another kind of brake system—disc brakes—the friction pad moves toward a metal disc. When these parts connect, friction results—and the vehicle stops.

The amount of pressure applied to the brakes creates the amount of force the shoes apply to the drum. In your personal vehicle, if you stomp on the brakes with a lot of force, the vehicle stops quickly. If you just tap the brakes and allow the vehicle to slow to a stop, this light, smooth technique stops the car more slowly.

Q. What about the brakes needed to stop a truck?

A. On larger commercial motor vehicles, the brake shoes and linings are pushed toward the drum or disc, thanks to pressure—which can be one of three types:

- **Hydraulic pressure**—this is usually on straight trucks and buses; hydraulic brakes use fluid pressure.
- **Vacuum pressure**—vacuum brakes have a cylinder with a moving piston, much like hydraulic brakes. In vacuum brakes, atmospheric pressure is on one side and the vacuum is on the other. The pressure of the atmosphere trying to fill the vacuum pushes the piston into the vacuum.
- **Air pressure**—see Chapter 13.

Parking Brakes

The parking brakes are used when you park your truck. All commercial motor vehicles manufactured after 1989 are required to have parking brakes.

Q. How do I apply the parking brakes?

A. Simply pull the parking brake control. All braking systems use this kind of control, but on some vehicles, pulling a lever or knob controls the cable that pulls the parking brakes into position.

To release the brakes, push the control back in. When you push in the knob, it releases the cable and the brakes. In most trucks, it takes a little effort to pull the brakes on—sort of like the parking brake in your personal vehicle. It takes an extra pull to set the parking brakes.

On some vehicles, setting the parking brakes requires more strength than the average driver may have—and that's when the parking brake mechanism is set with the help of air pressure.

Fuel Systems

Almost all fuel systems are alike and have similar parts:

- **The fuel tank** holds the fuel.
- **The primary and secondary fuel filters** clean the fuel before it reaches the fuel pump.
- **The fuel pump** delivers the fuel to the engine.
- **The fuel lines** carry the fuel from the pump to the cylinders.
- **The fuel injectors** spray the fuel into the combustion chambers.

Fuel is highly flammable and must be handled with care in all situations.

OTR SAFETY
Fuel lines must not come in contact with hot surfaces. They must be supported and not allowed to drag on the ground.

Always Remember:

- While driving, remember that the fuel lines should be protected from debris on the highway, but there should be enough slack in the lines so they won't break as the vehicle moves.
- Check to make sure the fuel tanks are mounted and secure.
- Look for leaks when you do your pre-trip and mid-trip inspections. A leaking fuel system wastes precious and costly fuel, but it can also be a hazard. Dripping fuel on a hot surface could cause it to ignite.

Coupling and Towing Devices

According to federal regulations, there are two main methods for towing vehicles:

- When the tractor is pulling the trailer, and
- When a tractor or other towing vehicle is being towed as cargo—called a tow-away operation.

The following are brief descriptions of parts used to pull trailers. (See Figure 11-4.)

Figure 11-4   Coupling the tractor-trailer.

The Fifth Wheel

Some people know the term *fifth wheel* because it is used to describe a recreational vehicle with four wheels that hitches in the back of a pick-up (which serves as the "fifth wheel" for the trailer). In commercial motor vehicles, the fifth wheel is a device that allows the trailer to be connected or uncoupled from the tractor.

It's mounted on the rear of the tractor frame with brackets and fasteners. The lower half of the fifth wheel (called the mounting assembly) must be kept free of bent parts or loose bolts.

The fifth wheel controls how much weight is distributed on each axle of the tractor.

If weight distribution is not equal, it can impact steering and can also cause tires to wear unevenly.

Fifth wheels can also be found on converter dollies as well as tractor frames. A converter dolly converts a semi-trailer to a full trailer—which is how it got its name.

The Locking Device

The fifth wheel has a locking device that keeps the towed trailer and towing tractor together until you're ready to uncouple them. This locking device is called the "locking jaws" and it locks around the shaft of the trailer's kingpin. This makes the connection secure for the trip.

Tow Bars

Trailers must have tow bars—and there must be locking devices on the towing vehicles.

This is how two trailers coupled with a converter dolly are kept from separating.

Aside from tow bars, safety chains, or a cable with the tow bar connection to the towing vehicle, are also used.

Saddle Mounts

A saddle mount is a steel assembly that couples a towed vehicle (trailer or semi-trailer) with the towing vehicle. The saddle mount has a kingpin that fits into the locking jaws of the fifth wheel of the vehicle towing the trailer. Then, a set of U-bolts or clamps secures the coupling to the front axle of the trailer.

Tires

Although they're often taken for granted, tires are an essential part of the rig because they provide traction, reduce vibration, and absorb shock.

Q. **What should I know about tires?**
A.   First of all, tires have to be good enough to provide traction—in all kinds of weather. But they also have to be able to transfer braking and driving force to the road.

As you know, today's market offers numerous different tire designs. But the fact is, all tires are made about the same.

All tires have:

- **Plies**—separate layers of rubber-cushioned cord. Plies make up the body of the tire and are tied into bundles of wire called bead coils. Plies can be bias, belted bias, or radial. (See Figure 11-5.)
  - ◆ **Bias plies** are placed at a criss-crossed angle. This makes the sidewall and the tread very rigid.
  - ◆ **Belted bias plies** cross at an angle and there's an added layered belt of fabric between the plies and the tread. Belts make the tread more rigid than on bias ply tires and the tread will last longer because the belts reduce tread motion when the tire is rolling.

Radial tires have plies that do not cross at an angle but are laid from bead to bead, across the tire. Radial tires have a number of belts and their construction means the sidewalls have less flex and less friction—thus, they require less horsepower and save fuel. Plus, radial tires also hold the road, resist skidding, and give a smoother ride than the bias types.

Other Parts of the Tire

- **Bead coils and beads**—bead coils form the bead—the part of the tire that fits into the rim. Bead coils provide the hoop strength for the bead sections, so the tire will hold its shape when being mounted on a wheel.
- **Sidewalls**—layers of rubber covering that connect the bead to the tread. Sidewalls also protect the plies.
- **Tread**—the part of the tire that hits the road. Treads are designed for specific jobs, such as extra traction and high speed. Tires on steering axles should be

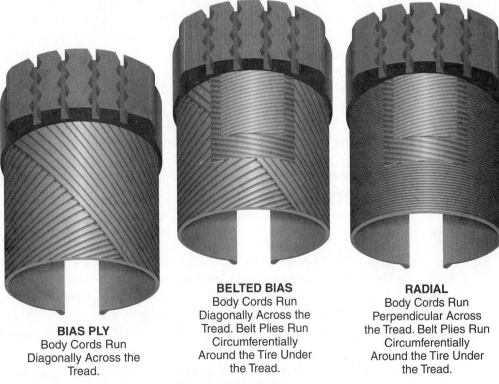

BIAS PLY
Body Cords Run
Diagonally Across the
Tread.

BELTED BIAS
Body Cords Run
Diagonally Across the
Tread. Belt Plies Run
Circumferentially
Around the Tire Under
the Tread.

RADIAL
Body Cords Run
Perpendicular Across
the Tread. Belt Plies Run
Circumferentially
Around the Tire Under
the Tread.

Figure 11-5   Bias ply. Belted bias ply. Radial ply.

able to roll and provide good traction. Drive tires must provide good traction for braking and acceleration. Tires for trailers should roll well. Drive wheel position tires need maximum traction—in all conditions.

- **Inner liner**—the sealing material that keeps air in the tire.

Q. What should I know about tire size?

A. Tire size is usually shown by a number or a series design designation on the sidewall of the tires. For example, in the number 10.00 × 22, the first number is the tire's width. This means an inflated tire of this size will measure ten inches from the farthest point outside on one sidewall to the farthest point outside the other sidewall.

The second number is the rim size. In 10.00 × 22, the tire will fit a 22-inch-diameter rim.

The series design designation came about because of the low-profile tire—a tire wider than its height. These tires are measured in millimeters rather than inches.

If the sidewall reads 295/75 R 22.5, it means:

- The section width is 295 millimeters.
- The aspect ratio (height compared with width) is 75.
- The "R" tells the type of tire—a radial.
- The rim is 22.5 inches in diameter.

Government regulations require tire manufacturers to label all tires with several items of information. Some of these items include: (1) the brand, (2) the manufacturer, (3) the load rating, and (4) the maximum load pressure.

Load rating refers to the strength of the tire. This can be rated from A to Z—with Z being the strongest. The maximum load rating is shown in pounds.

FMCSR Part 393 does not permit the use of a tire that cannot support the load, and the load rating makes certain you have the right tire for the job. *Maximum pressure* is designated in pounds per square inch (psi). This measurement is given for cold tires that have been driven less than one *mile*. This is why you should check tire pressure *before* you drive—and don't check tire pressure by kicking them! Tires have come a long way since your great grandpa's day, when kicking actually told you something.

Use a tire gauge instead. And measure tread depth with the proper instrument, not your fingernail.

OTR SAFETY

According to FMCSR Part 393, a motor vehicle cannot use tires that:

- Have fabric exposed through tread or sidewalls.
- Have less than 4/32 of an inch of tread measured at any point in a major tread groove on the front axle.
- Have less than 2/32 of an inch of tread measured at any point in a major tread groove on all other axles.
- Have front tires that have been regrooved, if tires have load capacity equal to or greater than an 8.25-20 eight-ply tire.

Regrooved tires are not allowed in most states. Be aware of any local regulations regarding these tires.

The following are a few more items to help you do a good job each time you perform a pre-trip inspection of your tires:

- When measuring depth of tread, don't measure at the tie bar, hump, or fillet. The best place to measure is on a major tread groove.
- The hump is a pattern of tire wear that has the same appearance as a cupped hand—the hump is at the edge or higher part of the cup.
- Tie bars and fillets are design factors, not wear patterns. So is a sipe, which is a cut across the tread to improve traction.

OTR SAFETY

You may use regrooved tires, recaps, and retreads on drive wheels and trailer wheels. They *cannot* be used on steering—or front—wheels on most trucks or tractors, however.

Note: If you've just had a tire changed, stop after you've driven it for awhile and make sure its lug nuts have not loosened.

Wheels and Rims, Hubs and Lugs

Tires are mounted on wheels and the wheel connects the tire to the axle. There are spoke wheels and disc wheels.

Q. What's the main difference between spoke wheels and disc wheels?
A. Spoke wheels clamp onto wheels with wheel clamps and if these are not installed properly, the wheel will soon be out of round. That means it will wobble when it rolls.

On a disc wheel, the rim and center portions are a single piece. The rim is part of the wheel and the wheel is bolted to the assembly for the hub and brake drum. With a disc wheel, there is less chance for the wheel to be out of round.

Q. What purpose does the rim serve?
A. The rim supports the tire bead and supports the lower sidewall.

When inspecting this area, make certain that the wheel and the rim are not damaged—cracked or broken—in any way. A cracked or broken wheel or rim can cause an accident. If a rim is damaged, there's a chance the tire could lose pressure or even come off.

The bolt holes and the studs should be perfectly round. If they're egg-shaped, they are out of round and are signs of defects.

OTR SAFETY

All nuts and bolts should be in place, tightened, and free of rust. Use a wrench to check tightness. Never use your hands—it's not a good test.

Missing clamps, spacers, studs, and lugs could cause problems. So could mismatched, bent, or cracked lock rings—they're dangerous, too.

When inspecting, if you see evidence that wheels or rims have been welded in the past, note these welds as defects.

One more thing to check on the tires and wheels—make sure there are no leaks around the hubs and be certain the hubs have a good supply of oil.

You can check the oil level mark on the window of the hubcap.

The Suspension System

Every wheeled vehicle's weight is supported by the suspension system. You are probably familiar with the suspension system—struts and shocks—in personal vehicles. It keeps the ride, smooth, right?

The same applies in a CMV. The suspension system prevents the frame of the vehicle from riding right on the axles and provides a smoother ride for the driver and the cargo.

Today's suspension systems come in four major types:

- **Leaf spring**—in this design, layers of pliable metal are bolted together and the axle is located on the middle of the spring. The front and rear of the spring are attached to the frame.
- **Coil spring**—a spiral of heavy-duty metal is placed at each wheel and the top of the spiral is attached to the frame. The bottom is indirectly connected onto each wheel.
- **Torsion bar**—made of heavy-duty metal that returns to its original shape after it has been twisted, torsion bars absorb shock by twisting. On the highway, the metal contracts, extends, or twists in response to the various levels of the road. The torsion bar allows the wheel to move in and out of low places and over high places while the frame remains stable and level.
- **Air bag**—made of rubber fabric and supplied with compressed air. The supply of air allows the bag to expand or shrink—much like springs contract and expand in response to road shocks.

Q. What do shock absorbers do?
A. They are attached to the springs and are partially filled with hydraulic fluid.

When the piston moves up and down in the cylinder as the spring moves over high and low places, the shock absorber minimizes the spring's motion that's eventually transmitted to the driver.

To maintain the suspension system, keep the springs in good condition, because any cracks, rust, breaks, or other damage often reduce the driver's ability to control the vehicle.

If you have an air bag suspension system—watch for leaks and valve problems. You should also know that the braking system should get charged with air before the air bag suspension system—and the braking system must have at least 55 psi before the air pressure valve on the air bag lets air in. The air bags should also fill all the way around, otherwise the vehicle will not be level.

OTR SAFETY
There should be no air leakage more than three psi over five minutes when the vehicle's air pressure gauge reads "normal." If there's more than three psi over five minutes, get the system fixed before going on the road.

The Steering System

A good driver understands the steering mechanism of his or her truck, the parts of the mechanism, and how it all works.

The steering system allows the driver to make the necessary maneuvers to move the truck from Point A to Point B. This may include turning corners, moving around barriers, and entering and exiting highway ramps—without slipping, sliding, or rolling over.

The steering system begins with the steering wheel—the hand control of the wheels connected to the steering axle. Between the steering wheel and the steering axle are the parts that make steering possible:

1. The **steering wheel** is connected to the **steering column** with a nut. The steering wheel translates the driver's movements to the steering system. When the steering wheel turns, the steering column turns in the same direction.
2. This motion continues through the **U-joint** to the **steering gear shaft.** From there, the driver's motion continues through another U-joint to the steering gear box.
3. The **steering gear box** is also called the **"steering sector."** It changes the rotating motion of the steering column to a back-and-forth motion on the Pitman arm.
4. The **Pitman arm** is a lever attached to the steering gear box and a **drag link** joins the Pitman arm and the steering lever.
5. The **steering lever** is the first part of the **steering (or front) axle** and it performs two separate jobs—it carries a load and it steers the vehicle.
6. The steering lever turns the front wheels left and right when the Pitman arm pulls it back and forth.
7. The steering lever connects to the **steering knuckle** (the moveable connection between the axle and the wheel that allows the wheels to turn left or right). There is a **steering knuckle** at the end of each axle. They contain the **seals, bushings,** and **bearings** that support the vehicle's weight.
8. The steering knuckles translate the motion from the driver to the **cross-steering lever** and the **cross-steering tube** (the tie rod).
9. **Spindles,** which are parts of the **steering axle knuckles,** are inserted through the wheels. Spindles are also called **stub axles** and are attached to the kingpin.
10. The **tie-rod** holds both wheels in the same position. As the left wheel turns, the right wheel follows in the same direction. A **kingpin** in the steering knuckle gives each wheel its own pivot point.

When hydraulic pressure assists in steering a vehicle, a hydraulic unit replaces the steering gear box and a hydraulic pump is added to the engine to supply the pressure used to help turn the wheels.

With hydraulic pressure to help turn the wheels, when the steering wheel is turned to the right, the hydraulic valve senses it, opens, and fluid pressure helps turn the wheels to the right.

You've just completed reviewing the major systems found in most commercial motor vehicles—the wiring and electrical systems, braking systems, fuel systems, coupling devices, tires, emergency equipment, body components, suspension, and steering.

Each of these systems and all of this equipment have been deemed "necessary for safe operation" of a commercial motor vehicle according to the Federal Motor Carrier Safety Regulations.

OTR SAFETY

A vehicle with a power-steering system uses hydraulic pressure or air pressure to assist in making the turn—this requires less strength on the part of the driver.

When Taking the CDL Test

When you take the CDL test, the examiner may ask you questions about any or all of these systems.

He may ask you to identify the parts on your truck, and you may be asked to explain how they work. You will be expected to recognize defects and describe how they impact safe operations.

We suggest you go back over the information in this chapter in a few days. Give it time to sink in, and then go back over the diagrams. Read over the areas that are least familiar to you.

Review the test questions a couple of times—or make up some of your own. The point being that: This chapter is *important*. The more familiar you are with this information— and the vehicle you'll use for the test—the better your score will be!

12

Loading, Securing, and Hauling Cargo

As a professional driver, you are not only skilled in operating a commercial vehicle but you are also knowledgeable about loading, securing, and moving cargo from Point A to Point B. Nobody in the business knows this area of the industry better than you, the driver.

That's what this chapter is about. You will learn about how to inspect cargo, how to secure a load, and how to handle specific cargo, as well as weight and balance guidelines.

OTR SAFETY

The following are some quick tips about moving cargo safely and efficiently:

- Never take another person's word for the condition of your cargo, how it's loaded, how it's balanced, and/or how it's tied down.
- Always check the load—even if you're just stopping to take a break (Figure 12-1).

- Remember—getting the cargo there in good shape is your job.
- Loading a device—such as tires, wheels, and suspension—beyond its manufacturer's weight rating is illegal and unsafe.
- Remember—legal size and weight limits are based on perfect weather and road conditions. In bad weather or on bad roads, it may not be safe to operate at the legal speed limit or at the legal maximum weight. In bad weather, it may be necessary to slow down, to increase the following distance, and to increase the distance you perceive it will take you to stop.
- When hauling cargo, adjust your driving to avoid cargo shift. That means don't make any sudden moves, don't swerve, and don't stop suddenly.

Figure 12-1   Inspect your cargo and make necessary adjustments.

- In poor conditions, drive under the "safe speed" limits, keep a safe distance from the vehicle in front of you, and give yourself space and time to maneuver.
- Don't pull off onto an uneven surface.
- Avoid parking on inclines.
- If you intend to haul hazardous material that requires your vehicle to be placarded, you will also need a hazardous materials endorsement.

Loose cargo is dangerous:

- It could fall off the truck and injure another driver on the road.
- It could fall off the truck, causing an accident.
- It could injure or even kill you during a quick stop.

And what if your vehicle is overloaded?

- If you are overloaded, it will affect how you steer or control the rig.
- If you are overloaded, you could damage your vehicle.
- If you are overloaded, your vehicle could damage the road.
- If you are overloaded, it is more difficult to stop, and the stopping distance increases.
- If you are overloaded, brake failure is more likely to occur—the additional weight makes brakes work harder because it exceeds their limits.
- If you are overloaded, you'll have to take upgrades slower and be ready to control faster speeds on downgrades.

Step One: Inspecting Cargo

When should you inspect your cargo and how it is secured? (Figure 12-1)

1. The inspection process begins while cargo is being loaded. If you or someone else loads cargo wrong or does not secure it properly, it can be a danger to you and others.
2. It continues as part of your pre-trip inspection—checking for overloads, poorly distributed and balanced weight, and cargo that is not properly secured.
3. Check again after you've driven fifty miles from the originating dock or terminal. It's a federal regulation—so make any adjustments needed.
4. Check again every three hours or every 150 miles that you drive.
5. Check every time you take a break during your trip.

Remember to protect yourself, your carrier, and your customer. Ask yourself, "Is the cargo in good order?" Federal, state, and local regulations governing weight, securing cargo, the covering of cargo, and truck routes vary across the country. Know the rules and regulations in the states where you will be operating your vehicle. If you're a cross-country driver, find out about all these regulations. It will be to your advantage.

Step Two: Loading Cargo

Before loading, look at the floor of the trailer and make certain there are no nails, splinters, or other obstacles that could damage the cargo. In vans, make certain the floor and walls are clean and dry.

Figure 12-2 It is the driver's responsibility to make sure the vehicle is not overloaded.

When cargo is loaded onto a trailer, the weight of the total cargo must be evenly distributed between all the axles.

It is the driver's responsibility to make sure that the vehicle is not overloaded. (see Figure 12-2).

Q. What is the legal weight limit?

A. That depends where you are—all states set legal weight limits and have maximums for gross vehicle weights and for axle weights. As you review legal cargo weights for the states you'll be running (find them in trucker's map books), it is important to know the following terms:

- **Gross vehicle weight** (GVW)—the total weight of a single vehicle and its load.
- **Gross combination weight** (GCW)—the total weight of a power unit, its trailer, and its load, such as a loaded tractor-trailer.
- **Gross combination vehicle weight rating** (GCVWR)—the maximum weight specified by the manufacturer for a specific combination of vehicles and their loads.
- **Center of gravity**—the point where weight acts as a force. A vehicle's center of gravity affects its stability.
- **Axle weight**—weight transmitted to the ground by one axle or one set of axles. Axle weight is not how much the axles themselves weigh! Axles support the vehicle and its load.

- **Tire load**—the maximum weight a tire can carry safely at a certain tire pressure. This information is stamped on the side of the tire. If tires are over-inflated or under-inflated, this rating may no longer apply—thus, an under-inflated or over-inflated tire may not safely carry the same load that it could with the correct inflation pressure.
- **Suspension systems**—all such systems have a manufacturer's weight/capacity rating. The manufacturer states how much weight these parts can carry safely.
- **Coupling device capacity**—all coupling devices are rated by the manufacturer for the weight they can safely carry.

- **Bridge weight**—because bridges can handle only so much weight at any one point, some states have bridge laws—a formula used to determine how much weight is put on any point of the bridge by any group of axles, such as one set of tandems. If the vehicle has more than one set of tandems, the formula takes into account how close the sets of axles are to each other. The resulting maximum axle weight for axles that are closer together may be lower for each axle in the group.

Weight Distribution on Tractor and Trailer Tractor

- Distribute Weight Properly over Axles
- Weight Distribution Depends on Position of Fifth Wheel

  - Single Axle—Slightly Forward of Centerline
  - Tandem Axle

    - Stationary—Just Ahead of Centerline
    - Sliding—Last Notch of Slider Adjustment
    - Fifth Wheel Moved Forward

- *More* of *Load* Shifted to Front Axle

Trailer

- Divide Load Evenly Between Front and Rear
- Adjust Load to Meet Axle Weight Limitations

  - Heavy Freight on Bottom
  - Properly Distributed

Balancing the Load

Some people in the trucking business have a sixth sense about how to achieve a balanced load. Others learn from experience. Figure 12-3 shows a well-balanced load.

Point One: Distribute the weight of the cargo over all axles and remember the center of gravity. You should put the load's center of gravity where it has the most support.

The height of the vehicle's center of gravity is important for safe handling of that vehicle. If cargo is piled up high on the trailer or in the trailer, or if heavy cargo is on top, this high center of gravity will cause the rig to tip over. This is especially true on curves or if you have to swerve suddenly to avoid an accident or a hazard.

It is best to distribute the weight of the load over all axles and keep the center of gravity as low as possible. Load the heaviest parts of the cargo under the lightest parts.

Here's another illustration. Picture your empty vehicle sitting on level ground.

Remember—the weight should be distributed over all the axles, including the front axles under the cab. Draw a line from wheel to wheel. When the center of gravity falls over the center of this rectangle, the vehicle will be most stable.

WEIGHT DISTRIBUTION ON TRACTOR AND TRAILER

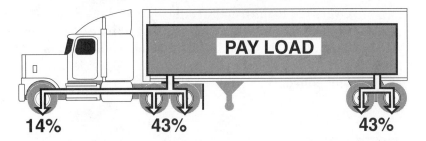

EXAMPLE OF A WELL BALANCED LOAD

TRACTOR
- Distribute Weight Properly Over Axles
- Weight Distribution Depends on Position of Fifth Wheel
  - Single Axle - Slightly Forward of Centerline
  - Tandem Axle
    - Stationary - Just Ahead of Centerline
    - Sliding - Last Notch of Slider Adjustment
    - Fifth Wheel Moved Forward
      - MORE of LOAD Shifted to Front Axle

TRAILER
- Divide Load Evenly Between Front and Rear
- Adjust Load to Meet Axle Weight Limitations
  - Heavy Freight on Bottom
  - Properly Distributed

Figure 12-3 Experienced drivers assure cargo is loaded in a balanced manner.

OTR SAFETY

It's important to balance the weight because:

- A poorly balanced load will make the vehicle tough to handle and unsafe. Also, damage to the suspension and axle are possible.
- Too much weight on the steering axle makes the vehicle difficult to steer—and can cause damage to the steering axle and tires.
- Underloaded front axles can cause the steering axle weight to be too light—making it difficult to steer safely.
- Too little weight on the driving axles means poor traction (in bad weather it will be difficult for the truck to keep going).
- If the center of gravity is too high, the possibility of rollover increases.
- If the center of gravity is too high on a flatbed load, it will shift to the side and may fall off.

Q. What about length and width?

A. All states have length and width regulations as well as weight regulations.

    If you are overloaded or if your cargo has been loaded unsafely, it is possible that you may be put out of service until the cargo has been reloaded in a safe configuration if you are inspected.

    Oversized loads usually require special permits, may be allowed on certain roads only at certain times, and may be asked to take "irregular" routes rather than the usual interstate routes. Some oversized loads are required to have escorts—either those provided by the carrier (a pilot car) or the police.

Step Three: Securing Cargo

Proper loading is an important part of moving freight safely and efficiently from one point to another. Securing the cargo is equally important for the same reasons: safety and efficiency.

    The following are step-by-step guidelines for properly securing all types of loads.

In the Cargo Compartment

Bracing is a method that prevents movement of the cargo in the trailer or any other cargo compartment. When you brace a load, you use various elements to steady the load, from the upper part of the cargo to the floor. You also place braces on the walls of the compartment to minimize movement.

    Blocking is another method, used in front, in back, and/or on the sides of a piece of cargo to keep it from sliding in the trailer (Figure 12-4). Blocking is usually shaped to fit tightly against and around the cargo and then is secured to the deck of the trailer to prevent the cargo from moving.

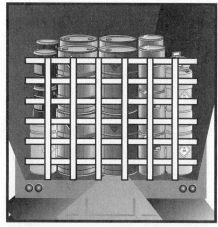

Right   Wrong

Figure 12-4 Blocking and bracing cargo protects it for the duration of the trip. (Photo courtesy of ATA Associates, Inc.)

Load locks are long poles that stretch from wall to wall in a trailer. These should be at the rear of the load to prevent cargo from falling. Place one at the top—and another halfway down.

Loading pallets make certain the pallets don't lean. Each should be placed tightly against the one ahead or in front of it. Leave space between rows of pallets and between the pallets and the walls of the trailer. However, leave as little space as possible between pallets and walls to prevent the cargo from shifting.

Cargo should have at least one tiedown for each ten feet of cargo. Make sure you have enough tiedowns to meet this need. No matter how small the cargo is, there should be at least two tiedowns holding it.

On the Flatbed Trailer

Tiedowns are used to keep cargo from moving in closed trailers as well as on flatbed trailers without sides (Figure 12-5). This secures the cargo, preventing it from shifting and/or eventually falling off the trailer.

When using tiedowns to secure cargo, they must be of the correct type and strength. Obviously, tying down a mammoth turbine with kite string will not secure the cargo.

Note: *Federal regulations require the aggregate working load limit of any securement system used to secure an article or articles against movement must be at least one-half times the weight of the article or articles. The aggregate working load limit is the sum of:*

1. One-half of the working load limit of each associated connector or attachment mechanism used to secure the cargo to the vehicle; and
2. One-half of the working load limit for each end section of a tiedown that is attached to an anchor point.

Note: *Proper tiedown equipment includes ropes, straps, and chains.*

Note: *Tension devices used in tiedowns include winches, ratchets, and cinching components.*

Cargo should have at least one tiedown for each 10 feet of cargo. Make sure you have enough tiedowns to meet this need. No matter how small the cargo is, there should be at least two tiedowns holding it .

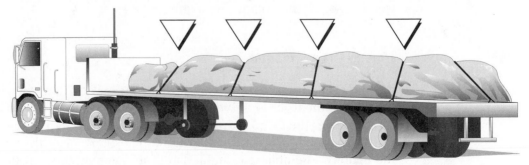

Figure 12-5   Adequate tiedowns keep cargo from shifting.

Note: All tiedowns—regardless of material—should be attached correctly to the vehicle using hooks, bolts, rails, and rings.

OTR SAFETY

All cargo must be secured by tiedowns every ten feet. It is important to have enough tiedowns to meet these requirements.

Don't damage the cargo by securing it too tightly!

No matter how small, the cargo must be secured to the trailer by *at least two tiedowns.* Various specialized cargo such as logs, dressed lumber, paper rolls, concrete pipe, and so on have special tiedown requirements. If you haul this kind of cargo, find out the specific requirements to tie down this special cargo.

What's a "Header Board?"

Header boards at the front end of the load are called "headache racks"—they protect the driver from the freight shifting or crushing the cab in an accident or a sudden stop. Headache racks are attached to the tractor frame between the rear of the cab and the fifth wheel. Front-end header boards protect the driver when the vehicle is carrying loads capable of shifting.

Covered Cargo: What You Should Know

In the past, when you've seen an eighteen-wheeler pulling big cargo pieces on a flatbed trailer, you probably thought it was covered to keep it clean.

According to regulations, cargo is covered for two reasons:

1. To protect people from spilled cargo, and
2. To protect the cargo from the weather.

In some states, the cargo must be covered to prevent spills—find out what the covering rules are in the states where you will be running.

Tarps (tarpaulins) are used to cover most freight and are tied down with rope, webbing, or elastic hooks. (See Figure 12-6.)

How to "Tarp" a Load

Lift the rolled up tarp to the top of the front racks. Then, unroll it over the bars to the back of the truck bed. Pull it tight. Tie it to the cross bars on the rack. If the tarp is placed over the cargo tightly and evenly, it will not flap.

To tarp a load that is uneven or of irregular shape, place the tarp on the cargo after the tiedown assemblies are tight. Then tie down the tarp so the wind and weather don't get inside. Longer ropes may be needed to tie down irregular configuration.

CARGO COVERS

SPILL PROTECTION
•TO PROTECT PUBLIC
•TO MEET STATE LAW REQUIREMENTS

CARGO PROTECTION
•TO PREVENT CORROSION OR OTHER WEATHER DAMAGE
•COMPANY CAN BE LIABLE FOR RUINED CARGO
•USE TARP WHEN NEEDED
•MAKE SURE TARP DOES NOT LEAK
•MAKE SURE TARP IS TIED PROPERLY SO IT WILL NOT TEAR OR LEAK

Figure 12-6   To protect cargo from spilling, covers should be tied down and secure throughout the trip.

Overlapping the front will help keep the wind and weather out.

To "smoke tarp" a load on a flatbed, cover the front part of the load to keep exhaust from the smokestacks from discoloring the load.

While on the road, professional drivers check the covering on a load after the first fifty miles and then every 150 miles or three hours, whichever comes first. If a cover pulls free, uncovers the cargo, and is flapping in the wind as your trailer pulls down the highway, you should stop and reattach it immediately so that the cover won't fly off and block your vision—or someone else's. In addition, a flapping tarp will eventually tear itself to pieces, and tarps are very expensive.

Spill Protection

- To protect the public
- To meet state law requirements

Cargo Protection

- To prevent corrosion or other weather damage
- The company can be liable for ruined cargo
- Use the tarp when needed
- Make sure the tarp does not leak
- Make sure the tarp is tied properly so it will not tear or leak

Cargo Covers

Loading Flatbed Loads—If a crane or forklift is to be used in placing or unloading a heavy piece of freight, place loose packing material (called "dunnage") for the load to ride on. This will allow the forklift at the receiving dock or destination to get under the load without a problem.

What About Sealed and Containerized Loads?—Container traffic—cargo that is placed in a container and sealed to be carried part of its journey by rail or ship—is one of the fastest growing components of the freight business in the country.

Some shippers prefer containerized shipments because they are easier to handle and more secure, especially if the cargo is traveling by ship or rail.

Containers—once they reach port—are loaded onto trucks and are on their way to the end-user. Containers may also be transported from the manufacturer or shipper from the shipper's location to the loading dock for rail or transoceanic movement.

Some containers have their own tiedowns that attach to a special frame for container loads.

Others are loaded onto flatbed trailers and are secured with tiedowns every two feet, just like any other cargo.

OTR SAFETY
You can't inspect a sealed load, but you should check to see that you are not exceeding the gross weight or axle weight limits.

Cargo that Requires Special Handling

- **Dry bulk tanks**—like liquid tankers, dry bulk tankers (Figure 12-7) have a high center of gravity, which means the driver must use special care, particularly when rounding curves and when entering or exiting a freeway ramp. When hauling a dry bulk tanker or any tanker, always drive at a speed well under the posted speed limit on curves, ramps, and in any kind of bad weather.
- **Swinging meat**—a side of beef or any other meat can be extremely unstable, when hanging in a refrigerated trailer (reefer). This type of load also has a high center of gravity (again, see Figure 12-7). Drive under the speed limit and use care on curves, turns, ramps, and in bad weather.
- **Livestock**—hauling live animals, such as beef, hogs, horses, sheep, goats, and so on creates the same problems as liquid loads. And these animals add a few additional challenges. Livestock trailers always have a high center of gravity (see Figure 12-7 also).

Live animals also have a tendency to lean while going around a curve—and this creates a problem similar to the liquid surge found in liquid tanks.

Note: If you don't have a full load, use portable bulkheads to keep the animals from moving around. The tighter the animals are packed, the less movement there will be.

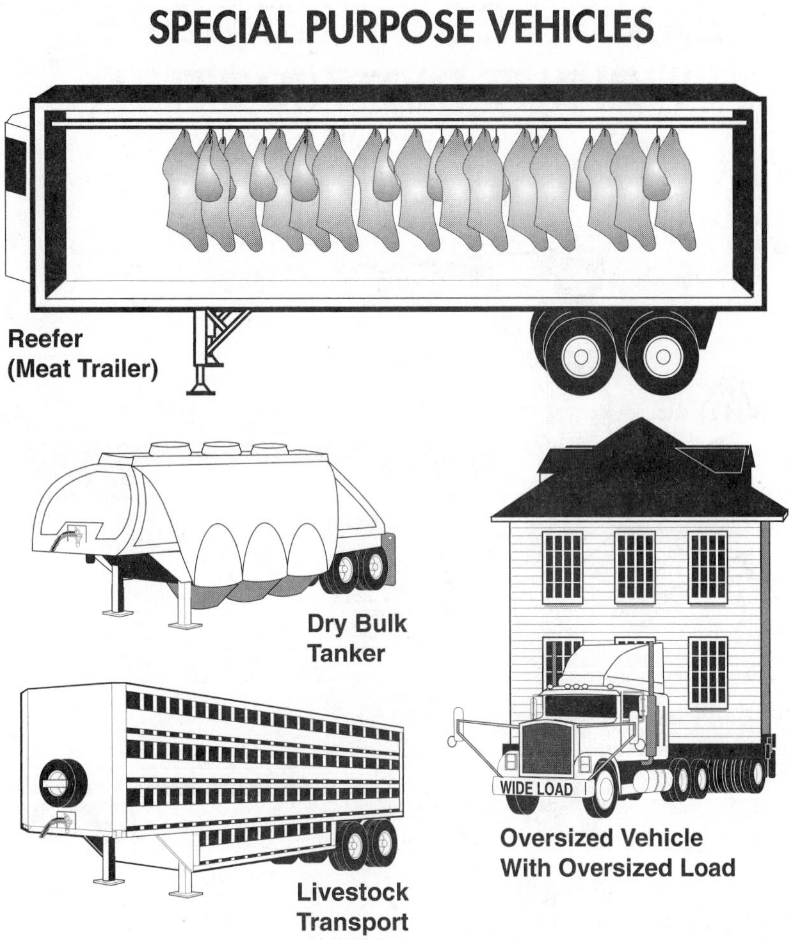

SPECIAL PURPOSE VEHICLES

**Reefer
(Meat Trailer)**

**Dry Bulk
Tanker**

**Livestock
Transport**

**Oversized Vehicle
With Oversized Load**

WIDE LOAD

Figure 12-7 Each special purpose vehicle has its own requirements for operation.

Remember the "nose factor." When you are parked in a truck stop or roadside rest area, park downwind. Otherwise, you will accumulate legions of enemies.

Step Four: Driving with a Load

The high center of gravity associated with some trailers and the way cargo is loaded has already been covered. Just remember, when you're loaded and have a high center of gravity, give yourself plenty of time and room to stop, and drive slowly on curves, entrance ramps, exit ramps, and into turns. A loose load will "surge" whether it's liquid in a smooth bore tank or swinging meat. This causes the center of gravity to change from moment to moment while the vehicle is in motion.

When you are loaded, remember that:

- A heavy load gives you better traction—which means you can stop faster and more safely.
- A light load or empty vehicle does not give good traction. You may be able to move faster but it also takes more distance to stop this type of vehicle.
- Poor distribution of cargo weight makes axles too light—this makes it easier to skid. (See Figure 12-8.)

EXAMPLES OF IMPROPER WEIGHT DISTRIBUTION

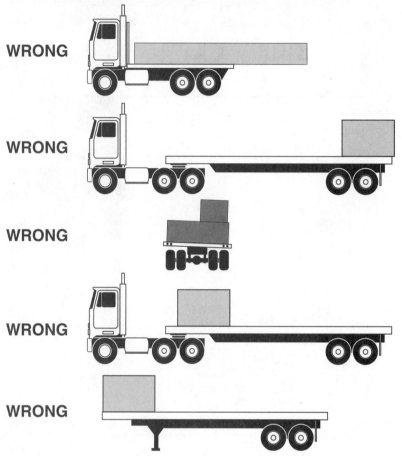

WRONG

WRONG

WRONG

WRONG

WRONG

Figure 12-8   Weight should be distributed evenly over all axles.

OTR SAFETY

When you are turning, remember that:

- A loaded trailer puts more weight on the axles, including the steering axle. The heavier the weight on the steering axle, the more difficult the rig will be to steer.
- Too much weight on the rear axles means there is not enough weight on the steering axle. This decreases steering control.

Driving Banks and Curves

A load with a high center of gravity will make driving banks and curves more hazardous. If the cargo is loaded incorrectly with a high center of gravity, the vehicle will tip when taking a steep bank or curve. (See Figure 12-9.)

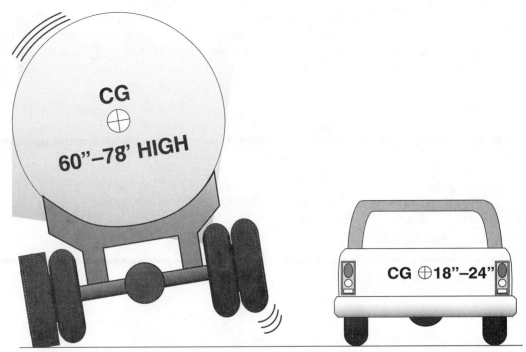

Figure 12-9 Tankers have a high center of gravity, which makes rollovers easier.

The same will happen if cargo is unbalanced when it is loaded.

If you're driving a flatbed on a bank or curve and your cargo is not secure, it may shift or fall off.

If you're hauling hanging sides of meat suspended from rails in the trailer, the swinging caused by the motion of the trailer may cause a problem. As the meat swings more and more, the load builds momentum, which can make the vehicle very unstable, especially on curves and ramps.

If you're hauling dry bulk, you'll be driving a tanker—which has a high center of gravity because of its design. Sometimes—on curves and sharp turns or ramps—the load will shift, creating a very dangerous situation.

Driving Upgrades and Downgrades

A properly secured load will not cause any problems, but the way that a vehicle is loaded will affect how it performs on upgrades and downgrades.

If the truck is overloaded, it will navigate a hill very slowly.

OTR SAFETY
Always use a climbing lane. Otherwise, be aware of traffic behind you and other drivers who may be apt to tailgate your vehicle.

On a downgrade, the loaded vehicle will pick up momentum at a greater rate than the same unloaded vehicle. If your speed on the downgrade becomes excessive, use your brakes. But remember: Trying to slow or stop a loaded vehicle while traveling at a high rate of speed on a downgrade may cause brake failure—a common accident, but one that is easily preventable.

OTR SAFETY

A common rule of thumb is to go down the hill or grade one gear lower than the gear used to climb the hill or grade.

13 Air Brake Knowledge Test

This chapter contains information for all CDL candidates who drive or who will be driving commercial motor vehicles equipped with an air brake system. Those individuals will be required to pass the CDL Air Brake Knowledge Test, which includes all Class A CDL candidates and many Class B CDL candidates.

Available information about air brakes is extensive, so we will cover only the key parts of the system and how it works in this chapter. If you want additional information, consult the Internet, the public library, or veteran drivers.

All air brake systems have three major braking systems (Figure 13-1). They are:

- **The service brake system**—this is the system that applies and releases the brakes as you apply and release pressure on the service brake. You'll use it every day. The service brake system works by applying pressure with your foot to the brake pedal.
- **The parking brake system**—this is the system used when applying the parking brake.
- **The emergency brake system**—this is the system that stops the commercial motor vehicle in an emergency situation—usually caused by failure of the

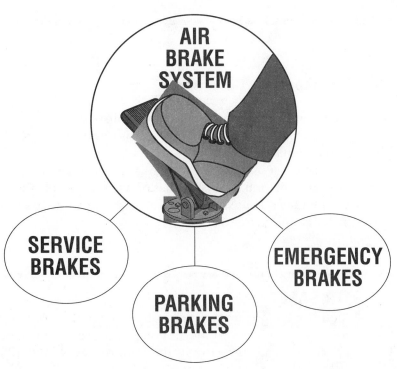

Figure 13-1   Three major braking components of air brake systems.

braking system. The emergency brake system uses parts of the service and parking brake systems.

Parts of the Air Brake System

Air Compressor

Air brakes use compressed air to brake the vehicle. The air compressor compresses air and pumps it into the air tanks (also known as the storage tanks or reservoirs).

Several types of air compressors are in use today. Some are air-cooled, while others are cooled by the engine's cooling system. Some are connected to the engine with gears. Others use V-belts—and if you use this system, you should check the condition of the belts during the inspection. If these belts are not in good condition, the air compressor will fail, which means there will be no air for the braking system.

OTR SAFETY

During the pre-trip inspection, always check the air compressor belts. Some are lubricated by engine oil. If the air compressor has its own oil, check it during this inspection.

The Air Compressor Governor

The air compressor governor maintains constant air pressure in the air tanks—normally between 100 psi and 125 psi. This number may be different from manufacturer to manufacturer.

The governor keeps air in the air tanks and regulates air pressure. The governor also makes sure the braking system has enough air for proper braking. This is done with the **cut-in level** (which turns the air compressor on) and **cut-out level** (which turns the air compressor off).

OTR SAFETY

When the air pressure in the tanks is below a certain level—usually 100 psi—the cut-in turns on the air compressor so the air pressure is built back up. When the air pressure in the tank reaches about 125 psi, the cut-out level is achieved and the compressor turns off.

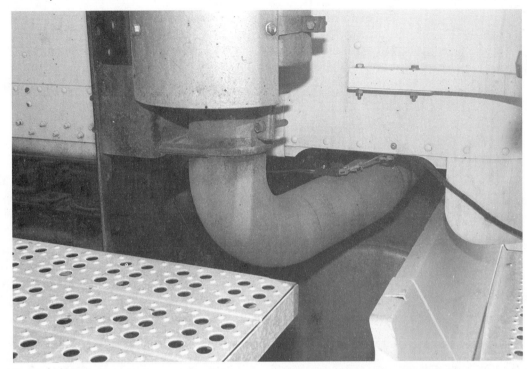

Figure 13-2 Air storage tanks. (Photo courtesy of ATA Associates, Inc.)

Air Storage Tanks

Air storage tanks are also called "air tanks" or "air reservoirs" (Figure 13-2). These tanks hold compressed air produced by the air compressor. They have enough air to stop the vehicle several times, even if the air compressor stops working. The size and number of air tanks in a system vary among vehicles.

Air Tank Drains

Air tanks are equipped with drains, which are usually located at the bottom of the tank. Oil and water accumulate in the tanks and must be drained daily.

- **The manual drain**—is operated by turning a knob (or petcock) a quarter turn—or by pulling a cable.
- **The automatic drain**—is activated automatically. You will hear these drains blow out the air and any accumulated oil and water from time to time.

Why is it important that air tank drains be drained daily, especially in winter? Because freezing temperatures will cause moisture in the lines to freeze, causing braking system problems.

Alcohol Evaporators

Some air brake systems have alcohol evaporators—they are designed to automatically inject alcohol into the system to reduce the chance that water in the system will freeze. However, even if the truck has an alcohol evaporator, you must still drain the air tanks daily. And during cold weather, you must check and fill the alcohol level daily.

Safety Valve (or Pop-Off Valve)

Located in the first tank into which the air compressor pumps, this valve will release excess air and protect the air system from exceeding psi limitations (and possibly damaging the system.) Most safety valves will release if the pressure reaches 150 psi.

Brake Pedal

A part of the service brake system, the brake pedal is also called "the foot valve" or the "foot brake" or the "treadle valve." When you press the brake pedal with your foot, you apply the brakes. How? By forcing air through the lines to the brakes. The more pressure you apply with your foot, the harder the brakes will be applied—and the more air will be used.

Take your foot off the pedal and the air that has been used will be released and the air in the air tanks will be reduced. The more times you press and release the pedal, the less air you will have in the system. When air pressure reaches about 100 psi—the cut-in level—the air compressor's governor will allow the air compressor to turn on and pump air into the system to replace the air that has been used.

OTR SAFETY
You must have adequate air in the air tanks in order for the service brake system to work properly. Use your brake pedal only when needed!

Low Air Pressure Warning Devices

All vehicles equipped with air brakes must have a "low air pressure" warning device.

These devices come on before air pressure goes below approximately 60 psi. Warnings are usually red lights, which are sometimes accompanied by a loud buzzer. If you see the red light or hear the buzzer, you've got a problem. If this occurs while you're driving, stop immediately when you find a safe spot. Don't attempt to drive the vehicle until the problem has been identified and repaired.

The **wig-wag** is another type of low air pressure warning device. This is a metal arm located above the driver's sight-line and attached at the top of the windshield near the visor. When air pressure reaches around 60 psi, the wig-wag will swing in front of the driver's face. Again, if this happens while you're driving down the highway, stop immediately.

The wig-wag can't be reset until the air pressure in the system is above 60 psi.

Foundation Brakes

Each wheel has a foundation brake. The foundation brake most often used is the S-cam brake. To pass the CDL test, you must know the parts of the S-cam brake and the major parts of the braking system.

- **Brake drums**—located at ends of the axle. The drum contains the braking mechanism and the wheels are bolted to the drums.
- **Brake shoes and brake linings**—the brake shoes and brake linings press against the drum, creating enough friction to slow or stop the vehicle.

Friction causes heat and the longer and harder the shoes and linings are held against the brake drum, the more heat is generated. If this heat becomes too intense, the brakes will begin to "fade" or lose their ability to stop the vehicle.

Too much heat will also eventually warp or crack the drum.

- **Brake chamber**—when the driver applies the brake, and air is applied to the braking system, air is pumped into the brake chamber and pushes out the push rod—which is attached to the "slack adjuster." When the driver takes his or her foot off the brake pedal, the air is released out of the brake chamber and the return spring pulls the brake shoes away from the drum.
- **Slack adjuster**—this is attached to one end of the push rod and on the other to the brake cam shaft. When it is pushed out, it causes the brake cam shaft to twist, which will cause the S-cam to turn. This forces the brake shoes away from each other and presses them inside the drum, causing the vehicle to stop.
- **Push rod**—this is attached to one end of the slack adjuster.
- **Return spring**—this pulls the brake shoes away from the drum when the brake pedal is released.
- **Brake cam shaft**—when the slack adjuster is pushed out, the brake cam shaft twists, causing the S-cam to turn, forcing the brake shoes away from each other to press against the brake drum.

The Supply Pressure Gauge

All air brake systems must have an air pressure supply gauge (Figure 13-3) to tell the driver the amount of air pressure (measured in pounds per square inch—psi) in the system. If the vehicle has dual air brakes, there will either be one gauge with two needles or two separate gauges.

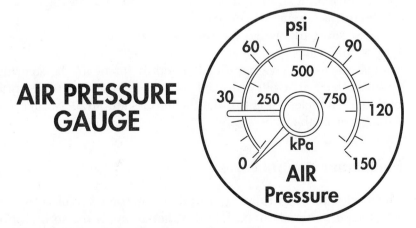

Figure 13-3 Air pressure supply guage.

The Application Pressure Gauge

The application pressure gauge lets the driver know how much air pressure is being applied to the brakes. The amount of air being applied is determined by the amount of pressure placed on the brake pedal. Be sure to know the difference between the supply pressure gauge and the application pressure gauge.

Stop Lamp Switch

Stop lights come on when the brake pedal is applied. The electrical switch that turns on the stop lights is activated by air pressure.

Spring Brakes ("Fail Safe Brakes")

Spring brakes are the most commonly used emergency brake and/or parking brake system on tractors and buses. These brakes must be mechanical because air can leak out.

When the parking brakes are applied, air is released from the brake chamber. This releases the springs and applies the brakes.

In an emergency—when air pressure has fallen to around 20 psi—the spring brakes will be automatically applied. When this happens, things can get a little more exciting than you planned! This is the reason for the low air pressure warning light/buzzer or wig-wag. Warning signals come on at about 60 psi—so you are only 30 to 40 psi away from the spring brakes locking up. When warnings come on, find a safe place to stop—quickly!

The spring brakes are effective only when the brakes are properly adjusted. The same goes for the service brake system.

When the vehicle is parked, the parking brakes are applied, so never apply pressure to the brakepedal as damage could result! The combined force of the spring brake and the brake pedal could create a real problem!

Parking Brake Controls

In older vehicles, the parking brake will be controlled by a lever. In newer models, the driver applies the parking brakes (spring brakes) using a yellow, diamond-shaped push-pull knob. You pull the knob out to apply the parking brakes and push it in to release them.

When you park, always use the parking brakes. This will guarantee you'll never have a roll-off.

Most tractors have a handle attached to (or near) the steering column called a "Johnson bar" or "trolley valve." It is used to apply the trailer brakes. Some drivers park their vehicles using this handle and locking trailer brakes only. *Don't do it!* It's a dangerous habit.

Modulating Control Valve

The modulating control valve is available on some vehicles. It is controlled by a handle located on the dashboard and is used to apply the spring brakes gradually. The more the handle is moved, the more the brakes are applied. This valve is designed to be used in case the service brakes fail while driving. Once you have stopped the vehicle, lock the handle in the "down" position with the locking device. Do not move your vehicle until the service brake problem is repaired.

Dual Parking Control Valves

Some vehicles (mainly buses) have auxiliary air tanks that can be used to release the spring brakes so the vehicle can be moved to a safe place. Vehicles with these *dual parking control valves* have two control knobs on the dash—one is a push-pull knob used to apply the spring brakes for normal parking. The other is spring-loaded in the "out" position. When you push it in, it releases air from the auxiliary tank and releases the air brakes. Because this is a spring-loaded knob, it must be held in while moving the vehicle. When you let go, it pops back out and reapplies the spring brakes. It can be used only a few times before running out of air.

Dual Air Brake Systems

Dual air brake systems are available on most newer models. Dual air brake systems offer more protection against brake failure. With these systems, the truck has two separate air brake systems, but only one set of controls—primary and secondary.

One system usually operates the brakes on the rear axle or axles. The second system usually operates the brakes on the front axle and maybe on one rear axle.

Before driving a vehicle with a dual air brake system, you must wait until the air pressure builds up to at least 100 psi. Normally, there is an air gauge for each system, but there may be only one gauge with two needles—one for each system.

With a dual air brake system, if the low air warning buzzer and light go on, you must stop as quickly and as safely as possible. Don't drive the vehicle again until you get the system fixed.

Inspecting Air Brake Systems

No professional driver would ever get into a vehicle without first checking its brakes—it's common sense. And it's your life you're putting on the line if you don't. The following are ten steps for checking the brake system. Learn them well.

1. **Check the air compressor belt and oil.**
2. **Check the manual slack adjusters on the S-cam brakes**—To do this, park the vehicle on level ground, put it in gear, turn off the engine, release the brakes, and chock the wheels (this will prevent the truck from moving). Locate the slack adjusters and pull them as hard as you can. If they move more than one inch where the push rod is connected, they are out of adjustment.

OTR SAFETY
Out-of-adjustment brakes are the most common problem found during state and DOT inspections—and they will cost you time and money if inspectors find this problem.

3. **Check the brake drums (discs), linings, and hoses**—If brake drums or discs have cracks longer than one-half the width of the friction area, they are out of service and the truck shall not be driven until they are repaired. Check the brake linings. They should not be loose or soaked with oil or grease. They also should not be too thin—this is dangerous. Hoses connected to the brake chambers should not be cracked, worn, or rubbing other hoses.

4. **Test the low-pressure warning signal**—With air pressure built up to the point that the buzzer or warning light has turned off, turn off the engine, and then turn the key to "On" but do not start the engine. Begin applying and releasing brakes until the low air buzzer warning light comes on. This should happen at about 60 psi. If it doesn't come on, get it repaired before beginning your trip.

5. **Check to make sure spring brakes come on automatically**—Use the same procedure as you did to test the low-pressure warning signal, except put the unit in gear or chock the wheels and release the parking brake. Continue pumping the brakes until the parking brake control knob pops out— between 20 and 40 psi.

6. **Check the rate of pressure build-up**—With the dual air system and engine idling, air pressure should build to between 84 to 100 psi within forty-five seconds. With single air systems, it could take three minutes to build the pressure to between 50 to 90 psi. If the air pressure does not build up within these time limits, there must be a problem.

7. **Test the air leakage rate**—With the air system fully charged and the gauge showing around 125 psi, turn off the engine. Then release the service brakes and allow time for the air pressure to drop. For a straight truck, the loss rate should be less than 2 psi in one minute. For a combination vehicle, the loss rate should be less than 3 psi in one minute. Apply 90 psi or more with the brake pedal. After the initial drop (don't count it), the air loss for straight trucks should not be more than 3 psi in one minute. In combination vehicles, air loss should not exceed 4 psi in one minute. If you are losing more than 3 psi for a straight truck or 4 psi for a combination, check the vehicle for air leaks (Figure 13-4).

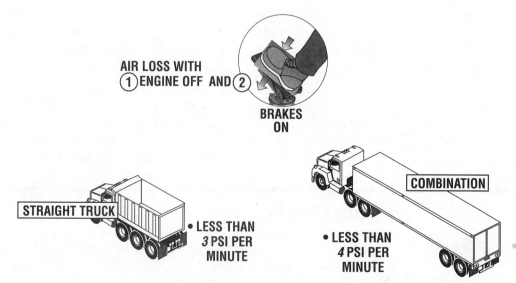

Figure 13-4   Always test the air leakage rate before starting a trip.

8. **Check the air compressor governor cut-in and cut-out pressure**—The governor should have the compressor cut in when the air pressure gets to about 100 psi and should cut out at about 125 psi. With the engine idling and air gauge at about 125 psi, begin pumping the brake pedal. When the pressure is pumped down to about 100 psi, the compressor should start. When it does, the needle on the gauge will begin rising, indicating a building of air pressure. When the gauge reaches 125 psi, the needle should stop rising, indicating that the governor has turned off the air compressor.

9. **Test the parking brake**—With the vehicle stopped, apply the parking brakes and *gently* attempt to move the vehicle into first gear. The parking brake must hold the vehicle in place.

10. **Test the service brakes**—After air pressure has built up completely, release the parking brakes and *slowly* begin to move forward. At 5 mph, apply the brakes using only the brake pedal. Brakes should stop the vehicle firmly.

Controlled Braking

If you are driving a combination vehicle (pulling a trailer), check the brakes on the trailer by *slowly* moving forward. At about 5 mph, pull the trailer hand valve down. The trailer brakes should lock firmly. If they don't, get them checked.

Using the Air Brakes

The use of air brakes must be learned and understood in three different situations. You must also learn the differences between each situation. These situations are:

- **Normal stopping**—in a normal stopping situation, you apply pressure to the brake pedal until the vehicle comes to a stop. Pressure is applied smoothly and steadily.
- **Controlled braking** (also called "squeeze braking")—this is accomplished by squeezing brakes firmly *without locking the wheels*. While squeezing the brakes, don't attempt to turn the wheels. If you need to turn the wheel or if the wheels start to lock up, release the brakes. Make the necessary adjustments in steering and then reapply the brakes. (See Figure 13-5.)
- **Stab braking**—used in emergency situations only, this is done in three steps:
  - Apply the brakes as hard as possible.
  - Release the brakes when the wheels lock up.
  - When the wheels start rolling again, reapply the brakes hard—and repeat these steps as often as you have to.

Note: If your truck is equipped with anti-lock brakes, this section may not apply. Read the vehicle manual for proper emergency procedures.

The purpose of stab braking is to lock the wheels.
You should also remember that:

- When the wheels are locked, there's no steering control.
- When you take your foot off the brake, it will take one second before the wheels begin rolling again.

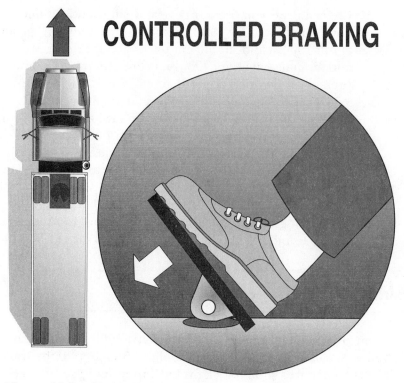

CONTROLLED BRAKING

Figure 13-5   Controlled braking is accomplished by squeezing brakes firmly without locking the wheels.

- Keeping the wheels locked for too long could make the vehicle slide sideways or begin to jackknife so *be careful when you perform stab braking!* (See Figure 13-6.)

Q. What should I know about stopping distance when using air brakes?

A. The stopping distance for a vehicle with air brakes is different than the stopping distance for a vehicle with hydraulic brakes.

With air brakes, there is an added time delay because of the time it takes for the air to travel to the brakes once the brake pedal has been pushed.

Four factors affect the stopping distance of a vehicle equipped with air brakes—and you should know them for the CDL test!

- **The perception distance**—The distance the vehicle will travel from the time the driver sees a hazard and the time the driver reacts (presses the brake pedal). The average perception time is 3/4 of a second—time enough for the vehicle to travel approximately 60 feet.
- **The reaction distance**—The time it takes for the driver's foot to move off the accelerator and stomp on the brake. Average driver reaction time is 3/4 of a second—time for the vehicle to travel another sixty feet—and the driver will just be beginning to brake at this point.
- **The brake lag distance**—The distance the vehicle travels once the brakes have been applied and begin to work. This takes another 1/2 second. Traveling at 55 mph, the vehicle will travel another forty feet in 1/2 second.
- **The effective braking distance**—The distance the vehicle travels once the brakes make contact with the drum. With good braking technique and perfectly adjusted brakes on good, dry pavement, the vehicle going 55 mph will travel 150 additional feet until it comes to a complete stop.

STAB BRAKING

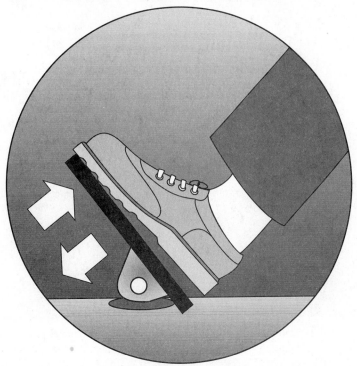

RELEASE AFTER WHEELS LOCK UP

Figure 13-6   Use "stab braking" only in an emergency.

Note: Taking all these distances into account, to stop a vehicle traveling 55 mph, it will require 310 feet—that's about the length of a football field!

Q. How do I brake properly on a downhill grade?

A. Brakes get hot when they're used. This heat comes from the friction between the shoes and the drum. The trick is to use the brakes so they don't get too hot—so they don't begin to "fade" or lose their ability to stop your vehicle. (See Figure 13-7.)

Q. How do I know if my brakes are "fading?"

A. When the brakes take more pressure to maintain the same speed, they are fading. So pull over. Be prepared to shift to the proper gear and brake carefully on downhill grades.

　　Then let the brakes cool. Once they cool down, they will regain some of their ability to stop your vehicle—and they may need to be adjusted, depending on how heated they became.

Q. How can I avoid brake "fade?"

A. There are several ways to avoid this problem:

1. Before driving a long downgrade, pull over and make sure the brakes are adjusted and in good working condition.
2. When beginning the downhill run, get into a gear that will allow you to maintain a safe speed by using the braking effect of the engine. This

Figure 13-7   Be prepared to shift to proper gear and break carefully on downhill grades.

effect is greatest when it is close to the governed rpm of the gear you have chosen—usually one or more gears lower than the climbing gear.

3. The "safe speed" is posted as the speed limit. Never exceed the posted speed.

4. Apply the brakes when you reach the "safe speed." Apply them enough to activate all brakes—you'll feel the vehicle slowing down. You'll need at least 20 psi braking pressure to accomplish this.

5. Keep the brakes applied until the vehicle speed is down to 5 mph under the "safe speed" and then release the brakes. If you're in the correct gear, brake application should last three seconds.

Q. What gear will help maintain the vehicle at the "safe speed" on a downgrade?

A. To go down the hill, choose a gear that is several gears lower than the one you used to climb the hill.

Q. What happens if my vehicle loses air pressure?

A. Stop the vehicle as soon as possible—and as safely as possible!

When the low air pressure warning comes on, it usually means there is a leak in the air system. When the pressure drops to approximately 60 psi, the warning buzzer and light will come on.

The brakes will lock when the air pressure drops to between 20 and 45 psi.

The time between the low-air-warning signals until the brakes lock is very short.

Pull over and stop as soon as possible after the low air warning comes on.

If you don't stop, the brakes may lock while you are traveling down the road and may lead to loss of control of the vehicle!

Parking Brakes

Whenever you park, never use the trolley valve or trailer handbrake. *Always* use the parking brake!

There are certain times when you should not use the parking brake—like right after coming down a long grade when the brakes are very hot. In this case, excessive heat can damage the brakes. You should also not use the parking brake when you are operating in cold weather—using the parking brakes may cause them to freeze and lock. Always park using *only* your parking brakes. If that's not possible because your brakes are hot after a downgrade or the temperature is freezing or below, use chocks.

Let's Review

Read each question and all of the answers provided. Place the letter of the correct answer in the space. Once you have answered all the questions, check your answers against the answer key that follows.

____ 1. The low air pressure warning will light or buzz at approximately:
  (A) 60 psi
  (B) 30 psi
  (C) 45 psi
  (D) 25 psi

____ 2. Air tanks should be drained:
  (A) On pre-trip and post-trip inspections
  (B) Every four hours
  (C) Every 150 miles
  (D) None of the above

____ 3. "Stab braking" is when you:
  (A) Brake hard until the wheels lock, and then release until the wheels begin to roll and repeat the process
  (B) Brake hard but not enough to lock the wheels
  (C) Brake gently and steadily by using pumping action
  (D) None of the above

____ 4. On a long downhill grade, it is recommended that you:
  (A) Gear down and keep your speed at 55 mph
  (B) Gear down three gears from climbing gear and keep your speed at 60 mph
  (C) Gear down and keep your speed 5 mph below the "safe speed"
  (D) All of the above

____ 5. The service brake system
  (A) Stops the vehicle in an emergency
  (B) Is the system used when you apply the parking brake
  (C) Applies and releases the brakes when you apply and release pressure on the service brake
  (D) None of the above

—— 6. When air pressure in the tanks falls below a certain level, the cut in:
  (A) Notifies the dispatcher at the carrier's headquarters
  (B) Turns on the air compressor
  (C) Turns off the compressor
  (D) Reads the gauge and gives you a digital read-out

—— 7. True or False. Air tanks collect oil and water when the air brakes are being used

—— 8. The application pressure gauge tells you to:
  (A) Stop and take a drug test
  (B) Stop the wig-wag
  (C) Let up on the brake pedal
  (D) None of the above

—— 9. "Brake fade" is where:
  (A) It takes more and more pressure on the brake pedal to slow the vehicle
  (B) It takes less and less pressure on the brake pedal to slow the vehicle
  (C) It takes more and more pressure on the accelerator to move the vehicle
  (D) None of the above

——10. True or False. Disc brakes are the most widely used brakes on commercial vehicles today.

Answers to Let's Review

1. A; 2. A; 3. A; 4. C; 5. C; 6. B; 7. True; 8. D; 9. A; 10. False.

14 Hazardous Materials and the HazMat Endorsement

Who Should Read This Chapter?

If you plan to transport hazardous materials in quantities that require hazardous materials placards on your vehicle, then you should read this chapter—and read it carefully, because you will need to pass the Hazardous Materials (HazMat) Endorsement for your CDL.

Training Guidelines

Federal law requires all drivers who transport hazardous materials to receive HazMat training. This regulation further requires that a record of the driver's training in hazardous materials be kept on file while that driver is employed with the company and for 90 days after the driver leaves employment.

The record must include (1) the driver's name, (2) the most recent training date, (3) a description of the training materials used to meet the requirements of the section, (4) the name and address of the person providing training, and (5) certification that the employee was trained and tested according to regulations.

Federal law also requires that all drivers involved in transporting hazardous materials receive (1) general awareness training, (2) function-specific training, (3) safety training, and (4) driver training.

This study manual meets the requirements for general awareness training, safety training, and driver training for HazMat drivers, including a test at the end of each Hazardous Materials and the HazMat Endorsement chapter. These can be placed in the driver's files and serve as testing the drivers in accordance with the HazMat regulations.

In order to certify that training and testing were conducted, the trainer must teach the general awareness portion of the training from this chapter. The Safety Training and Driver Training certification can be obtained by reviewing the appropriate chapters in this manual, along with the appropriate test.

The Hazardous Material Regulations (HMR) can be found in parts 171–180 of Title 49 of the Code of Federal Regulations—49 CFR 171–180.

Frequently Asked Questions (FAQ) About Hazardous Materials

Q. **Who needs HazMat training and testing?**
A. According to regulations, all drivers involved in transporting hazardous materials must receive training and testing. Your employer is required

Figure 14-1 HazMat regulations lessen any dangers to the public.

to provide this training for you and must keep a log (record) of this training as long as you work for the company and also for 90 days after you leave.

Regulations also require that employees receive updated HazMat training every two years.

Q. What is special routing?

A. Sometimes HazMat loads are required to take certain routes and some states require a special permit before certain hazardous materials are moved. Make sure you know about any special rules regarding hazardous materials in your state and in the areas in which you will be driving (Figure 14-1).

Q. Why so many regulations? Isn't this just freight or cargo?

A. Yes, it is freight and yes, it is cargo, but many hazardous materials can injure or kill people if allowed into the environment. So, the reason for the regulations is to lessen the danger.

HazMat rules exist for drivers as well as for shippers and the general public. These rules are very clear about how a material is packaged, loaded, hauled, and unloaded.

These are called **containment rules.** They are procedures to ensure that hazardous materials are contained and handled properly and to ensure that no leaking and no spillage occur.

Anyone dealing with hazardous materials—shippers and carriers—must tell drivers and others about the hazardous qualities, and drivers must warn motorists about the risk. Drivers must also warn others in case of an accident or spill.

Q. How do I warn motorists about hazardous materials and communicate the risks of these materials?

A. You use placards on all four sides of your vehicle to let drivers know the risk and also ensure the proper placement of shipping papers while HazMat cargo is being moved.

If you are hauling HazMat cargo and you don't have the HazMat Endorsement on your CDL, you will be fined and possibly jailed for noncompliance.

Q. Who is responsible for proper and lawful handling of HazMat cargo?

A. It is usually divided equally among the shipper, carrier, and driver.

Q. What is the shipper's role?

A. Anyone sending hazardous materials from Point A to Point B must understand and use HazMat regulations in order to decide the following for each HazMat product:

- The proper shipping name
- The hazardous class
- Identification numbers
- The correct type of packing
- The correct label and marking on the package
- The correct placard(s)

The shipper is also responsible for packing the HazMat cargo properly, labeling it properly, and identifying it properly on the package. The shipper is also responsible for supplying the proper placards and preparing the shipping papers.

The shipper must also certify on the shipping papers that the shipment has been prepared according to regulations. (The only exception is when the shipper is a private carrier, transporting its own products.)

Q. What's the carrier's responsibility when it comes to HazMat cargo?

A. The carrier plays a smaller but equally important role. The carrier must:

- Transport the shipment to the proper destination.
- Ensure that the shipper has correctly named, labeled, and marked the HazMat shipment.
- Report any accident or incident involving the HazMat cargo to the proper government agency.

Q. What is the driver's responsibility?

A. It is the driver's responsibility to:

- Double-check with both the shipper and carrier to make sure the load is properly identified, marked, and labeled.
- *Refuse* any leaking cartons or shipments.
- Communicate the risk by attaching proper placards to the vehicle.
- Deliver products as safely and quickly as possible and obey federal and state HazMat regulations.
- Keep all HazMat shipping papers in the proper place—a *requirement*.

Q. What is meant by the "Hazard Class?"

A. The "Hazard Class" of materials indicates the degree of risk associated with that material. The Hazard Class has nine classes or categories. They are found in Part 173 of the HMC and the provisions of Section 172.101.

Q. What do these class numbers mean?

A. The first number indicates the class of the hazardous material (that is, explosive, gases, flammable liquids, flammable solids, oxidizing substances, poisons, radioactive materials, corrosive material, and miscellaneous material).

   The second number indicates the division. In the number 1.3, the 1 tells you it's an explosive and the 3 tells you the division—which is explosive B. Table 14-1 lists the hazard classes and the divisions.

Q. What exactly do the different classes of explosives mean?

A. An explosive is any material or substance or item (like an explosive device) designed to operate through an explosive action or through a chemical reaction. Or this material may function in a similar manner, even though it was not designed to explode.

Q. Exactly what is the "shipping paper?"

A. The shipping paper is a form or document describing the HazMat cargo you are transporting, and may include bills of lading and manifests. Every cargo item listed on the shipping paper must show the hazardous materials hazard class(Figure 14-2).

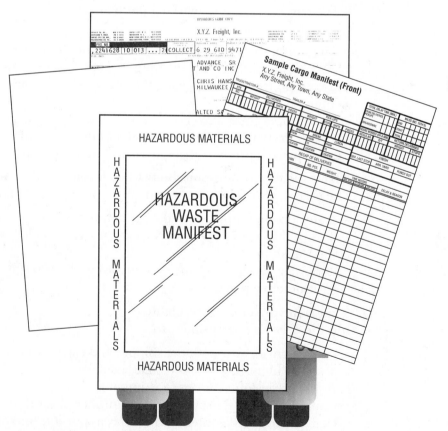

Figure 14-2   Every item of hazardous material must have a HazMat hazard class on all shipping papers.

Table 14-1
HM-181 Classes and Divisions

Class 1 (Explosives)	Explosives
1.1	Explosive Class A
1.2	Explosive A or B
1.3	Explosive B
1.4	Explosive C
1.5	Blasting Agent
1.6	
Class 2 (Gases)	Gases
2.1	Flammable Gas
2.2	Non-Flammable Gas
2.3	Poison Gas
Class 3 (Flammable Liquids)	Flammable Combustible Liquids
3.1	Flammable Liquid
3.2	Combustible Liquid
Class 4 (Flammable Solids)	Flammable Solids
4.1	Flammable Solid
4.2	Flammable Solid/Liquid
4.3	Flammable Solid—dangerous when wet
Class 5 (Oxidizing Substances)	Oxidizing Substances
5.1	Oxidizer
5.2	Organic Peroxide
Class 6 (Poisons)	Poisons
6.1	Poison B
6.2	Etiologic Agents (infectious substances)
Class 7 (Radioactive Materials)	Radioactive Material
Class 8 (Corrosive Material)	Corrosive Material
Class 9 (Miscellaneous Material)	ORM (Other Regulated Material)

Q. What else should be shown on the shipping paper?

A. Each copy of the shipping paper should have numbered pages, with the first page indicating the total number of papers for the shipment. The shipping paper should also contain the proper description of any hazardous material.

The shipper's certificate—signed by the shipper's representative—must be included as well. This certificate verifies that the shipment has been prepared according to all applicable regulations.

Q. Are there any exceptions to the shipping paper rules?

A. Yes—if the shipper is a private carrier that is transporting its own freight, the shipper does not need to sign a shipper's certificate.

Q. What if the shipment has a mix of nonhazardous and hazardous materials?

A. In this case, if the shipping papers show a mix of hazardous and nonhazardous materials, those items that are hazardous must be marked by:

- Describing the item first,
- Highlighting or printing in a different color,
- An "X" before the shipping name in the column marked HM,
- The letters RQ if the shipment is a reportable quantity.

OTR SAFETY

The description of the hazardous product must include the proper shipping name. It must also include the HazMat class or division and the Identification (ID) number, and must be written in that order—shipping name, hazard class, and ID number. No abbreviations!

The only abbreviations permitted are for the packaging type and the unit of measure—and these can appear on the shipping paper before or after the description.

If the shipment is hazardous waste, then the word "waste" must appear before the name of the material being shipped.

Also included must be the total quality and unit of measure (such as, drums, cylinders, or cartons). And if the HazMat shipment is a reportable quantity, the letters RQ must be marked on the shipping paper under HM (Figure 14-3).

Q. Why is the shipping paper so important?

A. The shipping paper is used for several reasons, but its primary purpose is to communicate what's being shipped and whether there's any risk involved.

Q. What happens if a truck carrying HazMat cargo is involved in an accident?

A. It may be necessary for law enforcement officials to obtain information quickly, and for this reason the following regulations also apply to the shipping papers:

- They must be tagged or tabbed and placed on top of all other shipping papers. This is the responsibility of the carrier and the driver.
- When the driver is out of the truck, the shipping papers must be placed on the driver's seat or in a pouch in the driver's door.
- While driving, the driver must place the shipping papers in a pouch in the driver's door or in clear view of the driver when the seatbelt is being used (Figure 14-4).

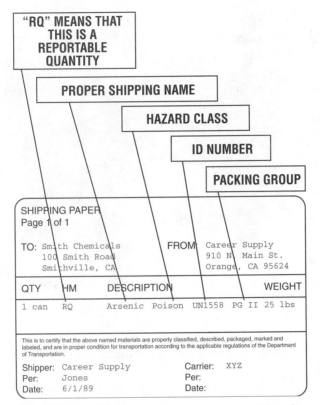

Figure 14-3 Shipping papers communicate items being shipped and any possible risk.

Figure 14-4 In case of accident, HazMat shipping papers provide law enforcement officials with necessary information.

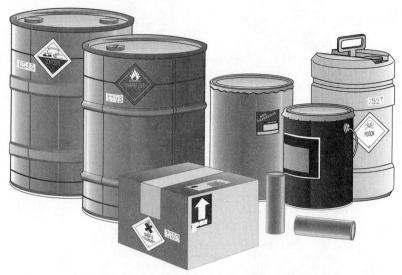

Figure 14-5 Paper labels are required for all HazMat items.

Q. Are there any other responsibilities—for the shipper or driver—regarding HazMat cargo?

A. The shipper must label the package properly, applying diamond-shaped labels indicating the hazardous materials within the package (Figure 14-5).

If the label cannot be placed on the package, the shipper must attach a tag or decal, indicating the hazard involved. In case of accidents, HazMat shipping papers provide law enforcement officials with necessary information.

Q. What is the difference between a HazMat placard and a HazMat label?

A. Both are diamond-shaped and both are used to communicate the contents and the hazards they involve.

The HazMat label is the responsibility of the shipper and goes on the shipment itself—whether it is a box, cylinder, or another type.

The HazMat placard is the responsibility of the driver and is a diamond-shaped sign that is placed on all four sides of the tractor—trailer carrying the hazardous materials. The placards must be readable in all four directions (Figure 14-6).

The placards must be placed on the rear of the trailer, both sides, and either the front of the trailer or the front of the tractor.

Placards must read from left to right and must be located at least three inches away from other markings. They must also be placed "on point." If a tanker is being used, the ID number of the HazMat shipment must be shown inside the placard or on an orange panel.

Q. Is there any time it is legal to drive an improperly placarded vehicle?

A. Only in an emergency to save or protect life or property.

Q. How will I know what placards are the correct ones to use?

A. This isn't always the easiest task, but following these three steps can help:

1. Check the shipping papers for the hazard class, the amount shipped, and the total weight of all hazardous materials in this shipment.

PLACARD LOCATIONS

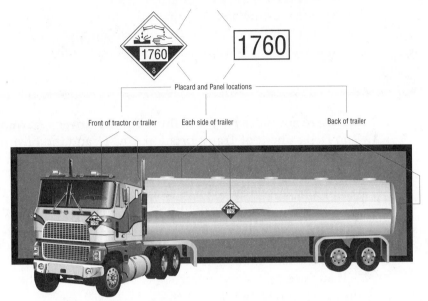

Figure 14-6   It is the driver's responsibility to properly placard all HazMat loads.

2. Check the shipment and make certain the packages match the hazard class listed on the shipping papers.
3. Once the labels have been matched to the shipping papers, check the placard tables to determine which placards should be used.

There are two placard tables—one requires placards for any amount of hazardous material being shipped. The other placard table requires placards if the amount being shipped is more than 1000 pounds.

OTR SAFETY

Once the HazMat cargo has been unloaded, it is the driver's responsibility to remove the placards! In most cases, HazMat placards are not allowed on empty trailers.

If the weight of the combined shipment is 1001 pounds or more, you'll be required to display the proper placard.

Q. Are there any other protections offered when hauling a HazMat load?
A. There are three main HazMat Lists for shippers, carriers, and drivers to use. These lists help each party involved determine the proper handling of any HazMat load.

- The Hazardous Materials Table
- The List of Hazardous Substances and Reportable Quantities
- The List of Marine Pollutants

OTR SAFETY

Before transporting any unfamiliar products or items, look for its name on each list. Each list will have the proper shipping name, hazardous class, identification number, and proper labeling required.

Q. Are there any more responsibilities for the driver regarding HazMat loads?

A. The Department of Transportation (DOT) and the Environmental Protection Agency (EPA) must be notified in the event of a leak or spill of certain hazardous materials.

The **Hazardous Substances and Reportable Quantities List** will tell you if the cargo is a reportable quantity. The product and the amount spilled determine whether or not it is reportable.

An asterisk (*) next to the name indicates that the product also appears on the HazMat table.

If any size spill of any hazardous materials occurs, the driver must report the spill to his or her employer.

Q. How much more do I need to know about HazMat?

A. As a driver, you must know the following information:

- You must be able to recognize that you are loading and will be hauling hazardous materials. How do you do that? First, look at the shipping papers. Then, determine if hazardous materials are being shipped.
- If hazardous materials are part or all of the cargo, check to make sure the shipping papers are properly filled out with the appropriate shipping name, hazard class, and ID number, listed in that exact order.
- You must also look for highlighted products or the letters "X" or "RQ" in the HM column.
- When accepting a delivery for shipment, the driver must be 100 percent sure the shipping papers are correct, the packages are properly labeled, and the vehicle is properly loaded and is displaying the appropriate placards.

OTR SAFETY

If you are not 100 percent certain that the process has been followed TO THE LETTER, you should contact the terminal dispatcher and make certain that the proper process has been followed.

OTR SAFETY

Never accept damaged or leaking HazMat shipments. If you have any questions, contact the dispatcher.

OTR SAFETY

If you pick up hazardous materials from more than one location, add the weight of the product you picked up to the product already loaded.

Classes and Divisions

Class 1—Explosives

- Division 1.1—Explosives that are a mass explosion hazard—if one goes, they all go—which makes for a bad situation. It's dangerous, to say the least.
- Division 1.2—Explosives that are not a mass explosion hazard but are a projection hazard.
- Division 1.3—Explosives that have a fire or minor blast or minor projection hazard—or both-but not a mass explosion hazard.
- Division 1.4—Explosive devices with a minor explosion hazard (can contain more than 25 grams of detonating material).
- Division 1.5—Insensitive explosives—they usually carry a mass explosion hazard but chances are remote. Under normal conditions, they would make the transition of being on fire and then exploding.
- Division 1.6—Items without mass explosion hazard—only very insensitive detonating substances which demonstrate little chance of accidental fire or explosion.

Class 2—Gases

- Division 2.1—This class of gases is any material that will ignite at 68 degrees Fahrenheit (20 degrees Celsius) and 14.7 psi pressure when mixed with air.
- Division 2.2—Nonflammable and nonpoisonous compressed gases. This includes compressed gas, liquefied gas, pressurized cryonic gas, and compressed gas, which is in solution. Any material in this division does not meet the definition of Division 2.1 or 2.3.
- Division 2.3—Known to be poisonous and to be toxic enough to be a hazard to human health—even if adequate data do not currently exist—but have been toxic to laboratory animals.

Class 3—Flammable Liquids

Class three has no divisions. A flammable liquid is one with a flash point of not more than 140 degrees Fahrenheit. This is true except for materials meeting the definition of any Class 2 material. And this class also includes a mixture having components that have a flash point greater than 141 degrees Fahrenheit or higher—if it makes up at least 99 percent of the total volume of the mix. Or it could also be a distilled spirit of 140 proof or lower, considered to have a flash point of lower than 73 degrees Fahrenheit.

Class 4—Flammable Solids

- Division 4.1—Includes three types of flammable solids. First, there are wetted explosives that when dry are explosives of Class 1, but there are some exceptions. Second, there are self-reactive materials that may undergo—at normal or elevated temperatures—a decomposition that could make them ignite. This can happen in high transport temperatures or through contamination. Any solids that are readily combustible can create fire through friction. This material shows a burning rate faster than 2.2 millimeters per second. The third type of flammable solid in this division includes metal powder that can ignite and react over the test area in ten minutes or less.
- Division 4.2—These are solid materials which, even in small quantities, ignite within five minutes of exposure to air under certain test procedures.
- Division 4.3—These are materials that can become spontaneously flammable on contact with water. This division also contains material that can emit (give off) flammable or toxic gases at a rate of 1 liter per kilogram per hour or greater.

Class 5—Oxidizing Substances

- Division 5.1—Because they emit oxygen, these materials can cause or increase the combustion of other materials.
- Division 5.2—This division includes organic peroxide—a derivative of hydrogen peroxide.

Class 6—Poisons

- Division 6.1—This division includes materials that are toxic to humans or so toxic that they pose a health hazard during transportation. The division also includes materials presumed hazardous to humans because of results in laboratory tests. This division also includes irritants, such as tear gas.
- Division 6.2—Infectious substances which may cause disease or death in animals or humans. This includes human or animal excretions, secretions, blood tissue, and tissue components.

Class 7—Radioactive Material

This class includes any radioactive material with a specific activity greater than 0.002 microcuries per gram.

Class 8—Corrosive Material

Includes materials—liquid or solid—that cause destruction/irreversible damage to human skin tissue on contact. These also have a high corrosion rate on steel and/or aluminum.

Class 9—Other Regulated Material (ORM)

Any material which presents a hazard during transport but is not included in any of the other classes—and that is subject to HazMat regulations.

Information About the Hazardous Materials Table

The following illustrates how to use the information contained in the Hazardous Materials Table. (See Table 14-2).

Column 1 has symbols that have a specific meaning. These include:

- **+** The designated proper shipping name and hazardous materials class must always be shown, even if the product doesn't match a hazard class definition.
- **D** The proper shipping name is appropriate for describing materials for domestic transportation but may not be proper for international transport.
- **A** Cargo is subject to the regulations only when transported by air, unless materials are hazardous substances and hazardous waste.
- **W** Cargo is subject to regulations only when transported by water, unless the material is a hazardous substance, hazardous waste, or marine pollutant.
- **G** Technical names of the hazardous materials must be listed in parentheses after the proper shipping name.
- **I** The proper shipping name is appropriate for use in international transportation.

Column 2 shows the name of regulated materials in alphabetical order. On this table, the proper shipping names are always shown in regular type. The names shown in italics are not proper shipping names and can only be used along with the proper shipping name

Column 3 shows the hazard class or division—or it may have the word "forbidden." When you see "forbidden," *never* transport this material.

The hazard class for the material is the indicator of what placards to use. To choose the proper placard, you must have three pieces of information: (1) the hazard class for the cargo, (2) the amount being shipped, and (3) the amount of all hazardous materials in all classes on the vehicle. If the words "inhalation hazard" appear on the shipping papers, you must use a poison placard in addition to the others that are required.

Column 4 shows the ID number for each proper shipping name. These ID numbers are preceded by the initials "UN" or "NA." The letters "NA" are used only in shipments between the United States and Canada. The ID number must also appear on the shipping paper, the package, the cargo tanks, and all other bulk packages.

Column 5 identifies the packing group that is assigned to the material.

Table 14-2
Part of the Hazardous Materials Table

Symbols (1)	Hazardous materials descriptions and proper shipping names (2)	Hazard class or division (3)	Identification Numbers (4)	PG (5)	Label codes (6)	Special provisions (7)	Packaging (§173.***) Exceptions (8A)	Non-bulk (8B)	Bulk (8C)	Quantity limitations Passenger aircraft/rail (9A)	Cargo aircraft only (9B)	Vessel stowage Location (10A)	Other (10B)
	Air bag inflators, compressed gas or Air bag modules, compressed gas or Seat-belt pretensioners, compressed gas	2.2	UN3353	—	2.2	133	166	166	166	75 kg	150 kg	A	
	Air bag inflators, pyrotechnic or Air bag modules, pyrotechnic or Seat-belt pretensioner, pyrotechnic	9	UN3268	III	9		166	166	166	25 kg	100 kg	A	
	Air, compressed	2.2	UN1002		2.2		306	302	302	75 kg	150 kg	A	
	Air, refrigerated liquid, (cryogenic liquid)	2.2	UN1003		2.2, 5.1	78	320	316	318, 319.	Forbidden	150 kg	D	51
	Air, refrigerated liquid, (cryogenic liquid) non-pressurized	2.2	UN1003		2.2, 5.1		320	316	318, 319.	Forbidden	Forbidden	D	51
	Aircraft evacuation slides, see Life saving appliances etc												
	Aircraft hydraulic power unit fuel tank (containing a mixture of anhydrous hydrazine and monomethyl hydrazine) (M86 fuel)	3	UN3165	I	3, 6.1, 8		None	172	None	Forbidden	42 L	E	
	Aircraft survival kits, see Life saving appliances etc.												
G	Alcoholates solution, n.o.s., in alcohol	3	UN3274	II	3, 8		None	202	243	1 L	5 L	B	
	Alcoholic beverages	3	UN3065	II	3	24, B1, T1	150	202	242	5 L	60 L	A	
		3		III	3	24, B1, N11, T1	150	203	242	60 L	220 L	A	
	Alcohols, n.o.s.	3	UN1987	—	3	T8, T31	None	201	243	1 L	30 L	E	
				II	3	T8, T31	150	202	242	5 L	60 L	B	
				III	3	B1, T7, T30	150	203	242	60 L	220 L	A	
G	Alcohols, flammable, toxic, n.o.s.	3	UN1986	—	3, 6.1	T8, T31	None	201	243	Forbidden	30 L	E	40
				II	3, 6.1	T8, T31	None	202	243	1 L	60 L	B	40
				III	3, 6.1	B1, T8, T31	None	203	242	60 L	220 L	A	
	Aldehydes, n.o.s.	3	UN1989	—	3	T8, T31	None	201	243	1 L	30 L	E	
				II	3	T8, T31	150	202	242	5 L	60 L	B	
				III	3	B1, T7, T30	150	203	242	60 L	220 L	A	
G	Aldehydes, flammable, toxic, n.o.s.	3	UN1988	—	3, 6.1	T8, T31	None	201	243	Forbidden	30 L	E	40
				II	3, 6.1	T8, T31	None	202	243	1 L	60 L	B	40

From 49 CFR 172—Part 172 Hazardous Materials Table. Available: www.access.gpo.gov/nara/cfr.

Column 6 shows the hazard label, which shippers must put on packages of hazardous materials. Some products require more than one label. If the word "none" appears, then no label is required.

Column 7 includes any additional provisions for this material—if you see a Column 7 entry, refer to federal regulations for specific information.

Column 8 is a three-part column which shows section numbers covering packaging for HazMat cargo.

Columns 9 and 10 do not apply to highway transport.

The Hazardous Waste Manifest

Any cargo containing hazardous waste must be accompanied by a hazardous waste manifest—and this must be signed by the driver.

Q. Who is responsible for preparing the manifest?
A. This manifest is the responsibility of the shipper. And the driver will treat the hazardous waste manifest as any other shipping paper.

The carrier who accepts the hazardous waste cargo must make certain that the hazardous waste manifest is properly completed, and a shipment labeled as hazardous waste may only be delivered to another registered carrier or to a facility that is authorized to receive and handle hazardous waste.

The carrier must maintain a copy of the hazardous waste manifest for three years following transport. Also, once the cargo is delivered to the authorized hazardous waste facility, the facility's operator must sign for the shipment.

Q. When can the "Dangerous" placard be used?
A. You can use the "Dangerous" placard if you have a load requiring a flammable placard and then pick up 1000 pounds of combustible material, instead of using two separate placards—like "flammable" or "combustible." There are two exceptions (1) if you have loaded 5000 pounds of HazMat cargo at one location, you must use the placard for that material, and (2) if the words "Inhalation Hazard" appear on the shipping papers, you must use the material's specific placard *and* a "Poison" placard.

Blasting agents (1.6), Oxidizer (5.1), and Dangerous placards are not required if the vehicle contains Class 1 explosives and you're using Division 1.1, 1.2, or 1.3 placards.

When the vehicle displays a Division 2.1 Flammable Gas or an Oxygen placard, you do not need to display a Nonflammable Gas placard if you pick up that material and add it to your load.

Note: If a vehicle carrying hazardous materials spills or leaks an RQ (reportable quantity), it must be reported to the carrier.

OTR SAFETY
Displaying the wrong placard is just as wrong as not displaying any placard.

The carrier reports it to the National Response Center (NRC), which has the ability to contact the proper law enforcement agency and the proper containment or clean-up personnel (Figure 14-7).

The carrier is required to call the NRC (800-424-8802) if an incident of leakage or spill occurs and if:

- Someone is killed
- Someone is injured and requires hospitalization

| NATIONAL RESPONSE CENTER (800) 424-8802 | CHEMTREC (800) 424-9300 |

CHEMICAL EMERGENCY

You need to know and understand what these agencies do and what they cannot do.

Figure 14-7 Agencies to call in case of accident or chemical involving a HazMat load.

- Estimated property damage exceeds $50,000
- One or more major roadways is closed for one hour or more
- Fire, breakage, spillage, or suspected radioactive contamination occurs
- Fire, breakage, spillage, or suspected contamination of etiologic agents occurs

When calling the NRC, give the following information:

- Name
- Name and address of carrier
- Phone number where carrier can be reached
- Date, time, and location of event
- The extent of injuries—if any
- The class, name, and quantity of the hazardous materials involved
- The type of incident and the nature of hazardous material involvement
- If a reportable quantity of hazardous substance is involved, the caller should also give the name of the shipper and the quantity of the hazardous materials discharged.

Q. What is CHEMTREC?

A. CHEMTREC is the acronym for the Chemical Transportation Emergency Center in Washington, DC. It has a 24-hour toll-free line and has evolved to provide emergency personnel with technical information and expertise about the physical properties of hazardous products. The NRC and CHEMTREC work closely together. If you call either CHEMTREC at 800-424-9300 or the NRC at 800-424-8802, whichever agency you call will notify the other about the problem.

　　In addition to calling the NRC or CHEMTREC, drivers are responsible for helping the carriers make a detailed written report. The driver is particularly valuable in completing these reports, so it is a good idea for the driver to write out a report, detailing what took place, as soon as possible.

Q. What should I know about loading, unloading, and hauling hazardous materials?

A. There are a few rules to always keep in mind when handling hazardous materials:

- No smoking at any time.
- Never load damaged or leaking packages or containers.
- Never open any packages during transport. If a package breaks open, call your dispatcher immediately.
- No overhangs or tailgate loads for explosives, oxidizing materials, or flammable solids.
- Rules forbid using cargo heaters or air-conditioning unless you know the rules for the cargo you're hauling. If in doubt, check with your company.
- When you park, set the brakes and chock the wheels.
- Do everything possible to protect the public.

Q. Are there any specific rules for loading HazMat cargo?

A. Unless otherwise stated, these materials must be loaded in a closed cargo space unless packages are fire- and water-resistant or covered with a fire- or water-resistant tarp:

Class 1 Explosives

- Before loading or unloading, turn off the engine.
- Disconnect heat power for cargo heaters and drain heater fuel tanks.
- Check the trailer or truck for any sharp points that could damage the cargo.
- Check the floorboards and sidewalls; you must use floor lining with Divisions 1.1, 1.2, or 1.3 explosives. The liner may not contain steel or iron.
- Never transfer explosives from one vehicle to another on a public highway. The only exception is an emergency situation.
- Never accept damaged packages or packages stained with oil or dampness.
- Never transport Division 1.1 explosives in triples.
- Never transport Division 1.2 and 1.3 explosives in combination if there's a placarded cargo tank in the combination or if you're hauling initiating explosives, radioactive materials (Class 7) or Class 6 poisons or hazardous materials in a portable tank.

Q. What do I need to know about corrosive liquids?

A. If you're loading by hand, handle containers one at a time—don't drop, turn over, or top load them unless the weight can be stabilized by freight on the bottom of the stack. Keep containers right side up—no ifs, ands, or buts. Never load nitric acid above anything else—and never more than two stacks high.

Never load corrosives with explosives, flammable solids, or oxidizing materials.

If you are loading cylinders (compressed gases or cryogenic liquids) and the vehicle doesn't have built-in racks, then the cylinders must be kept upright or braced lying down or in boxes to prevent them from turning over. If you are handling poisons, never mix loads with foodstuffs and never load these materials in the driver's cab or sleeper.

Q. What about radioactive materials? Are they handled any differently?

A. No matter how well radioactive materials are packaged, radiation escapes from each package. Look at Class 7 HazMat for the number of packages that can be transported. This is the "transport index." This tells the degree of control necessary during transportation—the total transport index of all packages in a single vehicle cannot exceed 50.

Q. How should mixed loads be handled?

A. Federal regulations—the Segregation and Separation Chart—demand that certain hazardous materials be loaded separately. (See Table 14-3).

Q. Are there any rules for actually hauling HazMat cargo?

A. As soon as the shipping papers have been checked and the truck has been properly placarded, there are a few reminders for drivers:

- Never park within five feet of the traveled part of the road if you're hauling explosives.
- When hauling explosives, never park within 300 feet of a bridge, tunnel, or building; places where people gather; or an open fire.

Table 14-3
Segregation and Separation Chart

Don't Load . . .	In the Same Vehicle With . . .
Poison—Class 6	Animal or human foodstuff, unless the poison package is over-packed in an approved way. (Foodstuff can be anything you swallow—except mouthwash, toothpastes, and skin cream, which are not foodstuffs.)
Poison—Division 2.3	Oxidizers, flammables, corrosives, organic peroxides.
Charged Storage Batteries—Division 1.1	Explosives.
Detonating Primers	Any other explosives, unless in authorized containers or packages.
Cyanides or Mixtures	Acids, corrosive materials, or other acidic materials which could release hydrocyanic acid from cyanides. Cyanides are materials with the letters "cyan" as part of their shipping name, like acetone cyanohydrin, silver cyanide, or trichloroisocyanuric acid, dry.
Nitric Acid	Other corrosive liquids in carboys (a container holding 5 to 15 gallons of liquid, often cushioned in a wooden box), unless separated in an approved manner.

- Someone—the shipper, the carrier, or the consignee—should be in attendance of the vehicle at all times when hauling explosives.
- The vehicle can be left unattended on a government-approved safe haven—a location approved for parking unattended vehicles loaded with explosives.

If you're hauling HazMat cargo—but not explosives—you may:

- Park within five feet of the road, only if the job requires it and someone is with the vehicle at all times and that person understands the hazards involved.
- Never uncouple the trailer and leave it on a public street.
- Set out reflective triangles within ten minutes, if you park along the roadway.
- Never park within 300 feet of an open fire.

Q. What's the difference between an "attended" and "unattended" vehicle?
A. If you have someone watch the vehicle for you, that person must be in the vehicle and must be alert—or they must be within 100 feet from the vehicle (not smoking) and within clear view.

   That individual must know what to do in an emergency and must be able to move the vehicle if necessary.

Q. Can flares be used in an emergency?
A. Never leave flares or any burning signal device around tankers used for flammables, explosives, flammable liquids, or flammable gas.

Q. What about refueling?

A. Always turn off the engine before refueling. Someone must be in control of the fuel at the nozzle.

Q. Where should I keep the shipping papers while on the road?

A. They must always be in clear view in the pouch on the driver's door or where the driver can reach them while the seatbelt is buckled. Shipping papers regarding HazMat information should be tagged and placed on top of all other papers.

Q. Where should shipping papers be when I am out of the truck?

A. This is a review question—they should be placed on the driver's seat or in a pouch inside the driver's side door.

Q. Are there any special inspections required when hauling HazMat Cargo?

A. Other than the pre-trip and en-route checks, you must check your tires at the beginning of each trip and each time the vehicle is parked. If you find a tire that is overheating you must immediately remove the tire and place it a safe distance from the vehicle. If you have a flat or a tire that is noticeably leaking, drive only as far as necessary to get it fixed.

Q. What about directions for hauling chlorine?

A. You should have an approved gas mask in the vehicle and must also know how to use an emergency kit for controlling leaks in dome lid plate fittings on the tank.

Q. What about railroad crossings?

A. *No matter what*, if you are in a placarded vehicle or carrying any amount of chlorine or have cargo tanks used to transport HazMat cargo (loaded or empty) you must stop at railroad crossings no closer than 15 feet and no further away than 50 feet from the nearest rail. *Don't* shift gears while crossing and turn on your four-way flashers when stopping at a railroad crossing.

Q. What about route restrictions?

A. Some areas of the country require permits and special routing for carriers transporting certain materials. As the driver, it is up to you to know about these special requirements, so check with your company and always check routes before beginning a trip—you want to be permitted to travel on the roads you'll be driving. Fines are costly—against the company and against you as the driver.

OTR SAFETY

Anytime you're hauling explosives (Division 1.1, 1.2, or 1.3), a written route plan is required—and you must follow that plan. The same applies when hauling radioactive materials—the carrier is responsible for telling the driver that the trailer is loaded with these materials.

HazMat Emergencies

The Emergency Response Guidebook (ERG) is used by fire fighters, police officers, industry safety personnel, and others in the event of an emergency involving hazardous materials. This book is available through the Department of Transportation (www.dot.gov), or you can download the forms at http://hazmat.dot.gov/ohmforms.htm.

When an emergency occurs, police and fire personnel must determine what type of hazardous material is involved. This is accomplished by checking the shipping papers, looking at the placards, and getting information from the driver. However, in some accidents, there may be no time to locate the shipping papers or talk to the driver. So, the only thing left is for them to look at the placards.

Once the type of hazardous material is determined, emergency personnel can then take steps to protect life and property—which is one more reason why the right placards must be used, the shipping papers must always be accurate, and the driver must be aware of what is being hauled.

Q. What do I do, as the driver, in case of an accident involving HazMat cargo?

A. The following is your responsibility at the scene of an accident involving hazardous materials:

- Warn people of danger and keep them away.
- Secure the accident scene as best you can (Figure 14-8).
- If you can do so safely, contain the spill.
- Contact the appropriate emergency response personnel (for instance, the police and fire departments) and tell them what has happened. Be prepared to provide the following information: the product's shipping

KEEP
PEOPLE
FAR AWAY
AND
UPWIND

Figure 14-8 In case of HazMat emergency, secure the accident area.

name, hazard class, and ID number, the extent of the spill and its location, when the accident/incident happened, and the phone number where you can be reached. Let them hang up first in order to make sure they have all the information they need, then contact your dispatcher and follow his or her instructions.

Q. What do I do in case of a fire?

A. Never attempt to fight a HazMat fire unless you have specific training on how to do it.

The power unit of a vehicle with placards must have a fire extinguisher with a UL rating of at least 10 B:C.

Q. What do I do in case of a leak or a spill?

A. First of all, don't touch it—because certain hazardous materials can kill you just by touching them or breathing the fumes. Determine what the HazMat cargo is by looking at shipping papers, but do not go near the spill or allow anyone else to go near it. Contact the local authorities and your dispatcher as quickly as possible. *Do not attempt to move the vehicle unless you have to due to safety concerns.*

- If you are driving and notice something leaking from the vehicle, pull as far off the road as you can, get the shipping papers, and get away from the vehicle. Then, send someone for help. Stay away from the truck but keep it in sight so you can keep others away.
- *Do not* drive to a phone if you spot a leak.
- When sending someone for help, write down your location, a description of the emergency, your name, and your carrier's name and phone number, as well as the shipping name, hazard class, and ID number of the materials.
- Never smoke or allow smoking around the vehicle.

If you see leakage or damage to a HazMat package while unloading, get away from the vehicle as quickly as possible and contact your dispatcher immediately. *Do not touch or inhale the material!*

Q. How should a tank be marked for HazMat cargo?

A. For *cargo tanks*—which are attached permanently to the vehicle—loading takes place with the tank on the vehicle.

On these tanks, placard requirements include an ID number that must appear on the vehicle—either black four-inch numbers on an orange panel, or a Department of Transportation placard on a white, diamond-shaped background. And don't forget, cargo tanks must also show re-test date markings.

For *portable tanks*—which are not permanently mounted to the vehicle—loading and unloading takes place with the tanks off the vehicle.

Portable tanks show the owner's or leaser's name. The shipping name and ID number must be on opposite sides. If the tanks hold 1,000 gallons or more, the ID number must be on all four sides—in black paint and at least two inches tall.

Q. Are there any rules and regulations about loading and unloading tanks?

A. Yes. Certain rules must be followed by the person unloading. That person must:

- Be within 25 feet and have a clear view of the tanks.
- Be aware of the hazards.

- Know the procedures for an emergency.
- Be authorized and have the ability to move the cargo tank if necessary.

When loading and unloading flammable gases into tanks:

- Don't smoke.
- Turn off the engine—use the engine only to run the pump, if necessary.
- The engine should be turned on only after the product hose is hooked up and turned off before uncoupling the hose.
- Secure the truck against movement.
- Secure the electrical ground wire correctly or have the ground wire attached before and after opening the fill hole.

Q. What is Performance Oriented Packaging (POP)?

A. This is a government term meaning that the packaging used for HazMat cargo must "perform" in such a way as to be safe, making it possible to handle and transport the cargo safely.

These standards require that each package be designed and produced so that when it is filled to capacity, sealed, and transported under normal conditions:

- The package will not release HazMat products.
- There will be nothing to reduce the strength or seal, or cause other changes due to fluctuation in temperature.
- The package itself should contain nothing that could ruin the packaging.

For additional information, check HMR, Part 173, "Shippers' General Requirements for Shipments and Packaging." To comply with governmental regulations, all packaging must meet the preceding requirements and must (1) contain the manufacturer's marking, (2) be marked with the proper shipping name and ID number, and (3) be tested and approved before use.

Let's Review

Read each question and all of the answers provided. Place the letter of the correct answer in the space provided or write your answers on a separate piece of paper so you can use these questions again as you review for the CDL. Once you have answered all the questions, check your answers against the answer key which follows.

_____ 1. When the driver is in the driver's seat with the seatbelt on, the shipping papers should be:
(A) In the glove box
(B) In a pouch in the driver's door
(C) In the driver's briefcase
(D) None of the above

_____ 2. If you are approaching a railroad crossing with a HazMat load, you must:
(A) Sound the horn before crossing
(B) Shift gears before crossing
(C) Stop five feet from the tracks
(D) None of the above

___ 3. True or False. Smoking is allowed around a HazMat load if you are smoking filtered cigarettes.

___ 4. If it is necessary for you to stop at a rest stop for a few minutes, you must put the shipping papers:
(A) On the driver's seat
(B) In your pocket
(C) Under the windshield wiper
(D) None of the above

___ 5. If you are hauling Division 1 explosives, you must not park your rig within how many feet of a fire?
(A) 300 feet
(B) 500 feet
(C) 50 feet
(D) 1,000 feet

___ 6. While hauling a HazMat load, you should do this every time the vehicle is parked:
(A) Check for leaks
(B) Check to make sure you have enough fuel
(C) Check the tires
(D) None of the above

___ 7. You are asked to pick up a five-pound container of "corrosives." The placards you should use are:
(A) Poison and Corrosive placards
(B) Poison only placards
(C) Poison and Dangerous placards
(D) No placards are required

___ 8. If you are a hauling a shipment containing chlorine, you should have a:
(A) Cell phone
(B) Gas mask
(C) Medical oxygen tank
(D) None of the above

___ 9. If you must park a vehicle loaded with hazardous materials and leave it unattended, the best place to park it is:
(A) The shipper's lot
(C) The consignee's lot
(B) The carrier's lot
(D) All of the above

___10. A driver of a vehicle carrying hazardous materials can communicate with authorities by:
(A) Using placards
(B) Calling before entering city limits
(C) Using the CB
(D) All of the above

Answers to Let's Review

1. B; 2. D; 3. False; 4. A; 5. A; 6. C; 7. A; 8. B; 9. D; 10. A.

15 Tanker Endorsement

If you are going to pull a tanker carrying a load of liquids or compressed gas, a Tank Vehicle Endorsement will be required on your CDL.

FMCSR Part 383 defines a "tank" as a vehicle carrying liquids and compressed gases in bulk.

FMCSR Part 383 offers an additional description: A tank vehicle can be a permanently attached tank or it can be a portable tank. Both types may hold 1,000 gallons of cargo or more.

A permanent tank is loaded or unloaded while attached to the vehicle. A portable tank can be taken off the vehicle to be loaded or unloaded.

These definitions make it possible for a tank vehicle to be:

- A straight truck with a permanently attached tanker
- A semi-trailer that is a tanker and can be coupled to a tractor
- A flatbed trailer carrying a portable tank

When you drive a tank vehicle, you must have the knowledge and skill to handle two problems: (1) a high center of gravity, and (2) liquid surge.

Q. What problems are caused by a high center of gravity?

A. Tank vehicles come in all sizes but they all have a high center of gravity (CG).

Translation: Most tank vehicles sit higher than other vehicles. Therefore, the load's weight is carried higher above the road. So, the load's center of gravity is always high in a tanker. And as you learned in the General Knowledge section, it is important to keep the center of gravity of a load as low as possible.

Why? To lessen the possibility of rolling over (Figure 15-1).

Q. What is liquid surge and what problems are caused by it?

A. Liquid surge happens when the liquid contents of partially filled tanks shift in a tanker.

In a partially filled tank vehicle, when the truck comes to a stop, the liquid contents will surge back and forth in the tank—from front to back and side to side. When the wave of liquid hits the end of the tank, it usually pushes the truck in the direction the wave is moving. So, when you are braking, the surge will push the truck forward and then pull it back until the liquid settles back down in the bottom of the tank. One more important point: The thicker the liquid, the less the surge will be. For example, if the tank is carrying lighter-weight liquids, such as milk or brine, the surge will be greater. If the cargo is a heavier liquid, like molasses or heavy oil, the surge will be less.

However, any liquid in a tank vehicle can cause very specific problems for the driver. Therefore, you should keep your movements gradual and slow. Why? Because the less sloshing that liquid cargo does, the less surge there will be—so make all shifts, turns, and stops slow and gradual.

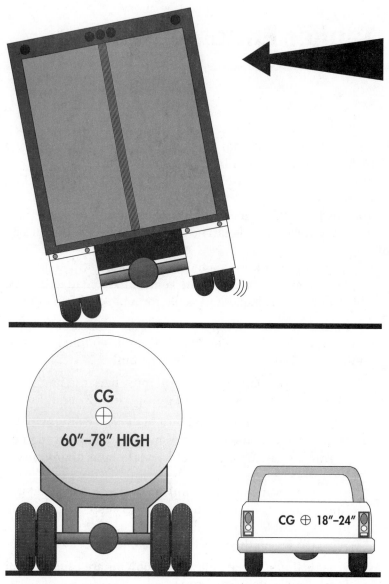

Figure 15-1   Tankers are built with a high center of gravity, making them prone to a rollover, especially on ramps and curves.

This requires planning on the part of the driver.
Table 15-1 shows densities of liquids measured at 60 degrees Fahrenheit.

OTR SAFETY
The higher the density of a liquid, the less the surge of the cargo there will be.

Table 15-1
Densities of Various Liquids at 60°F

Substance	Pounds per gallon
Alcohol	6.8
Asphalt (transport temperature)	7.8
Butane	4.88
Corn syrup	11.82
Crude oil	6.76
Diesel fuel	7.05
Jet fuel	12.2
Liquefied chlorine	4.88
Liquid petroleum gas	4.25
Lubricating oil	7.2
Molten sulfur	16.80
Sesame oil	7.6
Tar	9.00

Tankers

Three Basic Designs

Tankers come in three basic designs—bulkhead, baffled, and "smooth bore" (or unbaffled).

Bulkhead Tankers

Some tankers are equipped with bulkheads—a solid steel divider within the tank. These dividers create separate compartments within the tanker. Most gasoline tankers are equipped with bulkheads.

What is the advantage of these bulkheads?

- With these separate compartments, you can carry several different types of liquids at once. This makes it easy to service a customer who wants to buy different products at one delivery.
- Bulkheads reduce front-to-back liquid surge.

Baffled Tankers

Like bulkheads, baffles are dividers within the tanker itself. However, baffles have holes in them and do not create separate compartments.

So, why are baffles used in tankers? There is one main reason: Baffles slow down the front-to-back surge. By having holes, the baffles allow the product to move in the tank, but the partial partitions slow down the movement.

Does this mean you don't have to be as cautious when driving a baffled tank? *Absolutely not!*

"Smooth Bore" or Unbaffled Tankers

The smooth bore tank has no compartments. It is open, front-to-back, inside.

Smooth bore (or unbaffled) tank vehicles are used to transport food products and certain bulk chemicals. Smooth bore tanks are easier to clean than baffled or bulkhead tanks—which is why smooth bore tanks are almost always used when hauling food-grade products. So, in this type of tank, the surge factor is the most violent and powerful.

This means you must be very cautious in starting, stopping, turning, driving curves, or entering and exiting ramps (Figure 15-2).

EXAMPLES OF TANKERS

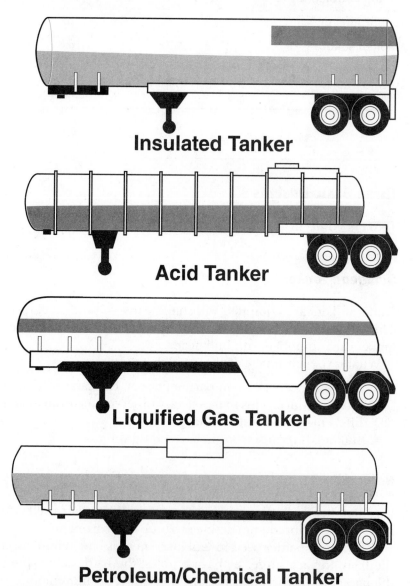

Insulated Tanker

Acid Tanker

Liquified Gas Tanker

Petroleum/Chemical Tanker

Figure 15-2 Various tanker styles are better suited to certain cargo.

What You Should Know About Driving Tank Vehicles

When you're driving a tank vehicle, it will be at its most stable when empty.

A tank vehicle that is 80-percent full will be the least stable (your tank will rarely be completely full, incidentally, which allows for the expansion of the products).

Legal Limits on Liquid Loads

Because a very dense liquid may exceed legal load limits if it fills the tank, often tank vehicle drivers only partially fill the tank with these heavy liquids. The way to know how much to load depends on (1) the outage of the liquid in transit, (2) the weight of the liquid, and (3) the legal weight limits of the tank vehicle.

Tank vehicles are required to have a liquid level-sensing device—a probe inside the tank wired to a controller. This controller is found near the other operator controls.

What You Should Know About Tank Vehicles and Brakes

In most cases, the brakes are designed to work best when a vehicle is fully loaded.

The heavier the weight of the load, the better the traction will be.

If you're driving an empty vehicle, it will sometimes require twice the distance to stop the vehicle when you apply the brakes.

OTR SAFETY
Brakes are more likely to lock up when you try to make an emergency stop with an empty vehicle.

OTR SAFETY
With a partial load, you're giving up the traction you would have with a full load. The surge factor would also be high enough to overtake the braking power of the vehicle.

In other words, that partial load would make your vehicle travel quite a distance from the time you apply your brakes to the time the vehicle actually stops.

Tank Vehicles and Emergency Systems

Tank vehicles are specifically designed to avoid accidental leakage. Some emergency systems operate automatically in an accident. Others must be done manually by the driver. However, if the tank is damaged—by accident or by wear and tear—certain features are included to prevent loss of the cargo. For example:

- Fittings are attached in such a way so if they were to break off, cargo will not leak out.
- A heavy-duty rear bumper protects the tank and its piping from damage in a rear-end collision.

- Openings for filling and inspection, plus the manhole, are protected from damage in case of a vehicle rollover, and safety devices prevent manhole and fill covers from opening when the tank is pressurized.
- Piping that is not protected from damage must have a stop-valve and a shear section.

Portable tanks don't have the same type of emergency systems as cargo tanks. They do have excess-flow valves, however—and once the flow rate exceeds the manufacturer's designated limit, they will close automatically.

The Stop Valve

A stop valve—located on the loading and unloading outlets of the tank vehicle—stops the flow of the liquid cargo. These valves are held in position by their own power supply.

Internal stop valves are self-closing. External stop valves self-close in emergencies (like fire or a broken hose).

Each stop valve also has a remote control, located more than ten feet from the valve. These remote controls are part of the emergency system that the driver can operate manually with levers located in the operator's cabinet.

The Shear Section

A shear section will "fail" in an accident and will break away in a rollover. In doing so, the shear section will save the important part of a pipe and its attachments. This will prevent a leak.

Shear sections are located inside the accident damage protection device but outside the stop valve.

Tank Vehicles and Pressure Relief Systems

Pressure relief systems on tank vehicles monitor the internal pressure of the tank and prevent the cargo from leaking out while the vehicle is on the road.

- The primary pressure relief system has one or more reclosing valves.
- The secondary pressure relief system will back up or assist the primary valve.

Both are marked with the pressure at which they will discharge. Both are also marked with the flow rate. Their location depends on the tank's structural specifications.

What Tank Vehicle Drivers Need to Know About Department of Transportation Specifications

Hazardous materials may be carried only in authorized vehicles that meet Department of Transportation specifications.

What Tank Vehicle Drivers Need to Know About Marking

The month and year of the last test/inspection and the type of inspection is marked on the tank itself.

Tank Vehicles and Special Driving Instructions

The following are important driving instructions for tank vehicle drivers:

- Always maintain a safe following distance—one second for every ten feet of your vehicle's length for speeds up to 40 miles per hour—or more if necessary. Never tailgate—because of the danger of cargo surge and the amount of space required to stop with the surge factor.
- Increase your following distance on wet pavement by one second plus one second for each ten feet of vehicle.
- Always release the clutch after the surge has hit the rear of the tank when upshifting.
- When entering a freeway entrance or exit ramp, always slow down and downshift before entering. A slow speed will reduce the risk of rollover on a ramp or curve. (See Figure 15-3.) A minimum of 5 miles per hour below the posted speed limit is recommended.
- At the top of a long hill, always downshift and select the proper gear before you start down the grade and use light pressure on the brake pedal. Pumping the brakes will cause the vehicle to rock, increasing the slosh and surge of the liquid cargo.

Figure 15-3   A slow speed will reduce the risk of a rollover on a ramp or a curve.

- When hauling liquid loads, never make sudden or sharp changes in direction at any speed—especially at high speeds. This sudden action will only increase the surge factor.
- It is almost always safer to steer to avoid a problem than to use your brakes. But if brakes are necessary, use controlled braking, releasing the brakes as soon as the wheels lock up and then applying the brakes hard a second time.

Let's Review

Read each question and all of the answers provided. Place the letter of the correct answer in the space provided. Once you have answered all the questions, check your answers against the answer key which follows.

____ 1. Liquid surge can be defined as:
  (A) When the tanker is filled with too much liquid
  (B) When the liquid cargo is expelled from the tank
  (C) When the liquid cargo moves back and forth as the vehicle comes to a stop
  (D) All of the above

____ 2. A professional driver needs special skills to drive a tanker because of:
  (A) The cargo surge factor
  (B) The tanker's high center of gravity
  (C) The careful handling of liquid cargoes required on curves and ramps
  (D) All of the above

____ 3. Outage is:
  (A) The room required in the tank for expansion of the liquid cargo
  (B) The amount of time it takes to empty the tank
  (C) The rate of leakage from the tanker
  (D) All of the above

____ 4. A smooth bore tanker is:
  (A) Usually used to carry food
  (B) Has no bulkhead
  (C) Has no baffles
  (D) All of the above

____ 5. Baffles make handling a liquid tank vehicle slightly easier because they:
  (A) Control forward and backward surge
  (B) Are easier to clean
  (C) Control side-to-side surge
  (D) All of the above

____ 6. When taking a curve with a loaded tanker, the driver will prevent rollover by traveling
  (A) At the posted speed limit
  (B) With a rollover protector
  (C) Five miles per hour faster than the posted speed limit
  (D) At a speed below the posted speed limit

_____ 7. Higher density liquids:
   (A) Can be loaded faster
   (B) Will surge less than lower-density liquids
   (C) Have no side-to-side surge
   (D) All of the above

_____ 8. A high center of gravity means:
   (A) A majority of the load's weight is carried high off the ground
   (B) The vehicle will be more apt to roll over on freeway ramps
   (C) The vehicle will be more apt to roll over on curves
   (D) All of the above

_____ 9. The surge factor is worse when a tank vehicle is:
   (A) 40 percent full
   (B) 90 percent full
   (C) 20 percent full
   (D) 80 percent full

_____10. With a partial tanker load:
   (A) Traction is less
   (B) The surge factor may overwhelm the vehicle's braking power
   (C) The vehicle could travel a significant distance before stopping after the brakes are applied
   (D) All of the above

Answers to Let's Review

1. C; 2. D; 3. A; 4. D; 5. A; 6. D; 7. B; 8. D; 9. D; 10. D.

16 Driving Doubles and Triples and Preparing for the Combination Test

For professional drivers who want the flexibility to be endorsed to drive double- and triple-trailer rigs, this chapter provides the information you need to pass the CDL knowledge test for driving double and triple trailers safely (Figure 16-1).

Its purpose is to inform you of safe driving procedures, how to couple and uncouple double- and triple-rigs and how to inspect doubles and triples to assure your over-the-road safety.

Legal Combinations

In the United States, a three-axle tractor pulling a two-axle semi-trailer is the most popular over-the-road vehicle. These "18-wheeled" combinations carry most of our freight today.

Double trailers (sometimes called "pups") are acceptable in most states, while triples are legal in some states and outlawed in others.

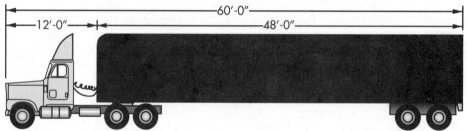

Typical dimensions of a tractor-semitrailer with a 48-foot semitrailer

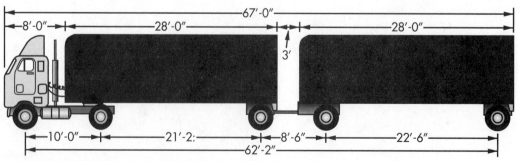

Typical dimensions of a twin trailer truck (Note: Use of conventional tractor adds 3 to 7 feet to total length.)

Figure 16-1 Driving doubles and triples requires unique driving skills.

Pulling Double and Triple Trailers Safely

Professional drivers must exercise extreme caution when pulling doubles and triples. The key words are "plan ahead," because planning becomes extremely important when you are pulling combinations.

There's no doubt about it—the law of averages tells you that more can go wrong when you are pulling two or three trailers than if you are pulling only one trailer. Moreover, doubles and triples have proved to be less stable. Because of this, there are several areas to be aware of and concerned with at the same time.

How to Inspect Doubles and Triples

Okay, let's get to work. Here, we are going to use the seven-step inspection procedure to begin the inspection, and then add the inspection points for doubles and triples.

Let's review what the seven-step inspection procedure includes:

Step One: On Approach

- Take a look at the general condition of the vehicle.
- Look for damage.
- Look at the ground under the vehicle. Do you see any oil, coolant, grease, or fuel leaks?
- Check around the vehicle for hazards such as low-hanging tree-limbs, wires, or anything that would be a problem when you move the vehicle.
- Review the last vehicle inspection report. Have the reported problems that would impact the safe operation of the vehicle been repaired?
- Inspect the vehicle to see if the problems have been fixed.

Step Two: Check the Engine

- Check that the parking brakes are on and/or the wheels are chocked.
- Raise the hood, tilt the cab (remember to secure all loose objects), or open the engine compartment door. Inspect the following:
  - Engine oil level
  - Coolant level in the radiator and the condition of the hoses
  - Power steering fluid level and hose condition (if necessary)
  - Windshield washer fluid level
  - Battery fluid level (if not maintenance-free), connections, and tiedowns (particularly if the battery is located elsewhere)
  - Automatic transmission fluid level
  - Belts and these components: alternator, water pump, air compressor. (Most air compressors today are gear-driven, so if necessary, make sure you also inspect the air-compressor gears.)

  ◆ Look for leaks in the engine compartment coming from fuel, coolant, oil, power steering fluid, hydraulic fluid, and battery fluid.
  ◆ Look for cracked and worn electrical wiring insulation.

Once this inspection is complete, lower the hood, cab, or engine compartment door and secure.

Step Three: Inspect the Inside of the Cab and Start the Engine

- The parking brake should be on.
- Always depress the clutch when engaging the starter.
- The gearshift should be in neutral (if automatic transmission, it should be in park).
- Listen for any unusual noises.

Look at the gauges:

- Oil pressure should register normal within a few seconds after the engine is on.
- The ammeter and/or voltmeter should be in normal ranges.
- Coolant temperature should begin gradually rising to the normal range.
- Engine oil temperature should begin gradually rising to the normal range.
- Warning lights and buzzers—all warning lights should turn off immediately except for the low air pressure gauge, which will turn off at about 60–80 psi.

Check the condition of the controls—look for looseness, sticking, damage, or any improper settings:

- Steering wheel
- Clutch
- Accelerator
- Brake controls
  ◆ Foot brake
  ◆ Trailer brake (if available)
  ◆ Parking brake
  ◆ Retarder controls (if available)
- Transmission controls
- Interaxle differential lock (if available)
- Horn
- Windshield wiper/washer
- Lights
  ◆ Headlights
  ◆ Dimmer switch
  ◆ Turn signals
  ◆ Four-way flashers
  ◆ Clearance, identification, marker light switches
- Check the mirrors and windshield—look for cracks, illegal stickers, or other visual obstructions. Clean and adjust where necessary.
- Check the emergency equipment.
  ◆ Spare fuses, three reflective triangles, and a properly charged/rated fire extinguisher should be present.

- Check for optional items
  - Tire chains (required in certain areas in the winter)
  - Tire changing equipment
  - List of emergency phone numbers
  - Accident-reporting packet

Step Four: Turn Off the Engine and Check the Lights

- Make sure the parking brake is on, turn off the engine, and remove the key. Then turn the headlights on low beams, turn on the four-way flashers, and get out, taking the key with you.
- Step to the front of the vehicle
- Check that the low beams are on and both four-way flashers are in working order.
- Get back into cab, push the dimmer switch, and then check that the high beams work.

Step Five: Perform a Walkaround Inspection (Done by Getting Back into the Cab and Changing the Lights)

- Turn off the headlights and four-way flashers.
- Turn on the parking, clearance, side-marker, and identification lights.
- Turn on the right turn signal—then get out of cab and begin walkaround inspection.

General inspection:

- Walk around and inspect the vehicle.
- Clean all lights, reflectors, and glass as you walk around.

For double- and triple-trailers:

- Shut-off valves should be open at the rear of the front trailer and closed at the rear of the last trailer.
- The converter dolly air tank drain valve should be closed.
- Check air lines—are they supported and the glad hands properly connected?
- If the spare tire is riding on a dolly, make sure it's secure.
- Check that the pintle-eye of the dolly is in place in the pintle hook of the trailer(s).
- Check that the pintle hook is latched and that the safety latch is in place.
- The safety chains should be secured to the trailer(s).
- Check that light cords are firmly in sockets on the trailers.
- Check to make sure the dolly fifth wheel is secure.

Check the left front:

- The driver's door glass should be clean.
- The locks should be in working order.
- Check the condition of the wheels, rims, and tires.
  - There should be no missing, bent, or broken studs, clamps, or lugs.
  - Tires should be properly inflated, and the valve stem and cap should be in place. The tired should show no serious cuts, slashes, bulges, or signs of tread wear.

- ◆ Test rust-streaked lug nuts for looseness.
- ◆ Hub oil level should be good with no leaks.

- Check the left front suspension
  - ◆ Make sure springs, spring hangers, shackles and U-bolts, and shock absorbers are in good condition.
- Be certain the left front brake drum and hoses are in good condition.

Check the front:

- Check the front axle for cracks or other problems.
- Check for loose, worn, bent, damaged, or missing parts of the steering system and test for looseness.
- The windshield should be clean and free of damage. Wipers should be in good working order—check for proper spring tension in the wiper arms. Check blades for stiff rubber and make sure they are secure.
- Parking, clearance, and identification lights are clean, operational, and of the proper color—amber in front.
- The right turn signal light must be clean, operational, and the proper color—amber or white.

Check the right front:

- Check all items on the right front just as you did for the left front.
- If you have a cab-over-engine model, all primary and safety locks should be engaged and working.
- The right fuel tank should be securely mounted, with no leaks. Make sure fuel crossover lines are secure, and that there is adequate fuel in the tank for the trip. Caps should be on and secure.
- Check the condition of visible parts.
  - ◆ Make sure there are no leaks in the rear of the engine or transmission, and that the exhaust system is secure and not leaking or touching wires or lines.
  - ◆ No cracks or bends should be visible in the frame and cross members.
- Check the air lines and electrical wiring to make certain there is no visible snagging, rubbing, or wearing.
- The spare tire carrier should not be damaged and the spare tire/wheel should be the correct size and properly inflated.
- The cargo should be secure—in other words, make certain it is blocked, braced, tied, and chained. The header board should be secure, side boards and stakes should be free of damage and properly placed, and the canvas or tarp should be secured to prevent tearing, billowing, or blocking mirrors.
- Oversized loads must have required signs properly mounted and all required permits must be in the driver's pouch.
- Curbside cargo compartment doors should be closed and latched, with all required security seals in place.

Check right rear:

- Check the condition of the wheels, rims, and tires. Look for any missing, bent, or broken spacers, studs, clamps or lugs. Make sure tires are evenly matched, are of the same type (no mixing of radial and bias types), and are properly inflated with valve stems and caps in place. There should be no cuts, bulges, or signs of tread wear. Tires should not be rubbing, and should be clear of debris and be properly spaced.

- Wheel bearing/seals should not be leaking.
- The suspension—springs, spring hangers, shackles, and U-bolts—should be in good condition, the axle should be secure, and the powered axle(s) should not be leaking gear oil.
- Check the condition of the torque rod arms and bushings.
- Check the condition of the shock absorber(s).
- If there is a retractable axle, check the lift mechanism. If it is air-powered, check for leaks.
- Make sure the brake drums are in good condition and hoses have been checked for wear, rubbing, and so on.
- Lights and reflectors—make sure side-marker lights are clean, operational, and red at the rear—others should be amber. The same goes for side markers.

Check the rear:

- Rear clearance and identification lights should be clean, operational, and red at the rear. Reflectors should be clean and red at the rear. Make sure taillights are clean, operational, and red at the rear. The right turn signal must be operating and of the proper color—red, yellow, or amber at rear.
- License plates should be present, clean, and secure.
- Splash guards must be properly fastened, undamaged, and not dragging or rubbing on tires.
- Check that the cargo is secure—that it is properly blocked and braced, tied, and chained.
- Tailboards should be up and secure. End gates must be free of damage and secured in stake sockets. If there is a lift gate, make sure it is also secure.
- Make sure the canvas or tarp is secured in order to avoid billowing, tearing, blocking the rearview mirror, or covering the rear lights.
- For over-length or over-width loads, have all signs and additional flags/lights in the proper position and have all required permits.
- Rear doors must be closed and locked.
- Secure all trailer doors and check the seal numbers.

Check left side:

Check everything you checked on the right side—and also the following:

- Batteries (if not located in the engine compartment)—make sure the battery box is securely attached and that the cover also is secure.
- Make sure batteries are not damaged or leaking and that they are secure.
- Check battery fluid levels (except in maintenance-free types).
- Make sure cell caps and vents are in place, are free of debris, and are secure.

Step Six: Check the Signal Lights

- Get in and turn off all the lights.
- Turn on the stop lights (apply the trailer hand brake).
- Turn on left turn signals.

Get out and check the lights:

- Check the left front turn signal—make sure it is clean, operational, and of proper amber or white on signals facing the front.
- Check the left rear turn signal and stoplights—make sure they are clean, operational, and of the proper red, yellow, or amber color.

Step Seven: Start Engine and Check Brake System

- Get in and turn off those lights not needed for driving.
- Check all required papers, trip manifests, permits, and so on.
- Secure all loose articles in the cab.
- Start the engine.
- Test for hydraulic leaks—if you have hydraulic brakes, pump them three times. Then apply pressure to the pedal and hold for five seconds. The pedal should not move—if it does, there might be a leak or other problem. Fix it before beginning your trip.
- Test the air brakes.
- Test the parking brake—fasten your seatbelt, allow the vehicle to move forward slowly, and apply the parking brake. If it doesn't stop the vehicle, get it fixed.
- Test the service brake stopping action—move the vehicle forward at about five miles per hour and push the brake pedal firmly. If the vehicle pulls to one side, this could mean brake trouble. Any unusual feel of the pedal or delayed stopping action could signal a problem.

Check the air brakes on doubles and triples like any other combination vehicle.

Rollovers

To prevent rollovers, steer combination rigs gently and go slowly around corners, on and off ramps and around curves. Watch your speed on curves. A safe speed for a single tractor-trailer combination is probably too fast for a set of doubles or triple trailers.

OTR SAFETY
A fully loaded rig is ten times more likely to roll over in a crash than an empty rig.

This fact, in itself, is reason enough to drive a combination rig slowly and carefully.

Avoiding the Crack-the-Whip Effect

Kids on roller skates like to form chains and then "crack the whip" or make a turn so that the last person in the chain moves twice as fast as those in the center. Believe it or not, this same effect occurs when pulling doubles and triples.

In the crack-the-whip effect when combinations are involved, the last trailer of the combination is most likely to roll over. When you drive combinations, be aware of this because doubles and triples are more likely to turn over than tractor-trailer rigs.

OTR SAFETY

To avoid the last trailer being "whipped" and turning over, you must steer gently.

So what does "steer gently" actually mean? Just what it says. Avoid jerky movements, sudden veers, or other knee-jerk maneuvers. Turn corners easily and steadily, take the ramp slowly and back off the accelerator when taking the curve.

Keep Your Eyes on the Road and Allow Plenty of Room

It's not rocket science. When you pull double- or triple-trailers, your rig is going to need a lot of room for any maneuver, whether it's changing lanes or stopping at an intersection. Allow for this additional space for any maneuver. When you're entering a freeway, make sure you allow enough room between oncoming vehicles before pulling into the driving lane.

Smooth driving is required when pulling doubles and triples. Exercise defensive driving tactics. Look as far ahead as possible and slow down or change lanes slowly, steadily, and gradually when necessary.

Manage Space

When you pull doubles and triples down the highway, whether you realize it or not, you are probably causing difficulties for other motorists. Doubles and triples take longer to pass. There are also situations where the triple combination could make it difficult for other motorists to enter or exit the roadway. Why? Because the triple combination may be blocking the entrance or exit ramps.

There's also something called "aerodynamic buffeting." As you drive your double or triple rig down the highway, you are cutting through the wind and, as you cut through, a "draft" is created behind you. When a smaller vehicle comes up beside you, this draft hits them and it's like getting hit by a crosswind.

OTR SAFETY

Remember! Doubles and triples take more time to change lanes, so you need to plan so as not to "cut off" a fellow motorist in the lane you want to enter.

Bad Weather Driving

In bad weather, take twice the precautions with doubles/triples. If the highway is wet or icy and you are pulling doubles and triples, remember that the hazards of these kinds of conditions double and triple for you, depending on what you're pulling. Greater length and more dead axles to pull with your drive axles increase the likelihood of skidding or losing traction.

OTR SAFETY

When driving combinations, you have greater length and more dead axles to pull with your drive axles than other drives. Therefore, there is a greater chance of skids and loss of traction. Keep your speed aligned with safe driving in current conditions at all times.

Parking Doubles and Triples

Always park so you can pull your rig straight through. Be aware of parking lots and their arrangements so your combination rig will not get hemmed in by other parked vehicles.

OTR SAFETY

For the sake of safety, the heavier of the loaded trailers should always be in the first position, directly behind the tractor. The trailer with the lighter load should always be in the rear position. This is true for doubles and triples.

Coupling and Uncoupling

The coupling and uncoupling process isn't difficult, but it is imperative that it is done correctly every time (Figure 16-2).

It is important to know how to couple and uncouple correctly for several reasons:

1. Time—which you never have enough of, especially when you have to go back and redo something that was done incorrectly.
2. If coupling and uncoupling are done incorrectly, a very dangerous situation is created.

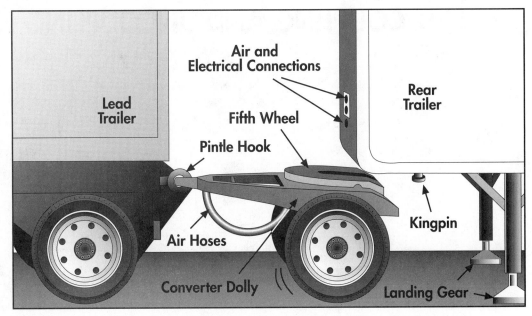

Figure 16-2　Pay close attention to step-by-step details when coupling and uncoupling.

OTR SAFETY

Take time to do these procedures correctly—no short cuts. Follow every step of the procedures to the letter.

Steps for Coupling Doubles

There are differences between rigs, so learn the specifics for the vehicles you will be operating.

1. Before beginning a coupling procedure, walk around the trailers and the tractor. Make sure the path is clear of anything that could damage the tractor or the trailers.
2. Check the trailer kingpins—they should not be bent or broken.
3. (This step is only needed for trailers manufactured before 1975) Secure the rear trailer—To set the emergency brakes on the second trailer:

   - Drive the tractor close to the trailer.
   - Connect the emergency line, charge the trailer air tank.
   - Disconnect the emergency line. This will set the second trailer's emergency brakes if the slack adjusters are correctly adjusted.

COUPLING AND UNCOUPLING HAZARDS

VEHICLE

HAZARD	RESULT
• Tractor Not Secured	• Damage to Brake Lines
• Trailer Brakes Not Functioning	• Trailer Pushed Into Obstruction
• Jaws Not Securely Fastened	• Trailer Breaks Loose on the Road
• Ground Not Firm for Uncoupling	• Trailer Falls and Is Damaged
• Trailer Wheels Not Chocked	• Is Pushed or Rolls Into Obstruction

DRIVER

HAZARD	RESULT
• Climbing on Tractor	• Falls From Slippery Surface
• Working Under Unsupported Trailer (No Jackstand or Tractor Under Trailer Nose)	• Injury When Landing Gear Collapses and Trailer Drops to the Ground

Figure 16-3   Coupling and uncoupling hazards.

4. Inspect the fifth wheel.

   • Look for damaged/missing parts.
   • Check that the mounting to the tractor is uncracked and secure.
   • Be sure the fifth wheel plate is greased. (Failure to keep the fifth wheel plate lubricated may cause steering problems due to friction produced between the tractor and trailer.)
   • Check that the fifth wheel is in the proper position for coupling:

     ◆ The wheel should be tilted down toward the rear of the tractor.
     ◆ The jaws must be open.
     ◆ The safety unlocking handle should be in the automatic locking position.

OTR SAFETY

If using a sliding fifth wheel, it should be in a locked position.

5. Chock the trailer wheels. If the trailer has spring brakes, make sure they are on.

6. Make sure the cargo is secured against movement during coupling.

7. Position the tractor directly in front of the trailer.

   • Never couple a trailer by backing under it at an angle. This could shove the trailer sideways and break or damage the landing gear.

   • Check the position, using outside mirrors—look down both sides of the trailer.

8. Back under the trailer slowly. Back until the fifth wheel touches the trailer, then stop. Don't hit the trailer!

9. Secure the tractor—put on the parking brake and shift the transmission into neutral.

10. Check the kingpin and fifth wheel—they should be aligned.

11. Check the trailer height—if it is too low, the tractor could hit and damage the nose of the trailer. If it's too high, it may not couple correctly. The trailer should be low enough to be raised slightly when the tractor backs under it.

12. Connect the air lines to the trailer.

    • Check glad hand seals and connect the tractor's emergency air lines to the trailer emergency glad hand.

    • Check glad hand seals and connect the tractor's service air line to the trailer service glad hand.

    • Check that air lines are safely supported and won't be crushed when the tractor is backing under the trailer (Figure 16-4).

13. Get into the cab and supply air to the trailer.

    • Move the tractor protection valve control from "emergency" to "normal" position—or push in the "air supply" knob.

    • Wait until the air pressure reaches "normal."

    • Check the brakes for crossed air lines by shutting off the engine so you can hear the brakes. Apply and release the trailer brakes—listen to hear the brake move and air escape when it's released.

    • When the brakes are working, start the engine.

    • Check to see that the air pressure is normal.

14. Lock the trailer brakes—pull out the "air supply" knob or move the tractor protection control from "normal" to the "emergency" position.

15. Back under the trailer *slowly*—using the lowest reverse gear—to avoid hitting the kingpin too hard. Stop when the kingpin is locked into the fifth wheel.

Figure 16-4   Connecting air lines to the trailer. (Photo courtesy of ATA Associates, Inc.)

16. Check the connection for security by raising the trailer landing gear slightly off the ground and pulling the tractor *slowly* forward while the trailer brakes are still locked.

17. Secure the rig—shift the transmission into neutral with the parking brakes on. Then, shut off the engine and take your key with you as a safety precaution (so someone else can't move your truck while you're inspecting the coupling).

18. Inspect the coupling—use a flashlight at night.

   • Ensure there is no space between the upper and lower fifth wheel. If you see space, something is wrong—the kingpin may be on top of the closed fifth wheel jaws and the trailer could come loose in transit. Check to find the problem.

   • Get under the trailer and look back to the fifth wheel—make sure the jaws are closed around the shank of the kingpin.

OTR SAFETY
Whenever you are working around or under your rig, be sure to remove keys and put them in your pocket. This will avoid someone getting into the cab and moving the rig while you're working around or under it.

   • The locking lever should be in the "lock" position, and the safety catch should be in position over the locking lever.

   • On some fifth wheels, the catch must be positioned over the locking lever by hand.

OTR SAFETY

If the coupling isn't done correctly or if coupling devices are damaged, don't drive the unit. Get it fixed!

19. Connect the electrical cord and check air lines:

  - Plug the electrical cord into the trailer and fasten the safety catch.
  - Check both the air lines and the electrical line for damage.
  - Check to make sure the air and electrical lines will not hit moving parts of the rig.

20. Raise the front trailer landing gear—if available, begin with the low gear range and when free of the weight, change to the high gear range.

  - Raise the landing gear all the way—never move a rig with landing gear partially up. It could catch on railroad tracks or other elevated portions of the roadway.
  - When the full weight of the trailer is held by the tractor, check for turning clearance between the rear of the tractor frame and the landing gear.
  - Make sure there is enough clearance between the top of the tractor tires and the nose of the trailer.

21. Position the converter dolly in front of the second or rear trailer:

  - Open the air tank petcock and release dolly brakes. (If dolly has spring brakes, use the dolly parking brake control.)
  - Wheel the dolly into position so it is in line with the kingpin (if it is a short distance away).
  - If the distance is too great, use the tractor and first trailer to pick up the converter dolly.
  - Position the tractor and the first trailer as close as possible to the converter dolly.
  - Move the dolly to the rear of the first trailer and couple it to the trailer:
    - Lock the pintle hook.
    - Secure the dolly support in the raised position.
    - Position the dolly as close as possible to the nose of the second trailer.
    - Lower the dolly support.
    - Unhook the dolly from the first trailer.
    - Wheel the dolly into position in front of the second trailer, aligned with the kingpin.

22. Connect the converter dolly to the front trailer. Back the first trailer in front of the dolly tongue. Hook the dolly to the front trailer. Then, lock the pintle hook and secure the converter gear support in the raised position.

23. Connect the converter dolly to the rear trailer.

Checking the Coupling

Check the trailer brakes—they should be locked.

- Make sure the trailer height is correct—slightly lower than the center of the fifth wheel so that the trailer is raised when the dolly is pushed under.
- Back the converter dolly under the rear trailer.
- As a precaution, raise the landing gear slightly off the ground to prevent damage if the trailer moves.
- Test the coupling by pulling against the pin of the second trailer.
- Take the transmission out of gear. Set the brakes and get out.
- Visually check the coupling—there should be no space between the upper and lower fifth wheel and the locking jaws closed on the kingpin.
- Connect safety chains, air hoses, and light cords.
- Close the converter dolly air tank petcock.
- Close the shut-off valves at the rear of the second trailer (service and emergency).
- Completely raise the landing gear.
- Push the "air supply" knob in and check for air at the rear of the second trailer. To do this, open the emergency line shut-off. If there is no air pressure, the brakes won't work and something is wrong.

Uncoupling Combination Trailers

Uncoupling the Rear Trailer

To uncouple double or triple trailers, begin with the rear trailer and use the following steps, working slowly and surely to avoid damage to vehicles or injury to yourself and others:

1. Park the rig on level ground and in a straight line.
2. Apply the parking brakes.
3. Lower the landing gear of the second trailer—enough to take some of the weight off the dolly.
4. Close the air shut-offs at the rear of the first trailer and on the dolly. Then, disconnect all the dolly air and electric lines and secure them.
5. Release the dolly brakes, either by pushing the brake release button or draining all the air from the dolly air tank.
6. Release the converter dolly fifth wheel latch.
7. Slowly pull the tractor and first trailer and dolly from under the rear trailer.

Uncoupling the Converter Dolly

1. Lower the dolly's lan]ding gear.
2. Disconnect the safety chains.
3. Chock the wheels or apply converter gear spring brakes.
4. Release the pintle hook on the first trailer and pull clear of the dolly.

OTR SAFETY

When the dolly is still under the rear trailer, never unlock the pintle hook. This may cause the dolly tow bar to fly up, which is dangerous in itself. However, it may also make it difficult to recouple.

Doubles and Triples Air Brake Checks

Check the brakes on combination rigs as you would any combination vehicle. Make sure the following checks on doubles and triples are completed prior to going on the road:

Test the Air Flow to All Trailers in the Combination

Use the tractor's parking brake to hold the vehicle.

1. Wait for the air pressure to reach "normal" readings.
2. Push in the red "trailer air supply" knob. This will supply air to the emergency (supply) lines.
3. Use the trailer handbrake to provide air to the service line.
4. Go to the rear of the rig and open the emergency line shut-off valve at the rear of the last trailer. You should hear air escaping, which shows the entire system is charged.
5. Close the emergency line valve.
6. Open the service line valve to check that the service pressure goes through all the trailers (this test assumes the trailer handbrake or the service brake pedal is "on").
7. Close the valve. If you do not hear air escaping from both lines, check that the shut-off valves on the trailers and dollies are in the "open" position. You must have air all the way to the back for all the brakes to work.

Test the Tractor Protection Valve

1. Charge the trailer air brake system by building up normal air pressure and then pushing the "air supply" knob in.
2. Shut off the engine.
3. Step on and off the brake pedal several times to reduce the air pressure in the tanks.
4. The trailer air supply control (also called the tractor protection valve control) should pop out (or go from the "normal" to the "emergency" position) when the air pressure falls into the pressure range specified by the manufacturer (usually within a range of 20 to 45 psi).

OTR SAFETY

If the tractor protection valve doesn't work properly, an air hose or trailer brake leak could drain all the air from the tractor. This would cause the emergency brakes to come on, with a possible loss of control.

Test the Trailer Emergency Brakes

To test the trailer emergency brakes, do the following:

1. Charge the trailer air brake system and check that the trailer rolls freely.
2. Stop and pull out the trailer air supply control (also called the tractor protection valve control or the trailer emergency valve), or place it in the "emergency" position.
3. Pull gently on the trailer with the tractor to check that the trailer emergency brakes are on.

Test the Trailer Service Brakes

To test the trailer service brakes, do the following:

1. Check for normal air pressure.
2. Release the parking brakes and move the vehicle slowly forward.
3. Apply the trailer brakes with the hand control (trolley valve)—that is, if your rig is equipped with one.
4. You should feel the brakes come on. This tells you the trailer brakes are connected and working properly.

OTR SAFETY

The trailer brakes should be tested with the hand valve, but controlled in normal operation with the foot pedal, which applies air to the service brakes at the wheels.

17 Driving Passenger Vehicles

Drivers operating buses, vans, or limousines that seat more than fifteen people, including the driver, must have a CDL (see Figure 17-1). The exception would be those driving family members for personal reasons, not for a salary or for profit.

Bus drivers are also required to have a Passenger Endorsement on their CDL. This includes passing the General Knowledge Tests, the Skills Test, and the Air Brakes Endorsement—if the bus has air brakes—plus the written Passenger Endorsement.

Vehicle Inspection

This is an important part of any professional driver's job but particularly if you are directly responsible for the safety of passengers.

Before beginning any trip, be sure the vehicle is safe. Review the inspection report made by the previous driver. Only if the problems reported earlier have been corrected should you sign the previous driver's report and attempt to operate the vehicle. This is your certification that defects reported earlier have been corrected.

Vehicle Systems

During each pre-trip check, the driver should ensure the good working order and safe function of the following items:

- The parking brake
- All lights and reflectors
- The horn

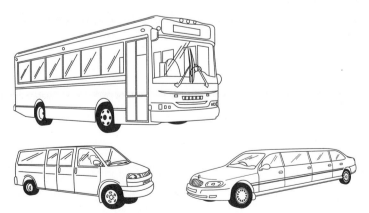

Figure 17-1　To drive a transit bus, passenger van, or a limousine you will need a CDL.

- The windshield wiper(s)
- The rear-view mirrors
- The steering mechanism
- The tires (no recapped or regrooved tires on the front wheels)
- The wheels and rims
- The service brakes (including hose couplings if bus has a trailer/semi-trailer)
- Coupling devices
- Emergency equipment
    - Close all open emergency exits
    - Close access panels (for engine, restroom service, baggage)

Interior Check

Drivers should check the interior for safety and working order of the following:

- Aisles and stairwells are clear.
- Floor coverings have no gaps or tears.
- Handholds and railings are intact.
- All emergency exit handles are secure.
- All signs/signaling devices are operational—including the restroom emergency device.
- All seats are securely fastened to the floor (one exception—a charter bus for farm workers may have up to eight temporary folding chairs).
- All emergency exit doors and windows are closed.
- All emergency exits are clearly marked with signage.
- Red emergency light must be working and clearly visible—drive with it on at night or any time you use outside lights.
- Roof hatches should be locked in partly open position, but do not leave them open as a general rule.
- The fire extinguisher and emergency reflectors are present, as required by law.
- Unless the bus is equipped with circuit breakers, it must have spare electrical fuses on board.

OTR SAFETY
The driver's seat should have a seatbelt. Always use it. It's the law!

Loading Passengers and Cargo

- Passengers must be seated and all baggage must be stored under the seats.
- No carry-on baggage is allowed in the stairwell or the aisle.
- All carry-on baggage must be stored to allow free movement about the bus and must not block emergency exits or windows. Carry-on baggage should be stowed to protect riders from injury if carry-ons fall or shift.

- No passenger should stand in the area adjacent to the driver. Most buses have a marked "standee line" that is placed even with the rear of the driver's seat. All riders should stand behind this line.

OTR SAFETY

When on the road, mention the company's safety rules and regulations, including "No smoking," "No drinking," and other rules designed for the comfort of passengers, such as the use of computers, cell phones, radios, and tape or CD players.

When You Arrive at the Destination

Once you've arrived at the destination, the driver's job is to:

- Announce the location.
- Announce the reason for stopping.
- Announce the next departure time.
- Announce the bus number.
- Remind passengers to watch their step.
- If aisles are on a lower level than the seating, remind passengers to step down when they are disembarking.
- Remind riders to take carry-ons with them.
- To prevent theft, don't allow preboarding riders on the bus until departure time.

Post-Trip Vehicle Inspection

After passengers have disembarked, inspect the bus. Interstate carriers require a written inspection report from each driver at the end of every shift. These reports list any problems with the bus systems or any damage done during the last shift.

Double-check areas that passengers may have damaged in transit, such as loose handholds, seats, emergency exits, and windows.

Report this damage at the end of the shift so repairs can be completed before the next trip.

If you drive for a mass transit organization, also look to see if the following are in working order:

- Passenger signaling units
- Brake-door interlocks

Hazardous Materials

It is the driver's responsibility to watch for cargo or baggage containing hazardous materials. Most hazardous materials cannot be carried on a bus.

OTR SAFETY

Some travelers may board a bus with unlabeled hazardous materials. They may not realize how unsafe it is to carry these materials. Do not allow passengers to carry on common hazardous materials like batteries or gasoline.

The Federal Hazardous Materials Table

The Federal Hazardous Materials Table designates which materials are hazardous to transport. They have been designated as "hazardous materials" because they endanger the health, safety, and property of those around them during their transport.

Federal rules require the originating shipper to mark any hazardous materials with the material's name, ID number, and hazard label.

There are nine different hazard labels. They are about four inches square and are diamond-shaped.

When you see the diamond-shaped labels on a container of material to be shipped, don't allow that container on your bus unless you are sure the material is allowed.

OTR SAFETY

Buses may carry small-arms ammunition labeled ORM-D, emergency hospital supplies, and drugs. You can also carry small amounts of other hazardous materials if the shipper cannot send them by any other means of transportation.

Buses May Never Carry Any of the Following:

- Division 2.3 poison gas, liquid Class 6 poison, tear gas, irritating material
- More than 100 pounds of solid Class 6 poisons, which include pesticides and arsenic
- Explosives in the space occupied by people, except for small-arms ammunition
- Labeled radioactive materials in the space occupied by people
- More than 500 pounds total of allowed hazardous materials, and no more than 100 pounds of any one hazard class

Prohibited Practices

When driving a passenger vehicle, avoid the following:

- Fueling bus with riders on board unless absolutely necessary.
- Never refuel in a closed building while riders are on board.

- Don't talk with riders or engage in other distracting activities while driving.
- Do not tow or push a disabled bus with riders onboard—unless getting off would be unsafe. Then, only tow or push the bus to the nearest point of safety where passengers can disembark.
- Follow the employer's guidelines regarding towing or pushing disabled buses or other passenger vehicles.

Brake-Door Interlocks and How They Are Used

Mass transit coaches often have a brake and accelerator interlock system that applies the brakes and holds the throttle in an idle position when rear door is open. The interlock system releases when the rear door closes.

OTR SAFETY
Never use this safety feature in place of the parking brake.

18 Driving School Buses

School buses are the safest form of highway transportation. There are about 440,000 public school buses that travel approximately 5 billion miles each year. Each day, school buses carry around 20 million students to school and school-related events (see Figure 18-1). (Accident Facts 1996, National Safety Council)

OTR SAFETY
About two-thirds of school bus-related fatalities happen outside the bus.

Danger Zones

What Are the Danger Zones Found Around Your Bus?

The danger zone is the area on all sides of the bus where children are at the greatest risk of being hit, either by another vehicle or their own school bus. These danger zones extend as much as 30 feet from the front bumper, ten feet from the left and right sides of the bus, and ten feet behind the rear bumper of the bus.

Figure 18-1 To get your CDL to drive a school bus, you must first learn the specific school bus regulations.

OTR SAFETY

In addition to the traditional danger zones around a school bus, the area to the left of the bus is always considered dangerous for the passengers because of passing cars and trucks.

How to Use the Mirrors on Your Bus

Correct Mirror Adjustment

It is vital—to the safety of your passengers and yourself—to adjust and use all mirrors properly. Make sure you can see all danger zones and the students riding your bus as well as traffic and other objects within the school bus's environment.

Always check each mirror before operating the school bus so you will have maximum viewing of the area around your bus. If necessary, have these mirrors adjusted.

Outside Left- and Right-Side Flat Mirrors

These mirrors are mounted to the left and right front corners of the bus at the side or front of the windshield. They will help you monitor traffic and check clearances and students to the side and rear of the bus.

There are two key blind spots to take note of:

- There is a "blind spot" immediately below and in front of each mirror and directly in back of the rear bumper.
- The "blind spot" directly behind the bus extends as much as 400 feet, depending on the width of the bus.

Adjust these mirrors so you can see:

- At least 200 feet or four bus lengths behind the bus
- Both sides of the bus
- The rear tires—where they touch the ground

Outside Left- and Right-Side Convex Mirrors

These mirrors are located below the outside flat mirrors and are used to monitor the left and right sides at the wide angle.

They give the driver a view of the traffic, clearances, and students at the side of the bus, but don't accurately depict the size of the people or their distance from the bus.

Position these mirrors so you can see:

- The side of the bus up to the mirror mounts
- The front of the rear tires where they touch the ground
- At least one traffic lane on either side of the bus

Using Outside Left- and Right-Side Crossover Mirrors

There mirrors can be found on both the left and right front corners of the bus. They are used to see the front bumper danger zone directly in front of the bus, which is not directly visible from the driver's seat. These mirrors also provide the driver with a view of the left side and right side of the bus, including the front wheel area and the service door. This area also provides a view of people and objects but does not give an accurate reflection of their size and distance from the bus. Always make sure these mirrors are properly adjusted before driving the bus so you can see the following:

- The entire area in front of the bus—from bumper to ground level—and make sure your direct vision and your mirror view overlap.
- The right and left front tires touching the ground.
- The right side of the bus from the front of the bus to the service door.
- These mirrors should be viewed in logical sequence to ensure a child or object is not in any of the bus's danger zones.

Using the Overhead Inside Rearview Mirror

The overhead inside rearview mirror is mounted directly above the windshield on the driver's side of the bus and is used to monitor passenger activity inside.

It may offer limited visibility of the back of the bus, so use the exterior side mirrors to monitor passenger traffic entering this area of the bus.

Place the mirror so you can easily see:

- The top of the rear window in the top of the mirror.
- All students, including the heads of students seated immediately behind the driver.

Loading and Unloading Passengers

According to safety statistics, the most dangerous part of a school bus ride for students is during the loading and unloading procedure.

Numerous measures have been employed to increase student safety during this part of their transportation to and from school. For example, federal mandates require all new buses to be equipped with an eight-lamp warning system and stop signal arm. In 1994, new school buses were also required to meet new standards for mirrors that will increase visibility around the school bus.

To increase student safety, training for drivers and students should be conducted on loading and unloading procedures at the beginning of the school year and throughout the school year as a reminder. The driver should repeat these procedures to students regularly.

The recommended procedures are:

1. Activate warning flasher system at least 100 feet prior to making a stop.
2. Approach the loading zone slowly and carefully. Direct students to wait in an orderly fashion safely back from the roadway.
3. Stop the vehicle 10 or 15 feet (if space is available) from students before loading (direct students to walk to the bus when the door is opened and the driver signals them to load).

4. Place the vehicle's transmission in neutral and set the parking brake before opening the door to load or unload.
5. Ensure that traffic is stopped in both directions before allowing the pupils to approach or exit the bus.
6. Unload those pupils who cross the street prior to those who do not cross.
7. Count students to know how many are loading on or unloading from the bus, where they are, and where they are going. If the count is lost, do not move the bus. If necessary, shut off the bus, secure it, and check underneath before moving the bus.
8. Ensure that students cross far enough in front of the bus so that the driver can see them even if they drop something. Require students to maintain eye contact with the driver.
9. Instruct students to look to the driver for a signal and check for traffic before continuing across the roadway. All drivers in the fleet should utilize the same signal—confusion could lead to tragedy.
10. Establish a prearranged danger signal, such as the horn, in case a vehicle does not stop for the bus while children are loading or unloading. Make sure students know exactly what to do if they hear the danger signal—for instance, "Go back to the side of the road you started from." All drivers should utilize the same danger signal and instructions.
11. Load and unload at designated pick-up and drop-off points.
12. Back up only at approved turnarounds if backing is necessary near a bus stop. Prior to backing up, ensure that all students are inside the bus. For instance, load children before backing up in the morning and unload children after backing up in the afternoon.
13. Do not unload children at corners immediately before making a right turn. Discharge children after making the turn.
14. Pick up and drop off pupils on their own side of the street if possible.
15. Instruct pupils never to cross behind the school bus.
16. Double-check all crossover and side mirrors for students and traffic before leaving the bus stop.
17. Do not put the bus in motion until all students outside are at a safe distance from the bus and all students inside are properly seated.
18. Before moving the bus after loading or unloading students, look and listen for any last-second warnings from others nearby that a child might be near the bus. A parent, teacher, motorist, another bus driver, or students on the bus might see a child near or even under the bus. Turn off noisy equipment and silence passengers so warnings can be heard.
19. Instruct students in the proper procedure for loading and unloading within the first week of school and throughout the school year.
20. Be cautious when students are carrying loose papers or books which they might drop near the bus—encourage students to use a book bag.
21. Be aware of the dangers of clothing, book bag, back pack, and jacket strings/straps that could become entangled in the doorway of the school bus.
22. Upon completion of the route, walk through the bus to check for sleeping students, vandalism, and forgotten articles.
23. Report the license number of vehicles passing a stopped school bus with an operating stop signal arm and/or warning light system.
24. Examine stops regularly and report unsafe conditions to the supervisor.

When Approaching a Stop, the Driver Should:

1. Approach at a slow rate of speed.
2. Be on the lookout for pedestrians, traffic, or other objects.
3. Continue to check mirrors.
4. Activate alternating flashing amber warning lights at least 200 feet before stopping.
5. Turn on the right turn signal about 100–300 feet before pulling over to stop.
6. Check mirrors constantly to make certain students are safe as they enter and exit the bus.
7. Bring the bus to a full stop at least ten feet from students waiting at the school bus stop.
8. Place the transmission in park or neutral and set the parking brakes.
9. Open the service door to activate alternating red lights.
10. Perform a final check to make sure all traffic has stopped completely before opening the door and signaling students to enter the bus.

When Students Have to Cross the Roadway:

The driver should know what students need to do to exit the bus and cross the roadway safely. Students should be informed how to exit and cross the roadway safely, although the driver should also be aware students do not always do what they have been instructed to do.

Students should follow these procedures when having to cross the roadway:

1. Walk approximately ten feet away from the side of the school bus to a position where the driver is able to see them.
2. Walk to a spot at least ten feet in front of the right corner of the bus bumper.
3. Stop at the right edge of the roadway. The driver should be able to see the student's feet at this point.
4. After reaching the edge of the roadway, students should stop and look in all directions, making sure the road is clear of traffic and is safe to cross.
5. Check to see if the red flashing lights on the bus are still flashing.
6. Students should wait for the driver's signal before they cross the street.

Dangers During Loading and Unloading School Buses

Objects that have been dropped—Always focus on students as they approach the bus and watch for any who suddenly disappear because they are stooping to retrieve a dropped object near the bus. Students should be told to leave any dropped object and, before retrieving the object, telling the driver so he or she can be watching for the student.

Handrail safety—In the past, students have been severely injured or killed when their clothing or backpacks get caught in the handrail or the door as they leave the bus. Watch students leaving the bus closely to make sure they are in a safe location prior to moving the bus forward.

Post-Trip Inspections

Once the run has been completed—in the mornings and afternoons—the driver should walk through the bus, looking for:

- Articles left on the bus
- Sleeping students
- Open doors and windows
- Mechanical or operational problems with the bus, such as mirrors, flashing warning lamps and stop signal arms
- Any damage or vandalism

Any problems or damage should be reported immediately to the transportation supervisor or school authorities.

Emergency Exits/Evacuation Procedures

Emergencies happen any time, anywhere, and any day of the week. Whether it's a collision or a stalled school bus at a railroad crossing or busy highway intersection, a student's medical emergency or a fire in the bus, itself, it is important that you—the professional—knows what to do in case of an emergency. Be sure you understand the entire evacuation procedure—it can mean the difference between life and death.

How to Determine the Need to Evacuate the Bus

Your number one consideration when determining whether or not to evacuate the bus is that you recognize a hazard. If time permits, contact your dispatcher and let them know the situation before deciding whether or not to evacuate the bus.

Maintain student safety and control by keeping students on the bus during an emergency or in case of an impending crisis—but only if keeping them on the bus does not pose any danger, unnecessary risk, or injury to the students.

When making a decision about evacuating the bus, consider the following:

- Is there a fire or a danger of fire?
- Is there a smell of fuel?
- Could the bus be hit by another vehicle?
- Is the bus in the path of a sighted tornado?
- Is the bus in the path of rising waters?
- Are there downed power lines nearby?
- If you evacuate students, would they be exposed to speeding traffic, severe weather, or dangers such as downed power lines?
- Would evacuating the students complicate any existing injuries, such as neck, head, or back injuries or fractured limbs?
- Is there a hazardous spill involved?

When Is It Mandatory to Evacuate the Bus?

Drivers must evacuate their buses when:

- The bus is on fire or there is a risk of fire.
- The bus is stalled on or close to a highway-railroad crossing.

- The bus's position may change and, therefore, increase the danger to the students.
- There is the risk of collision.
- There is a need to quickly evacuate because of a HazMat spill.

Evacuation Procedures

Planning ahead—if possible, before any hazards occur, assign two older student assistants at each emergency exit. Show them how to assist other students as they leave the bus. Give another student assistant the responsibility of leading evacuees to a safe place.

If there are no older students on the bus, explain the emergency evacuation procedures to all the students. This training includes knowing how to work the various emergency exits and how important it is to listen to, and follow, all your instructions.

How to Determine a "Safe Place" After Evacuation:

- The spot must be at least 100 feet off the road. This will help students avoid being hit by debris if another vehicle collides with the bus.
- Students should be led upwind of the bus if there's a fire.
- Students should be led as far away from railroad tracks as possible—and in the direction of the oncoming train. This places them as far as possible from a possible collision point.
- If there is a HazMat spill, students should be led upwind at least 300 feet from the problem.
- If there is an oncoming tornado, escort students to the nearest ditch, culvert, or building, if one is available. Direct every student to lie don, hands covering their heads—they should be far enough away from the bus so it can't fall—or be blown over onto them. Avoid dry creek beds and areas subject to flash floods.

General Evacuation Instructions

If you determine that evacuation is necessary for passenger safety:

- Determine the best method of evacuation: (1) front-, rear-, or side-door evacuation, or a combination of doors; (2) roof or window evacuation.

Secure the Bus

- Place the transmission in park or in neutral.
- Set the parking brakes.
- Shut off the engine.
- Remove the ignition key.
- Activate hazard warning signals.

If Time Allows

- Notify the dispatcher of the evacuation location, the conditions, and any assistance needed.
- Hang the radio microphone out the driver's window for later use.
- If no radio is available, dispatch a passing motorist to call for help.
- As a last resort, send two older students for help.

Order the Evacuation

- Evacuate the students from the bus.
- Do not move students who may have suffered neck or spinal injuries—special procedures are needed to move neck/spinal injury victims to prevent further damage.
- Direct student assistance to lead evacuees to the nearest safe place.
- Walk through the bus to make certain all students have been evacuated.
- Retrieve any available emergency equipment and join the evacuated students.
- Check to make sure all passengers are accounted for.
- Set out any emergency devices.
- Prepare information for emergency responders, according to school policies.

Railroad-Highway Crossings

There are two types of railroad crossings over roadways:

- **The passive railroad crossing**—a crossing without any type of traffic control device, such as a bell, a flashing light, or gates. These crossings may have yellow circular advance warning signs, pavement markings, or white crossbucks with black lettering. You must stop at these crossings, but the decision to proceed is entirely in your hands. At a passive crossing, you must stop, look for trains using the track and decide when it is safe to cross over the tracks.
- **The active railroad crossing**—has a traffic signal device to regulate traffic. These include flashing red lights and may be accompanied by bells or gates.

Warning Signs and Other Warning Devices

Advance Warning Signs

The round black-on-yellow warning sign is placed ahead of a public railroad-highway crossing. This signs indicate you should slow down, look, and listen for an oncoming train—and be prepared to stop at the tracks if a train is coming.

Pavement Markings

Pavement markings, which usually consist of an X with the letters RR and a no-passing marking on two lane roads, mean the same as an advance warning sign.

There is also a no-passing zone sign on two-lane roads. There may be a white stop line painted on the pavement before the railroad tracks. In such cases, the school bus must remain behind this line while stopped at the railroad crossing.

Crossbuck Signs

The white crossbuck sign requires you to stop and yield right-of-way to all trains. If there is no white line painted on the pavement, school buses must stop before the crossbuck sign. When the roadway crosses more than one set of tracks, a sign below the crossbucks indicates the number of tracks to be crossed.

Flashing Red Light Signals

Some crossings have a crossbuck sign as well as flashing red lights and bells. When the red lights flash, stop the bus at once because a train is approaching. Always yield the right-of-way to a train. Never try to race a train to a crossing. If there is more than one track to cross, make sure all tracks are clear before starting across.

Gates

Some crossings have flashing red lights, bells, and gates. Stop when the lights begin flashing and before the gate lowers. Never try to race past a gate as it is lowering. Your bus should remain stopped until the gates go up and the red lights have stopped flashing. If the gate remains down after the train passes, do not attempt to go around. Instead, call your dispatcher for instructions.

Recommended Rail Crossing Procedures

Every state has laws regulating how school buses should operate at railroad-highway crossings. Understand and obey these laws. Generally, school buses are required to stop at all crossings and drivers must make certain it is safe to cross the tracks before proceeding forward.

Because of a train's size and usual speed, school buses are no match for trains at any time. Always proceed with care and follow these procedures:

When Approaching a Crossing

- Slow down. Shift into a lower gear if using a manual transmission and test your brakes.
- Activate hazard lights 200 feet before the crossing.
- Scan the environment and check for traffic behind you.
- Stay to the right of the roadway.
- Choose an escape route in the case of brake failure or problems behind you.

At the Crossing

- Stop no closer than 15 feet and no farther than 50 feet from the nearest rail. This provides the best view of the tracks.
- Shift into park, or if there's no park, place the bus in neutral and press the service brake or set the parking brakes.
- Turn off all radios and silence passengers.
- Open the service door and driver's window. Look and listen for any approaching train.

Crossing the Track

- Check crossing signals again before proceeding.
- Stop only before the first set of tracks at multitrack crossings. When you are certain no train is approaching on any track, proceed across all tracks and keep going until you have completely cleared then.
- Use low gear when crossing tracks and do not attempt to change gears as you cross them.
- If you have started across and the signal gate on the opposite side begins to come down, keep going—even if it means breaking the gate.

Unusual Scenarios

When the bus stalls or becomes trapped on the tracks—get everyone out and away from the tracks immediately.

When there is a police officer at the crossing—obey her directions. If the signal appears to be malfunctioning, call your dispatcher, report the problem, and ask for instructions before proceeding.

When your view of the tracks is blocked—always select a route that gives you maximum view at every highway-railroad crossing. Never attempt to cross tracks unless you can see enough to be absolutely certain no trains are coming. Be especially careful at crossings where there are no signals or warning devices. Always stop-look-and-listen for trains before crossing any tracks.

Determining if your bus will fit in storage/containment areas at highway-railroad crossings—when determining if there is enough room on the other side after your bus clears the railroad tracks, add 15 feet to the length of the school bus to determine if the amount of containment/storage space is adequate.

Managing Student Passengers

In order to get students to and from school and other destinations safely and in a timely manner, concentrate on driving. Don't try to deal with on-bus problems while driving the bus.

When loading and unloading students, don't take your eyes off the environment outside the bus. But, if behavior problems occur among students riding the bus, wait until the students unloading are safely off the bus and have them move away before pulling the bus over to handle the problem.

What to Do if Serious Problems Occur

- Follow the school district's procedures for discipline or the refusal of rights for a student or students to ride the bus.
- Stop the bus, if necessary, in a safe location off the roadway. Parking lots or driveways work well for these stops.
- If you leave your seat, take the ignition key. This secures the bus.
- Speak respectfully and in a courteous manner to the offender(s). Stand up and use a firm voice.
- Remind offender(s) of expected behavior. Do not show anger or frustration, but do communicate that you mean business.
- If a change in seating is needed, request the student move to a seat near you.
- Never put a student off the bus except at school or her designated stop.
- If you feel the offense is serious enough that you cannot continue to drive safely, call a school administrator, dispatcher, or the police to come and remove the student.
- Always follow the school's procedures for requesting assistance.

Anti-Lock Braking Systems (ABS)

The Department of Transportation (DOT) requires anti-lock braking systems be on:

- Buses, trucks, trailers, and converter dollies built after March 1998.
- Hydraulically braked trucks and buses with a gross vehicle weight rating (GVWR) of 10,000 pounds or more if they were built after March 1, 1999.

Many buses built before these dates have been retrofitted with ABS. Your bus should have a yellow ABS malfunction lamp on the instrument panel if it is equipped with ABS.

The Benefits of ABS

Braking hard on slick roadways without ABS may cause the vehicle's wheels to lock.

- When steering wheels lock, you lose steering control of your vehicle.
- When other wheels lock, your vehicle may spin or skid.

ABS helps you maintain control of your vehicle while avoiding wheel lock-up. ABS does not allow you to stop faster, but you should be able to steer around obstacles while braking and avoid skidding caused by over-braking.

When You Brake with ABS

Driving a vehicle with ABS is no different than driving a vehicle with any other type of brakes. Brake as always, only using the braking force necessary to stop safely and maintain control of the vehicle.

OTR SAFETY
When braking in an emergency using ABS brakes, don't pump the brakes.

As you slow down, monitor the vehicle and back off the brakes to maintain control—if it is safe to do so.

Braking if ABS Is Not Working

You will still have normal brake function if your ABS is not working (which is indicated by the yellow ABS malfunction lamp on the instrument panel of your bus).

On newer vehicles, the malfunction lamp comes on when you start the bus for a bulb check and then quickly goes out. On older buses, the lamp stays on until you have increased the driving speed to 5 mph.

If the ABS malfunction lamp stays on after the bulb check or comes on when you are underway, you may have lost ABS control of one or more wheels.

OTR SAFETY
If your ABS malfunctions, you still have regular brakes. Drive as usual, but make sure the ABS system is serviced soon.

Some ABS Safety Reminders

- Just because you have ABS is not a reason to drive faster or to take chances.
- ABS won't prevent power skids or skids during turns.
- ABS should prevent brake-related skids but not skids caused by spinning the drive wheels or going too fast in a turn.
- ABS won't lessen your stopping distance—at any speed.
- ABS doesn't change the way you should brake your bus. It will stop as it normally does, but ABS does come into play when a wheel would normally have locked because of over-braking.
- ABS won't compensate for bad brakes or poor brake maintenance.

OTR SAFETY
The best vehicle safety feature is still a safe driver, so drive in a manner where you'll never need to use your ABS. However, if you need them, ABS could prevent a serious crash.

Special Safety Topics

Strobe Lights

Some school buses come with roof-mounted white strobe lights. If your bus is equipped with these, the overhead strobe light should be used when you have limited visibility in front of, or around, your bus. In all instances when strobe lights are used, comply with state or local regulations regarding use of these lights.

Driving in Windy Conditions

Strong winds can push a school bus sideways, and windy weather conditions affect how a school bus is handled . . . because the side of the bus acts much like the sail of a sailboat. Winds can also push a school bus off the road or, in high winds, can tip a bus over.

If you are driving in strong winds, do the following:

- Keep a firm grip on the steering wheel.
- Try to anticipate wind gusts.
- Slow your speed to lessen wind effects.
- Pull off the highway and wait for the winds to die down.
- Call your dispatcher to get information on how you should proceed.

Backing up a School Bus

Backing up a school bus is strongly discouraged and the bus should be backed only when there is no other safe maneuver available.

OTR SAFETY
Never back up a school bus when students are outside of the bus.

Backing is dangerous and increases your risk of collision, but if you have no choice, follow these safety procedures:

- Post a lookout to warn you about any obstacles as you back out the bus. The lookout should not give any directions about how to back up the vehicle.
- Signal for quiet on the bus.
- Check all mirrors and rear windows constantly as you maneuver the bus.
- Back up slowly and smoothly.
- If no lookout is available:
  - Set the parking brake.
  - Turn off the motor and take the keys with you.
  - Walk to the rear of the bus to determine if your backing path is clear.

- If you are required to back up the bus at a student pickup point, pick up the students before backing the bus—and watch for any latecomers during the entire maneuver.
- Be sure all students have boarded the bus before backing.
- If you must back up at a student drop-off point, be sure to unload students after backing up—not before.

OTR SAFETY

A school bus can have up to a three-foot tail swing. Check all mirrors before and during any turns to monitor the tail swing.

19 Review Questions for Endorsement Tests

To help you prepare for the various Endorsement Tests, a number of review questions are included. These are not the actual test questions, but they are similar to those you will see on the written Endorsement Tests. You may write the answers next to each question or use an additional sheet of paper, putting the answers next to the number corresponding to the question. This way, you can use these tests several times if necessary.

Review Questions for Air Brakes Endorsement

The following statements are either true or false. Mark your answer in the blank provided, and then check your answers with the key at the end of the chapter.

___ 1. Fanning air brakes increases the air pressure.

___ 2. Even if your air compressor stops working, you should have air pressure stored in the air tanks.

___ 3. The air brake system safety relief valve opens at 60 psi.

___ 4. If your air brake system safety relief valve opens a couple of times, you should have your system repaired.

___ 5. When the brakes are hot, you should not set the parking brake.

___ 6. Spring brakes should come on automatically if you pump the air pressure down to 60 psi.

___ 7. When the low air pressure warning device comes on, you should do nothing until you get to a service station.

___ 8. The breakaway valve is also called the tractor protection valve.

___ 9. When your brakes are out of adjustment, your service, parking, and emergency braking power will be poor.

___10. Spring brakes are not affected by air pressure.

___11. Air brakes of most large vehicles have spring brakes that are part of the emergency brake and parking brake system.

___12. The trailer hand brake can also be used as a parking brake.

___13. If you have one, a front brake limiting valve control should be in the "normal" position under all road conditions.

___14. The service brake system is the pump and check valves that keep the air tank pressure in check.

___15. In a single brake system that has a fully charged air system, the air pressure should not drop more than 5 psi per minute after the initial drop.

___16. Brake drums or discs should not have cracks longer than half the width of the friction area.

___17. Slack adjusters never need adjustment.

___18. The service brake glad hands are color-coded blue.

___19. You should have your vehicle's single brake system adjusted if the governor stops between 100 and 125 psi.

___20. The emergency brake glad hands are color-coded blue.

___21. Unless you have a dual air system, the spring brakes will come on if the emergency brake air lines rupture.

___22. Unless you have a dual air system, the spring brakes will come on if the service air lines break.

___23. To adjust the slack, you should always apply the service and parking brakes.

___24. To test the brakes on a single air system, start the engine and let it run at a fast idle to charge the air system—you should see an increase in pressure from 50 to 90 psi in three minutes.

___25. When testing the brakes on a dual air system, start the engine and let it run at a fast idle to charge the air system—you should see an increase in pressure from 85 to 100 psi in 45 seconds.

The following statements are multiple choice. Mark your answer in the blank provided, and then check your answers with the key at the end.

___ 1. Air brakes take more time to activate than hydraulic brakes because:
(A) It takes air longer to flow through the lines.
(B) Air brakes use a different type of brake drum.
(C) Air brakes are located further from the wheels.
(D) An air brake system comprises of multiple systems.

___ 2. Why is the stopping distance for air brakes longer than hydraulic brakes?
(A) Reaction time.
(B) Brake lag distance.
(C) Effective braking distance.
(D) All of the above.

___ 3. What affects the power of spring brakes?
(A) The condition of the emergency brakes.
(B) The adjustment of the spring brakes ensures the power.
(C) Weather conditions.
(D) The condition of the parking brakes.

___ 4. When the driver uses the brake pedal, which brake system applies and releases the brakes?
(A) Parking.
(B) Service.
(C) Dual.
(D) Emergency.

___ 5. A combination of service, parking, and _____ systems comprise modern air brakes.
(A) Hand.
(B) Emergency.
(C) Drum.
(D) Dual.

___ 6. What does the air compressor governor control?
(A) The air pressure applied to the brakes.
(B) The air compressor speed.
(C) The brake chamber release pressure.
(D) The air pumped into the air tanks.

___ 7. You should drain water from compressed air tanks because:
   (A) Water mixed with oil can cause brakes to slip.
   (B) Water cools the compressor excessively.
   (C) Water can get into the oil of the compressor.
   (D) Water can freeze and cause brake failure.

___ 8. In cold weather, what should you do to an alcohol evaporator?
   (A) Remove the alcohol.
   (B) Check the alcohol for oil.
   (C) Check and fill the alcohol level.
   (D) Clean the evaporator air filter.

___ 9. In an air brake system, a brake pedal:
   (A) Connects the shock adjuster.
   (B) Controls the air pressure applied to the brakes.
   (C) Joins the service and parking brake systems.
   (D) Joins the parking and emergency brake systems.

___10. What do all air brake-equipped vehicles have?
   (A) An air supply pressure gauge.
   (B) A hydraulic system.
   (C) At least one brake heater.
   (D) An air use gauge.

___11. The air supply pressure gauge indicates:
   (A) The pressure going to the brake chamber.
   (B) How much air has been used during the trip.
   (C) The pressure in the air tank.
   (D) The amount of air the air tank can hold.

___12. The purpose of dual parking control valves is:
   (A) To balance pressure to the brakes.
   (B) To utilize the service brake system when parked.
   (C) To balance parking power.
   (D) To release the spring brake in an emergency.

___13. On a long downgrade, how can you tell if your brakes are fading?
   (A) You begin to hear squeaking noises when you apply the brakes.
   (B) You have to push harder to control your speed.
   (C) The brakes don't cool sufficiently between applications.
   (D) All of the above.

___14. How should the free play of manual slack adjusters on S-cam brakes be checked?
   (A) Park on level ground and set the emergency brake.
   (B) Park on level ground, chock the wheels, turn off the parking brakes.
   (C) Set the parking brake and drain off air from the service brake.
   (D) Park on an incline and set only the emergency brake.

___15. What does the application pressure gauge show?
   (A) The pressure in the air tanks.
   (B) The amount of air in the air tank.
   (C) How much air pressure you are applying to the brakes.
   (D) The pressure applied to the brake pedal.

___16. The air pressure warning light should come on before the pressure gets below:
   (A) 60 psi.   (C) 30 psi.
   (B) 90 psi.   (D) 100 psi.

____17. What are spring brakes held back by?
   (A) Water pressure.
   (B) Air pressure.
   (C) Springs.
   (D) Centrifugal force.

____18. If there is a leak in the air brake system, the parking or emergency brake can be held in position only by:
   (A) Spring pressure.
   (B) Water pressure.
   (C) Foot pressure.
   (D) Centrifugal force.

____19. With the engine off and the service brake released, a straight truck air brake system should not leak at a rate greater than:
   (A) 0 psi per minute.
   (B) 1 psi per minute.
   (C) 2 psi per minute.
   (D) 3 psi per minute.

____20. You have a problem if you are testing the service brakes and notice that:
   (A) They have an unusual feel.
   (B) The vehicle pulls to one side.
   (C) Stopping action is delayed.
   (D) All of the above.

____21. The dual air brake system operates on which axle(s)?
   (A) The rear axle.
   (B) The front axle.
   (C) The trailer.
   (D) All axles.

____22. What should you do if the secondary system of a dual air brake equipped vehicle fails?
   (A) Bring the vehicle to a safe stop and get the system fixed.
   (B) Slow down and continue using the primary system.
   (C) Drive to the nearest garage for repairs.
   (D) Continue to the next convenient place to stop.

____23. When checking to make sure the spring brakes come on automatically, the parking brake knob should pop out when:
   (A) You start the truck.
   (B) The air pressure falls to between 20 and 40 psi.
   (C) You step on the foot brake.
   (D) All of the above.

____24. During an emergency stop, how should you brake?
   (A) Use the full power of the emergency brakes and service brakes.
   (B) Brake so you can steer and stay in a straight line.
   (C) Always brake hard and fast.
   (D) Maintain constant pressure on the brakes.

____25. Emergency stab braking is:
   (A) The same as controlled braking.
   (B) Putting on the brakes hard without locking the wheels.
   (C) Repeatedly braking until the wheels lock, and then releasing pressure.
   (D) Braking lightly several times in a row.

____26. Why is controlled or stab braking better than short, light brake pedal pressure on long downhill grades?
(A) Steady pressure works better with a vehicle that is in low gear.
(B) Air usage is less with controlled or stab braking.
(C) Light pressure heats up the brakes.
(D) All of the above.

____27. When the low air pressure warning comes on, you should:
(A) Stop and park as soon as possible.
(B) Continue on to your destination.
(C) Use the parking or emergency brake to stop.
(D) Tap the air pressure gauge to see if it is working.

____28. When do you use the parking brake in an air brake-equipped vehicle?
(A) Only when parked on a hill.
(B) Only in an emergency.
(C) Any time you park.
(D) To inspect the service brake.

____29. If it is not done automatically in your vehicle, how often should you drain your air tanks?
(A) Every time you stop for more than ten minutes.
(B) At the end of each day of driving.
(C) Every two hours of driving.
(D) At least once a month.

Review Questions for Combination Vehicle/Doubles/ Triples Endorsement

The following statements are either true or false. Mark your answer in the blank provided, and then check your answers with the key at the end of the chapter.

____ 1. The dolly support carries the dolly air lines.

____ 2. It is impossible to check if the entire brake system of a triple is charged.

____ 3. Triples have the most rearward amplification.

____ 4. The first step to coupling is applying the trailer brakes.

____ 5. To finish the coupling process, begin in high gear to roll up the landing gear.

____ 6. Double and triple trailers should be inspected carefully because they have more parts.

____ 7. You might eventually get a service line air leak if your glad hand on your blue air line doesn't have a seal.

____ 8. Uncoupling is much easier if you park the trailer at an angle.

____ 9. When you finish coupling, always make sure there's no slack in the air lines.

____10. To prevent roll-over, make sure your load is low and centered between the trailer sides.

____11. A converter dolly should be treated as an axle with a fifth wheel and may have its own air tank.

____12. Your brakes will not work at all if you cross your air lines on a new trailer equipped with spring brakes.

____13. The tractor protection valve should close automatically when you reduce the air pressure to 60 psi.

____14. You can test the trailer emergency brake system if you charge the trailer brakes and then push in the blue round knob.

____15. To make a right turn with a long vehicle, you should use another lane to avoid hitting the curb.

____16. When coupling doubles, it is best to back the converter dolly under the second trailer.

____17. In double or triple trailers, you will find shut-off valves only in the emergency air lines.

____18. You can injure yourself if you unhook the pintle hook with the converter dolly still under the trailer.

____19. You can test the trailer service brakes by pulling the red, eight-sided knob.

____20. To make sure your air lines are not crossed, you should turn off your engine, apply and release the trailer brakes with the hand valve, and then listen for brake movement and air release.

____21. You are having problems when you turn a corner and your trailer wheels go a different way than your tractor wheels.

____22. Release the trailer brakes if your vehicle starts to skid.

____23. When coupling doubles, there is nothing you can do if the second trailer does not have spring brakes.

____24. You should check your path for hazards before you begin coupling.

____25. It is possible to damage your landing gear if you back under the trailer at an angle.

The following statements are multiple choice. Mark your answer in the blank provided, and then check your answers with the key at the end of the chapter.

____ 1. When driving doubles or triples, what should you remember about looking ahead?
   (A) Allow more following distance.
   (B) Look far ahead so you can slow down gradually.
   (C) Looking ahead increases your safety.
   (D) All of the above.

____ 2. To maintain safety when hauling a double or triple, you should:
   (A) Use special care in bad weather and mountain driving.
   (B) Be ready to stop at the last minute.
   (C) Watch only the brake lights of the car in front of you.
   (D) All of the above.

____ 3. You can prevent a roll over by keeping the cargo as close to the ground as possible and:
   (A) Steering hard and applying the brakes around curves.
   (B) Making sure your brakes function properly.
   (C) Going slow around curves.
   (D) Keeping your tires properly inflated.

____ 4. Why are "bobtail" tractors harder to stop?
   (A) The back of the vehicle is shorter.
   (B) The vehicle is lighter.
   (C) There are fewer wheels to stop the tractor.
   (D) There are less brake systems.

_____ 5. On a combination vehicle, to stop a jackknife:

    (A) Brake hard.

    (B) Do not use the trailer hand brake.

    (C) Turn the steering wheel in the opposite direction of the skid.

    (D) All of the above.

_____ 6. Offtracking is:

    (A) When the rear wheels follow a different path than the front wheels.

    (B) The process of taking the tracks off a tractor.

    (C) When a driver fails to keep the wheels on track.

    (D) An error in keeping track of the hours and miles driven.

_____ 7. When pulling a 100-foot double at 30 miles per hour, how many seconds of space should you keep between you and the vehicle in front of you?

    (A) At least two seconds.

    (B) At least five seconds.

    (C) At least seven seconds.

    (D) At least ten seconds.

_____ 8. When pulling a 100-foot triple at 50 miles per hour, how many seconds of space should you keep between you and the vehicle in front of you?

    (A) At least two seconds.

    (B) At least five seconds.

    (C) At least 11 seconds.

    (D) At least 15 seconds.

_____ 9. When the trailer wheels of a double go into a skid, what is likely to happen?

    (A) The trailer will tip over.

    (B) The trailer will jackknife.

    (C) The brakes will squeak.

    (D) The front wheels of the tractor will skid.

_____10. Which of the following is true about quick steering movements with doubles and triples?

    (A) Stab braking is always used in quick steering.

    (B) Double and triples tip over easily from quick steering.

    (C) Counter-steering is easier with doubles and triples.

    (D) None of the above.

_____11. When driving doubles and triples, which of the following is correct?

    (A) The rear trailer of a triple is less likely to tip over than a double.

    (B) Rearward amplification prevents a crack-the-whip effect.

    (C) A sudden steering movement can result in the rear trailer tipping over.

    (D) All of the above.

_____12. You need _____ times more stopping distance when stopping a combination at 40 miles per hour than at 20 miles per hour.

    (A) Three times.

    (B) Four times.

    (C) Eight times.

    (D) Ten times.

_____13. When emergency braking doubles or triples, what should you do?

    (A) Use only the tractor brakes.

    (B) Brake hard.

    (C) Use controlled or stab braking.

    (D) Use lock braking and steering.

____14. The trailer air supply:
    (A) Controls the tractor air supply.
    (B) Controls the air supply to the protection valve.
    (C) Supplies the trailer with air.
    (D) Supplies air to the tractor control.

____15. The service air line:
    (A) Controls the tractor air brakes.
    (B) Controls the air supply.
    (C) Carries air to the tractor brakes.
    (D) Carries air to the trailer brakes.

____16. What color are the emergency line couplers?
    (A) Red.   (C) Blue.
    (B) Yellow.   (D) Black.

____17. Why should you connect the air hose couplers together?
    (A) To maintain a constant air supply.
    (B) To keep the dirt and water out of the lines.
    (C) To keep the rubber seals from drying out.
    (D) None of the above.

____18. What happens when you cross the air lines of an older trailer without spring brakes?
    (A) The brake pedal will not work.
    (B) You will not be able to start the vehicle.
    (C) The hand valve will cause the trailer brakes to come on when you use the air brakes.
    (D) You could drive away, but have no trailer brakes.

____19. Why do many trailers built before 1975 have no parking brakes?
    (A) They don't have air brakes.
    (B) They don't have spring brakes.
    (C) They use the emergency brake for a parking brake.
    (D) Shut-off valves were not available then.

____20. If the service air line comes apart while driving but the emergency line is okay, what happens immediately?
    (A) The same thing as when there's a leak in the emergency line.
    (B) The emergency trailer brakes will come on immediately.
    (C) Nothing is likely to happen until you press the brakes.
    (D) The emergency tractor brake will come on.

____21. You should always grease the fifth wheel because:
    (A) It makes it easy to couple.
    (B) It makes it easy to uncouple.
    (C) It prevents steering problems.
    (D) It prevents rust and corrosion.

____22. What should you do just before the tractor is coupled?
    (A) Make sure the trailer and tractor line up.
    (B) Chock the trailer wheels.
    (C) Connect the emergency and service air lines.
    (D) None of the above.

____23. In coupling, where should the tractor be lined up?
    (A) In front of the kingpin.
    (B) Slightly to the right of the trailer.
    (C) Directly in front of the trailer.
    (D) None of the above.

____24. In coupling, the trailer is at the right height when:
   (A) The top of the kingpin is even with the top of the fifth wheel.
   (B) The kingpin is two inches above the fifth wheel.
   (C) The trailer landing gear is fully extended.
   (D) The trailer is lifted slightly when the tractor connects.

____25. During coupling, how do you lock the trailer brakes before you back under the trailer?
   (A) Push in the air supply knob.
   (B) Pull out the air supply knob.
   (C) Apply the air brakes.
   (D) None of the above.

____26. To make sure the kingpin and fifth wheel connection are secure, what should you do?
   (A) Slowly drive forward with the trailer brakes locked.
   (B) Back up slowly.
   (C) Pull ahead, steering left and right.
   (D) Jerk the vehicle forward.

____27. When coupling is complete, how much space should there be between the upper and lower fifth wheel?
   (A) About one inch.
   (B) At least two inches.
   (C) 18 inches.
   (D) No space.

____28. When the fifth wheel locking lever is almost in the locking position but will not lock, what should you do?
   (A) Have it repaired before driving.
   (B) It's not a problem—the locking lever is only a safety precaution.
   (C) Keep working with the lever.
   (D) None of the above.

____29. After the tractor is coupled, you should not move it until you push in the air supply knob and:
   (A) Hear a loud click.
   (B) Wait until the air pressure is normal.
   (C) The tractor protection valve.
   (D) Flush all moisture from the system.

____30. After coupling, you can make sure the air lines are not crossed because:
   (A) When you pump the brake you will hear the brakes move and air escape.
   (B) The tractor will move easily forward and back.
   (C) The tractor protection valve will pop out.
   (D) All of the above.

____31. When the engine and brake are off, the air leakage rate for combination vehicles must be less than:
   (A) 0 psi per minute.   (C) 6 psi per minute.
   (B) 3 psi per minute.   (D) None of the above.

____32. The maximum leakage rate for a combination vehicle with the engine off and brakes on is:
   (A) 1 psi per minute.
   (B) 2 psi per minute.
   (C) 4 psi per minute.
   (D) 10 psi per minute.

___33. You should use the trailer hand valve:
(A) To test the trailer brakes.
(B) Only when the trailer is fully loaded.
(C) To complete an emergency stop.
(D) In combination with the foot brake.

___34. Why do you need a tractor protection valve?
(A) It keeps air in the tractor if the trailer breaks away or develops a bad leak.
(B) It protects the tractor from damage.
(C) It is a backup for the trailer air supply control.
(D) All of the above.

___35. The tractor protection valve will close automatically when:
(A) You push in the trailer air supply control.
(B) The air pressure is low (20 to 45 psi).
(C) The air pressure is too high (70 to 90 psi).
(D) The emergency brakes are turned on.

___36. How do you keep the trailer from moving when hooking a combination to a second trailer?
(A) By using the trailer emergency brakes.
(B) By using the trailer spring brakes.
(C) By using wheel chocks.
(D) Any of the above will work.

___37. When connecting two or more trailers to the tractor, the heaviest trailer should be placed:
(A) In the front, closest to the tractor.
(B) In the rear, as the last trailer.
(C) Don't connect trailers that are not the same weight.
(D) None of the above.

___38. Which of the following statements is true about converter dollies?
(A) They usually need glad hand converters.
(B) They have little braking power because they're small.
(C) They do not have spring brakes.
(D) All of the above.

___39. During coupling, when you connect a trailer to a converter dolly, what is the correct height for the trailer?
(A) The locking jaws and the kingpin flange should be the same height.
(B) It must be slightly lower than the center of the fifth wheel.
(C) The trailer must be higher than the top of the dolly.
(D) The fifth wheel should be the same height as the kingpin.

___40. How can you supply air to the air tanks of the second trailer?
(A) Open the shut-off valve at the rear of the first trailer and close the valve at the rear of the second.
(B) Open the shut-off valve of both trailers.
(C) Close the shut-off valve of both trailers.
(D) None of the above.

___41. After coupling doubles, you can make sure air has reached the last trailer by:
(A) Opening the hand valve and listening to the air.
(B) Looking at the air gauge for each trailer.
(C) Opening the emergency line shut-off valve at the rear of the last trailer.
(D) There is really no way to tell until you begin driving.

——42. What will happen if you unlock the pintle hook with the dolly still under the rear trailer?

(A) The dolly may roll back.

(B) The dolly tow bar may fly up.

(C) The brake lights will come on.

(D) The pintle hook may break.

——43. During a walk-around inspection, what is the position of the pintle hook and the dolly air drain valve?

(A) Open, free.

(B) Closed, free.

(C) Open, latched.

(D) Closed, latched.

——44. What should you hear when you inspect the trailer brakes of a double, turn the hand valve on, and open the service line valve at the rear of the rig?

(A) A high-pitched whistle.

(B) The tractor protection valve open.

(C) Air escape from the open valve.

(D) Nothing at all, if things are okay.

——45. When testing the trailer emergency brakes, you should charge the air brake system, check that the trailer rolls freely, and:

(A) Open the emergency brake air lines.

(B) Pull out the trailer air supply control.

(C) Push in the trailer air supply control.

(D) None of the above.

——46. After you have turned the hand brake on, how do you check the trailer brakes?

(A) Bring the air pressure up to normal.

(B) Turn the parking brakes off.

(C) Move slowly forward to see if the vehicle slows down.

(D) All of the above.

Review Questions for Tank Vehicle Endorsement

The following statements are either true or false. Mark your answer in the blank provided. Then, check your answers with the key at the end of the chapter.

——— 1. Outage is dangerous.

——— 2. Retest markings are stamped on the tank itself.

——— 3. To avoid roll-over with a tanker, you should speed through a curve.

——— 4. A smooth bore tanker is one that is a long, hollow tube with no sharp corners.

——— 5. Because bulk liquid tankers have a high center of gravity, they are hard to handle.

——— 6. Baffles are located inside tankers that have openings at the top and bottom.

——— 7. Baffles eliminate side-to-side liquid surge.

——— 8. Cylindrical is the most stable liquid tanker shape.

____ 9. A retest marking reading of "12-01, P, V, L" says that in December 2001, the cargo tank received and passed a pressure retest, external visual inspection and test, and a lining inspection.

____ 10. In case of emergency, the stop valves will close in the cargo tanks.

The following statements are multiple choice. Mark your answer in the blank provided. Then, check your answers with the key at the end of the chapter.

____ 1. Why does hauling liquids in tankers require special care?
   (A) Because the center of gravity is low.
   (B) Because the center of gravity is high.
   (C) Because the center of gravity is wide.
   (D) Because the center of gravity is flat.

____ 2. When exiting the freeway with a tanker, you should drive below the posted speed because:
   (A) The exit speed posted may be too high for your particular load.
   (B) Your tanker may roll over.
   (C) Liquid surge may make your tanker hard to handle.
   (D) All of the above.

____ 3. Liquid surge in a tanker affects handling by:
   (A) Moving the vehicle in the direction of the surge.
   (B) Making cornering easier.
   (C) Increasing vehicle power downhill.
   (D) Causing the tanker to move slower.

____ 4. What should you do when loading a tanker equipped with bulkheads?
   (A) Nothing special.
   (B) Check your weight distribution.
   (C) Watch your power usage.
   (D) Don't drive unless they are all filled.

____ 5. The advantage of baffled bulkheads is:
   (A) There will be less side-to-side surge.
   (B) There will be more side-to-side surge.
   (C) There will be less front-to-back surge.
   (D) There will be more front-to-back surge.

____ 6. Baffles in liquid cargo tanks do not prevent surges:
   (A) Top-to-bottom.
   (B) Side-to-side.
   (C) Back-to-front.
   (D) In-and-out.

____ 7. What can happen when you are transporting liquids and have a side-to-side surge?
   (A) Engine overheat.
   (B) Tire failure.
   (C) Brake failure.
   (D) Rollovers.

____ 8. When can smooth bore liquid tankers be very dangerous?
   (A) When you are starting or stopping.
   (B) When you are driving against the wind.
   (C) When you are loading or unloading.
   (D) When you are going downhill.

___ 9. Why should you know the outage of your tanker load?
   (A) Liquids evaporate at different speeds.
   (B) Some liquids expand more than others when warm.
   (C) Some heavy liquids don't require outage.
   (D) You don't need to know the outage of your tanker load.

___10. How much liquid can you load in a tanker?
   (A) It depends on the weight of the liquid.
   (B) It depends on the amount the liquid will expand.
   (C) It depends on the legal limit.
   (D) All of the above.

Review Questions for Hazardous Materials

The following statements are either true or false. Mark your answer in the blank provided. Then, check your answers with the key at the end of the chapter.

___ 1. When loading and unloading cargo tanks, the person in attendance must be within 50 feet of the tanker.

___ 2. Column 1 of the Hazardous Materials Table shows how to ship an item.

___ 3. A driver is allowed to run the vehicle engine while loading explosives.

___ 4. Drivers carrying Class A or B explosives must have a floor liner that doesn't contain iron or steel.

___ 5. The Separation Distance Table explains how far packages of hazardous materials should be located from people and cargo space walls.

___ 6. When a consignee refuses a shipment of hazardous materials, the only thing you can do is return it to the shipper.

___ 7. The word "waste" is written before the name of the materials on the shipping papers.

___ 8. Anyone can drive a vehicle placarded for hazardous materials.

___ 9. Class A is the least dangerous type of explosive.

___10. ORM B is regulated because it can damage your vehicle.

___11. The Segregation and Separation Chart lists hazardous materials that are prohibited to be carried in combination.

___12. Smoking is prohibited within 25 feet of a vehicle loaded with hazardous materials.

___13. When hauling hazardous materials in a vehicle with dual tires, you should check the tires often.

___14. Drivers should always be aware that hazardous materials pose a risk to health, safety, and property during transportation.

___15. Tankers used to transport hazardous materials must be marked with a manufacturer's date.

___16. Black III indicates the highest level of radioactivity.

___17. You will need a "Dangerous" placard when transporting pressurized liquid oxygen.

___18. The Uniform Hazardous Waste Manifest must have a copy of the loading plan.

___19. A vehicle placarded for Class A or B explosives must never be left unattended.

___20. Proper shipping names are shown in plain type and in alphabetical order on the Hazardous Materials Table.

___21. When placarding a vehicle, you must put placards on the front, back, and both sides.

___22. To communicate risks, make sure the right shipping papers, package labels, and placards are included with hazardous materials.

___23. Always refuse shipments that are leaking hazardous materials.

___24. When an accident occurs on a trailer containing explosives, make sure to remove all the explosive material before pulling the vehicles apart.

___25. If your vehicle is leaking hazardous materials, stop the vehicle and go get help.

___26. If an accident occurs while transporting hazardous materials, your responsibility as a driver is to limit the spread of the material, even if it puts your safety at risk.

___27. The National Response Center should be called if someone is killed, injured, or sent to the hospital, or if property damages exceed $50,000 because of an accident involving hazardous materials cargo.

___28. The National Response Center is a resource center for police and fire fighters who must assist in a hazardous materials incident.

___29. Call the Department of Transportation if you are involved in a hazardous materials spill.

The following statements are multiple choice. Mark your answer in the blank provided, and then check your answers with the key at the end of the chapter.

___ 1. Who makes sure the shipper has correctly named, labeled, and marked a HazMat shipment?
   (A) Driver.   (C) Shipper.
   (B) Carrier.   (D) All of the above.

___ 2. What can drivers, shippers, and carriers use to find out if materials are regulated?
   (A) A List of Hazardous Substances and Reportable Quantities.
   (B) A Hazardous Material Table.
   (C) Both A and B.
   (D) Neither A nor B.

___ 3. Drivers who carry radioactive material or flammable cryogenic liquids must have special training within how many years?
   (A) One-half year.
   (B) One year.
   (C) Two years.
   (D) Five years.

___ 4. The shipper is not responsible for which of the following?
   (A) Labeling.
   (B) Packaging.
   (C) Placarding.
   (D) Preparing shipping papers.

___ 5. You cannot describe a nonhazardous material by:
   (A) Using a hazard class or ID number.
   (B) Slang words.
   (C) Abbreviations.
   (D) Code words.

_____ 6. What is the correct placard if you're carrying 500 pounds of class A and B explosives?
   (A) "Dangerous."   (C) "Explosive" B.
   (B) "Explosive" A.   (D) "Explosive and Dangerous."

_____ 7. What is the correct placard if you are carrying 600 pounds of organic peroxide and 500 pounds of oxidizer?
   (A) "Dangerous."
   (B) "Organic peroxide."
   (C) "Oxidizer."
   (D) None of the above.

_____ 8. What should you do when a common carrier transport material is classified as "Forbidden" on the Hazardous Material Table?
   (A) Transport it anyway and report it to the Department of Transportation.
   (B) Make sure the quantity does not exceed 500 pounds.
   (C) Transport it as a normal shipment, but be extremely careful.
   (D) Never transport the material.

_____ 9. What is the proper way to placard two liters of "Flammable Liquid" labeled "Poison-Inhalation Hazard" on the shipping paper?
   (A) Placard as a poison gas.
   (B) Use a poison placard and the proper hazard class placard.
   (C) Both A and B are correct.
   (D) Neither A nor B is correct.

_____10. What does it mean when you see an "X" or "RQ" in the HM column of a shipping paper entry?
   (A) The cargo will not be shipped.
   (B) The driver must report the shipment to the Department of Transportation.
   (C) The shipment is regulated by hazardous materials regulations.
   (D) None of the above.

_____11. The correct order of description of hazardous materials on the shipping paper is:
   (A) Shipping name, hazard class, ID number.
   (B) Hazard class, ID number, shipping name.
   (C) ID number, shipping name, hazard class.
   (D) The order does not matter as long as all three descriptions are present.

_____12. What special equipment should the driver carry when hauling chlorine in cargo tanks?
   (A) A kit that measures chlorine levels.
   (B) A cell phone.
   (C) A gas mask and emergency kit for leak control.
   (D) No special equipment is required.

_____13. The shipper certifies that he or she has packaged the material according to the regulations, except when:
   (A) The shipper is a private carrier hauling his own product.
   (B) The driver's cargo compartment is sealed.
   (C) The vehicle will not cross state lines.
   (D) The shipment is hazardous waste.

D 14. You know a shipment includes hazardous material if:
(A) You talk to the shipper.
(B) You inspect every package.
(C) You check the hazardous material table.
(D) You look at the shipping papers.

L 15. Why do you need a uniform hazardous waste manifest?
(A) It indicates you're carrying hazardous material.
(B) It acts exactly the same as a shipping paper.
(C) None of the above.
(D) All of the above.

B 16. A vehicle that is carrying hazardous materials must have _____ placard(s)?
(A) One.
(B) Four.
(C) Eight.
(D) Ten.

___ 17. When a vehicle carrying explosives is stopped on the side of the road, what type of emergency warning device can be used?
(A) Reflective triangles.
(B) Flares.
(C) Traffic cones.
(D) Any of the above.

___ 18. When a vehicle carrying flammable liquids or gas is stopped on the side of the road, what type of emergency warning device can be used?
(A) Reflective triangles.
(B) Flares.
(C) Traffic cones.
(D) Any of the above.

___ 19. When loading hazardous materials, you should always:
(A) Double-wrap wet boxes in plastic.
(B) Never smoke within 50 feet of explosives, oxidizers, and flammables.
(C) Never use hooks.
(D) Keep bystanders 100 feet away.

___ 20. When you are loading explosives, you should check the cargo space:
(A) To make sure there are no sharp objects or points.
(B) To make sure cargo heaters are working and ready.
(C) To make sure the floor liners are loose.
(D) All of the above.

___ 21. You cannot transport Class A explosives with:
(A) A large wheelbase trailer.
(B) A placarded cargo tanker.
(C) Two or more trailers.
(D) A vehicle containing food.

___ 22. You should load cylinders of compressed gas by:
(A) Putting them in boxes that won't allow them to turn over.
(B) Putting them in racks attached to the vehicle.
(C) Holding them upright or braced lying down flat.
(D) Any of the above.

____23. What does the transport index on the labels of radioactive II packages mean?

(A) It is used by Department of Transportation inspectors only.

(B) It means nothing and can be covered or removed.

(C) It indicates the correct placard to use.

(D) It indicates the degree of control needed during transportation.

____24. In a single vehicle, the total transport index of all radioactive material cannot exceed:

(A) 0.   (C) 25.

(B) 15.   (D) 50.

____25. A vehicle carrying animal and human food must not be loaded with:

(A) Poisons.

(B) Explosives.

(C) Oxidizers.

(D) All of the above.

____26. What should you immediately do before moving a cargo tank of hazardous material?

(A) Double-check the air brake system.

(B) Close all manholes and valves.

(C) Call CHEMTREC at (800) 424-9300.

(D) No other safety precautions are necessary.

____27. You must park at least _____ feet away from an open fire if your vehicle is placarded.

(A) 50.

(B) 100.

(C) 200.

(D) 300.

____28. When monitoring a placarded vehicle, you must:

(A) Be awake and in the vehicle, or within 100 feet of it.

(B) Be aware of the hazards of the load.

(C) Know what to do in an emergency.

(D) All of the above.

____29. When should you check the dual tires on a placarded vehicle?

(A) Twice per day.

(B) Once per day.

(C) At the beginning of the day.

(D) At the beginning of each trip and each time the vehicle is parked.

____30. When transporting Class A or B explosives, a driver must always have:

(A) Shipping papers.

(B) A copy of FMCSR Part 397.

(C) A written route plan and emergency instructions.

(D) All of the above.

____31. If a permit or special route is needed to transport a HazMat load, whose responsibility is it to get it?

(A) The Department of Transportation.

(B) The shipper.

(C) The driver.

(D) All of the above.

_____32. If you are transporting hazardous materials, when should you check your route about permits or restrictions?
  (A) Whenever you stop to fill up for gas.
  (B) As the need arises.
  (C) Before you start the trip.
  (D) When you see highway signs noting restrictions.

_____33. It is forbidden for a placarded vehicle to drive near an open flame unless:
  (A) It can pass safely without stopping.
  (B) It has a table 2 placard.
  (C) The cargo compartment is sealed.
  (D) The wind is blowing toward the road.

_____34. If transporting hazardous materials, when is a written route plan required?
  (A) Always.
  (B) When transporting class A and B explosives.
  (C) Only when the carrier is Class B.
  (D) Never.

_____35. If you are smoking, how close can you be to a placarded vehicle carrying explosives, oxidizers, or flammables?
  (A) You should never smoke around this cargo.
  (B) Not within 25 feet.
  (C) Not within 50 feet.
  (D) As close as you like.

_____36. When refueling a placarded vehicle with the engine off, always remember to:
  (A) Make sure you pay before you pump.
  (B) Have someone stand near the pump shut-off valve.
  (C) Be at the nozzle, controlling the fuel flow.
  (D) Watch for persons smoking.

_____37. In the power unit of a placarded vehicle, what type of fire extinguisher rating is required?
  (A) UL rating of 10 B:C or more.
  (B) UL rating of 25 B:C or more.
  (C) UL rating of 40 B:C or more.
  (D) UL rating of 100 B:C or more.

Review Questions for Passenger Transport

The following statements are either true or false. Mark your answer in the blank provided, and then check your answers with the key at the end of the chapter.

_____ 1. All buses should stop between 15 and 50 feet from a railroad crossing.
_____ 2. Stop at all drawbridges at least 10 feet before the draw of the bridge.
_____ 3. Hazardous materials are not allowed to be transported by buses.
_____ 4. All carry-on baggage must be stored to allow free movement about the bus and must not block emergency exits or windows.
_____ 5. Passengers must be seated and all baggage must be stowed under the seats.

_____ 6. When the bus is full, carry-on baggage is allowed in the stairwells or in the aisle.

_____ 7. Buses are required to slow down when the traffic light shows green.

_____ 8. A bus driver may engage another passenger in conversation while driving.

The following statements are multiple choice. Mark your answer in the blank provided. Then, check your answers with the key at the end of the chapter.

_____ 1. Curved (convex) mirrors on buses:
(A) Are against federal laws.
(B) Make things appear farther away than they are.
(C) Make things appear larger.
(D) All of the above.

_____ 2. During a pre-trip inspection, you should check:
(A) Rider signaling devices.
(B) Handhold railing.
(C) Emergency exit handles.
(D) All of the above.

_____ 3. When carrying farm workers, how many folding aisle seats can the vehicle have?
(A) None.
(B) Ten.
(C) Five.
(D) Eight.

_____ 4. Church buses can have how many unsecured seats?
(A) None.
(B) Ten.
(C) Five.
(D) Eight.

_____ 5. Bus emergency exits must:
(A) Have exit signs that are clearly marked.
(B) Be unlocked.
(C) Keep doors and windows closed.
(D) All of the above.

_____ 6. While operating a bus, you should always have which of the following emergency equipment?
(A) Emergency reflectors.
(B) At least one fire extinguisher.
(C) Spare electrical fuses.
(D) All of the above.

_____ 7. You should wear your seatbelt:
(A) During short trips.
(B) For highway driving.
(C) Always.
(D) During bad weather.

_____ 8. How should you secure baggage on a bus?
(A) Make sure allowable packages are only one-foot tall so when they are in the aisle they can easily be stepped over.
(B) You can secure luggage in front of the emergency exit.
(C) The packages should be stowed away so they don't fall on passengers.
(D) All of the above.

_____ 9. What type of cargo is prohibited on a bus?
   (A) Chickens.
   (B) Ammunition labeled ORM-D.
   (C) Irritating materials or tear gas.
   (D) All of the above.

_____10. The maximum weight of all hazardous materials that can be transported on a bus is:
   (A) 500 pounds.
   (B) 150 pounds.
   (C) 1000 pounds.
   (D) 50 pounds.

_____11. If a rider wants to board your bus and is carrying a closed gas can, what should you do?
   (A) Store the gasoline in the front of the bus.
   (B) Collect an extra fare for baggage.
   (C) Don't allow the rider to board.
   (D) It's okay to let the rider on board as long as the can is closed and kept away from the engine.

_____12. Passengers should not stand:
   (A) In the handicapped passenger space.
   (B) They can stand anywhere.
   (C) More than six deep.
   (D) In front of the standee line.

_____13. Disorderly or out-of-control riders should be discharged:
   (A) In a safe place.
   (B) Near a police station.
   (C) As soon as possible.
   (D) At the next bus stop.

_____14. Based on statistics, where do most bus crashes happen?
   (A) While the bus is parked.
   (B) On two-lane roads.
   (C) At intersections.
   (D) When the bus stops.

_____15. How do you keep control of the bus on curves?
   (A) Press hard on the brake and turn sharply.
   (B) Slow to a safe speed before the curve, then accelerate slightly.
   (C) Countersteer.
   (D) Brake all through the curve.

_____16. A bus driver should stop at a railroad crossing _____ feet before the nearest track.
   (A) 50 to 100.
   (B) 10 to 15.
   (C) 15 to 50.
   (D) 10.

_____17. You should stop _____ feet in front of a drawbridge that has no attendant.
   (A) 50.
   (B) 20.
   (C) 175.
   (D) 100.

_____18. A bus cannot be fueled while:
    (A) Near an open flame.
    (B) The engine is on.
    (C) Passengers are on board.
    (D) All of the above.

_____19. It is illegal to tow or push a bus with passengers unless:
    (A) The tow truck is larger than 20,000 VWR.
    (B) Discharging passengers would be unsafe.
    (C) Followed by an escort vehicle.
    (D) The distance is less than one mile.

_____20. When traveling at 50 miles per hour in a 40-foot bus, how many seconds of space should you keep between you and the vehicle in front of you?
    (A) Two seconds.
    (B) Eight seconds.
    (C) Five seconds.
    (D) Three seconds.

Check Yourself—Answers to Endorsements Tests

Air Brakes True/False

1. F; 2. T; 3. F; 4. T; 5. T; 6. F; 7. F; 8. T; 9. T; 10. F; 11. T; 12. F; 13. T; 14. F; 15. F; 16. T; 17. F; 18. T; 19. F; 20. F; 21. T; 22. T; 23. F; 24. T; 25. T.

Air Brakes Multiple Choice

1. A; 2. B; 3. B; 4. B; 5. B; 6. D; 7. D; 8. C; 9. B; 10. A; 11. C; 12. D; 13. B; 14. B; 15. C; 16. A; 17. B; 18. A; 19. C; 20. D; 21. D; 22. A; 23. B; 24. B; 25. C, 26. C; 27. A; 28. C; 29. B.

Combinations/Triples/ Doubles True/False

1. F; 2. F; 3. T; 4. F; 5. F; 6. T; 7. T; 8. F; 9. F; 10. T; 11. T; 12. F; 13. T; 14. F; 15. T; 16. T; 17. F; 18. T; 19. F; 20. T; 21. F; 22. T; 23. F; 24. T; 25. T.

Combinations/Triples/ Doubles Multiple Choice

1. D; 2. A; 3. C; 4. B; 5. B; 6. A; 7. D; 8. C; 9. B; 10. B; 11. C; 12. B; 13. C; 14. C; 15. D; 16. A; 17. B; 18. D; 19. B; 20. C; 21. C; 22. C; 23. C; 24. D; 25. B; 26. A; 27. D; 28. A; 29. B; 30. A; 31. B; 32. C; 33. A; 34. A; 35. B; 36. D; 37. A; 38. C; 39. B; 40. A; 41. C; 42. B; 43. D; 44. C; 45. B; 46. D.

Tank Vehicle True/False

1. F; 2. F; 3. F; 4. T; 5. T; 6. T; 7. F; 8. F; 9. T; 10. T.

Tank Vehicle Multiple Choice

1. B; 2. D; 3. A; 4. B; 5. C; 6. B; 7. D; 8. A; 9. B; 10. D.

Hazardous Materials True/False

1. F; 2. F; 3. F; 4. T; 5. T; 6. F; 7. T; 8. F; 9. F; 10. T; 11. T; 12. T; 13. T; 14. T; 15. F; 16. F; 17. T; 18. F; 19. F; 20. T; 21. T; 22. T; 23. T; 24. T; 25. F; 26. T; 27. T; 28. T; 29. F.

Hazardous Materials Multiple Choice

1. B; 2. C; 3. C; 4. C; 5. A; 6. B; 7. A; 8. D; 9. B; 10. C; 11. A; 12. C; 13. A; 14. D; 15. A; 16. B; 17. A; 18. A; 19. C; 20. A; 21. B; 22. D; 23. D; 24. D; 25. A; 26. B; 27. D; 28. D; 29. D; 30. D; 31. C; 32. C; 33. A; 34. B; 35. B; 36. C; 37. A.

Passenger Transport True/False

1. T; 2. F; 3. F; 4. T; 5. T; 6. F; 7. T; 8. F.

Passenger Transport Multiple Choice

1. B; 2. D; 3. D; 4. A; 5. D; 6. D; 7. C; 8. C; 9. C; 10. A; 11. C; 12. D; 13. A; 14. C; 15. B; 16. C; 17. A; 18. D; 19. B; 20. B.

Glossary

Accelerator   Located just under the steering wheel, you can operate this pedal with your right foot to control engine speed.

Access panels   Panels granting access to controls, vehicle parts and storage for tools, and other items.

Administrator   The Federal Highway Administrator, the chief executive of the Federal Highway Administration, an agency within the Department of Transportation.

Aerodynamic buffeting   As you drive your double or triple rig down the highway, you are cutting through the wind and, as you cut through, a "draft" is created behind you.

Air backflow   If the tractor air supply develops a problem, air from the trailer air supply would have a tendency to "back flow" and fill the tractor's air supply. If this happens, both tractor and trailer would be left powerless.

Air bag suspension   A trailer suspension system that uses air bags instead of traditional springs.

Air brakes   These brakes use air instead of fluid to stop or brake. They require special handling and an additional permit on your CDL.

Air compressor   Compresses air and pumps it into the air tanks. Air brakes use compressed air to brake the vehicle.

Air compressor governor   Maintains constant air pressure in the air tanks—between 100 psi and 125 psi.

Air leakage rate   The rate at which air leaks from the air brakes. Use the air leakage rate to test brake pressure.

Air pressure   Compacting air and storing it in a small space. Compressing it creates energy and this energy operates the air brakes.

Air storage tanks   Also called "air tanks" or "air reservoirs." These tanks hold compressed air produced by the air compressor. These tanks have enough air to stop the vehicle several times, even if the air compressor stops working.

Air tank drains   Air tanks are equipped with drains, usually located at the bottom of the tank. Oil and water accumulate in the tanks and must be drained daily.

Air tank petcock   A valve on a tank that can be opened to drain the tank.

Alcohol concentration (AC)   The concentration of alcohol in a person's blood or breath. When expressed as a percentage, it means grams of alcohol per 100 milliliters of blood or per 210 liters of breath.

Alcohol evaporators   Designed to automatically inject alcohol into the system to reduce the chance that water in the air brake system will freeze.

Alcohol or "alcoholic beverage"   Beer, wine, distilled spirits, or liquor.

Alternator   Keeps the battery charged and powers the truck's systems while it is running.

Ammeter   Used to measure the flow of electrical currents.

Amperage   The number of amperes generated by the vehicle's electrical system.

Amphetamines   Stimulant drugs used to stay awake. Also called "Bennies," "speed," or "pep pills"—they are illegal.

Application pressure gauge   Lets the driver know how much air pressure is being applied to the brakes.

Automatic drain   An air tank drain that is activated automatically. From time to time, you will hear these drains blow out the air and any accumulated oil and water.

Axle weight   Weight transmitted to the ground by one axle or one set of axles. Axle weight is not how much the axles themselves weigh! Axles support the vehicle and its load.

BAC   Blood alcohol level.

Backing   The process of putting a vehicle in reverse.

Backup lamp   One white light located at the rear of buses, trucks, and truck tractors. It is a signal to other drivers that you are backing up.

Baffled liquid tanks   Tanks with dividers designed to slow down front-to-back surge.

Baffles   Dividers in a tanker that keep the load from shifting.

Balanced load   Cargo that is evenly distributed from top to bottom, front to back, and side to side.

Bank   A sloped area that causes the highway or road to slant slightly.

Battery   Converts chemical energy to electricity. It is used to start the engine.

Belted bias ply   Tires on which the plies cross at an angle and there's an added layered belt of fabric between the plies and the tread. Belts make the tread more rigid than bias ply tires and the tread will last longer.

Bias ply   Tires in which the plies are placed at a criss-crossed angle. This makes the sidewall and the tread very rigid.

Binders   Used to bind down loads on flatbed trailers.

Black ice   A thin coating of ice that is usually invisible because you can see the roadway through it.

Bleeding tar   Tar that bleeds to the driving surface and can be very slippery.

Blind spot   An area that you can't see with your rearview mirrors—usually from the rear axle to midway up the trailer and from midway down the door to the ground.

Blocks   Also called "chocks." They prevent trucks from moving unexpectedly; used in testing brakes and loading and coupling trailers.

Bobtail tractor   The lead tractor and power supply when towing trailers or other tractors.

Braces and supports   Devices used to prevent the load from moving. Whether the vehicle is a flatbed or drybox, the load must be blocked or braced to prevent moving on all sides.

Bracing   A method that prevents movement of the cargo in the trailer or any other cargo compartment.

Brake cam shaft   The brake slack adjuster is attached to the push rod at one end and the cam shaft at the other end. When the slack adjuster is pushed, the cam shaft twists, forcing the brake shoes away from each other to press on the side of the brake drum.

Brake chamber   When the driver applies the brake and air is applied to the braking system, air is pumped into the brake chamber and pushes out the "push rod"—which is attached to the "slack adjuster." When the driver takes his or her foot off the brake pedal, the air is released from the brake chamber and the return spring pulls the brake shoes away from the drum.

Brake drums   Located at the ends of the axle. The drums contain the braking mechanism and the wheels are bolted to the drums.

Brake fade   When it takes more and more pressure on the brake pedal to slow the vehicle.

Brake failure   Brakes do not work.

Brake lag distance   Distance the vehicle travels once the brake has been applied and the brakes begin to work.

Brake linings   These press against the drum, creating enough friction to slow or stop the vehicle.

Brake pedal   Located just to the left of the accelerator and operated with your right foot. When you press down on the pedal, the brakes are applied and the vehicle slows down.

Brake reservoirs   For air or vacuum braking systems, the reservoirs (or tanks) store the compressed air until it is needed.

Brake shoes   These press against the drum, creating enough friction to slow or stop the vehicle.

Brake-door interlock   Applies the brakes and holds the throttle in an idle position each time the door is opened.

Brakes   Used to stop the vehicle.

Braking   Process of using brakes.

Braking distance   The perception time plus the reaction time plus the brake lag—needed to stop a rig. Usually calculated to include speed.

Braking force   A percentage of the GVWR or the GCWR.

Braking performance   A combination of how quickly the brakes stop the vehicle and how far the vehicle travels before it stops. Braking performance is also measured by how much force must be applied to the brakes before the vehicle stops.

Braking rate   The ability of a vehicle's brakes to stop the vehicle when traveling at a certain speed; these specifications are provided for the manufacturer and the vehicle must at least meet the required braking rate.

Bridge icing   In cold weather, bridges usually become icy before roads do. Drive slowly over bridges in cold weather.

Bridge traffic control officer   Individual stationed at a drawbridge to direct traffic and to stop traffic just prior to the bridge being raised.

Bulkhead   A solid steel divider within the tank.

Bus   Vehicle that carries more than 15 passengers.

Cab   The part of the vehicle where the driver sits.

Cables   Wires, chains, or other connectors from the tractor to the trailer.

Canceling the turn signal   Shutting off the turn signal.

Carboy   Glass, plastic, or metal container used to carry between 5 and 15 gallons of liquid.

Cargo doors   Doors located at the back or side of trailer where cargo may be loaded or unloaded.

Cargo heater   Heater used to keep cargo warm.

Cargo securement   Making sure that the cargo does not shift or fall.

Cargo securement devices   Tie-downs, chains, tarps, and other methods of securing cargo in a flatbed.

Cargo shift   Cargo moves from its original position.

Cargo tank   Tank used to hold liquid or compressed gas.

Carry-on baggage   Luggage, bags, and packages brought onto a bus by passengers. Carry-on baggage must be kept out of the aisle and not impede the movement of passengers. It is also imperative that carry-on baggage be stowed in a secure manner to avoid injuring passengers if the bus stops or lurches suddenly.

Center of gravity   The point where weight acts as a force. Center of gravity affects the vehicle's stability.

Centrifugal force   A natural force that pulls liquids or objects away from the center.

Chains   Used for tiedown to secure cargo.

Checklist   List of parts of the vehicle to check or inspect.

CHEMTREC   The acronym for the Chemical Transportation Emergency Center in Washington, DC. It has a 24-hour toll-free line and has evolved to provide emergency personnel with technical information and expertise about the physical properties of hazardous products. The number for CHEMTREC is 800-424-9300.

Chock   A block (usually made of wood) used to hold a tire in place and keep a vehicle from moving.

Clearance lights   Lamps that outline the length and width of the vehicle. These lights are found at the highest and widest part of the sides, back, and front of the vehicle.

Climbing lane   Extra lane used by slower vehicles trying to climb a hill.

Closed circuit   An electrical circuit in a completed loop in which electricity's positive and negative poles are connected. This allows the current to travel from the source to its usage point.

Clutch pedal   Located to the left of the brake pedal, the clutch pedal is operated with the left foot. You press the clutch pedal to disengage the clutch, and release the pedal to engage the clutch.

CMVSA/86   Commercial Vehicle Safety Act of 1986—requires all 50 states to meet the same minimum standards in testing and licensing of all commercial drivers and requires that all commercial motor vehicle drivers must pass and obtain the CDL.

Coil spring suspension   Dampens wheel vibration with coils that absorb "bounce" between the road and the tires.

Cold start and warm-up switch   Found on diesel engines. When the engine is cold, there's a start-up lag time. Turning the key allows the ejectors in the engine to warm up. A light comes on, letting you know the engine is warm enough to start.

Combustible   Any material that can ignite or burn.

Commerce   Any trade, traffic, or transportation within the jurisdiction of the United States between a place in a state and a place outside of that state, trade, traffic, and transportation in the United States, which affects any trade, traffic, and transportation.

Commercial driver's license (CDL)   A license issued by a state or other jurisdiction to an individual, which authorizes the individual to operate a specified class of commercial motor vehicle.

Commercial Driver's License Information System (CDLIS)   Established by FHWA pursuant to section 12007 of the Commercial Motor Vehicle Safety Act of 1986.

Commercial motor vehicle (CMV)   A motor vehicle or combination of motor vehicles used in commerce to transport passengers or property if the vehicle has a gross combination weight rating of 11,794 kilograms or more (26,001 pounds or more) inclusive of a towed unit with a gross vehicle weight rating of more than 4536 kilograms (10,000 pounds); or is designed to transport 15 or more passengers, including the driver.

Communicate the risk   Attaching proper placards to the vehicle.

Communicating with others   The use of lights, horns, and hand signals to let other drivers know your intentions.

Compartment   Enclosed space where certain items are kept.

Compressed gas   Gas held under pressure.

Containment   The ability to keep any situation or substance from moving from its original site; "containment" of a fire means restricting its movement from its origin; "containment of a liquid" means preventing liquid from spreading farther from its origin, as in a spill.

Controlled braking   Accomplished by squeezing brakes firmly *without locking the wheels.*

Controlled substance   Includes all substances listed on schedules I through V of 21 CFR 1308 (Secs. 1308.11 through 1308.15).

Converter dolly   Used to connect the trailer to the tractor or to another trailer.

Converter gear   Part of the converter dolly used to couple the tractor and the trailer, or the trailer to another trailer.

Conviction   A determination that a person has violated or failed to comply with the law in a court of original jurisdiction or a violation of a condition of release without bail, regardless of whether the penalty is rebated, suspended, or probated.

Coolant   Liquid used to keep the engine cool.

Corrosive   Includes materials that cause destruction or irreversible damage to human skin tissue on contact—can be liquid or solid.

Countersteering   Once you've steered around an obstacle in your path, you will turn the wheel back in the other direction.

Coupling   Connecting two sections of a vehicle or trailer.

Coupling device   A device—called a converter gear or dolly—that makes it possible to attach one trailer to another or to a tractor.

Cross-wind   Wind currents traveling from side to side—particularly dangerous on mountain roads.

Cryogenic   Maintaining materials by freezing.

Curves   Where the highway bends in another direction. Usually includes a slight bank, which may cause a load to shift; curves should be taken below the normal speed limit.

Cut-in/cut-out levels   Governor on the air compressor. When air pressure drops below a certain psi, the governor will cut in and build the pressure back to its necessary level. Then, the compressor will automatically cut out.

Cylinders   A pressurized tank designed to hold gases.

Cylindrical   In the shape of a cylinder—usually referring to anything long and round.

Dashboard   Control panel just beyond the steering wheel that houses all gauges, knobs, and other operating information so that the driver may operate the truck safely.

Dead axles   Axles pulled by the drive axle that do not give power to the wheels. Without the drive axle, these axles would be stationary.

Deceleration   Slowing the vehicle.

Defroster or defrosting device   An element associated with the vehicle's heating unit that clears the windshield of any ice or foggy distraction.

Departure   The time the vehicle is scheduled to leave the facility.

Destination   Arrival location.

Differential   Gears that allow each wheel to turn at a different speed on the same axle for easier manageability while turning.

Dimmer switch   Located on the floor to the left of the brake pedal (if it isn't on the dashboard). This switch allows you to move the headlights from low beam to high beam.

Disc brakes   Brakes that have a power screw, which is turned when air pressure is applied. This causes the power screw to clamp the disc between the caliper's brake lining pads.

Disqualification   The suspension, revocation, cancellation, or any other withdrawal by a state of a person's privilege to drive or a determination by the FHWA, under the rules of practice for motor carrier safety—that person is no longer qualified to operate a commercial motor vehicle.

Dolly support   The device that holds up the front end of a dolly when it is uncoupled from a tractor.

Dolly tongue   A part of the dolly converter that goes under the trailer, linking it to the tractor or another trailer.

DOT   Department of Transportation.

Double   A vehicle carrying two trailers or tankers.

Downgrade   A steep downward slant in the road, usually around mountains or hill country.

Downhill grade   See downgrade.

Drawbridge   Bridge that can be lifted to accommodate tall water vessels by pulling one-half of the bridge up, thereby interrupting traffic flow.

Drive axle   The axle that provides all of the power to the wheels and pulls the load.

Driveaway-towaway   A method of hauling in which the cargo is one or more vehicles with one or more sets of wheels on the roadway.

Driver applicant   An individual who applies to a state to obtain, transfer, upgrade, or renew a CDL.

Driver's license   A license issued by a state or other jurisdiction to an individual which authorizes the individual to operate a motor vehicle on the highways.

Driver's record of duty status   A form submitted by the driver to the carrier after completing a 24-hour period of work.

Driving a commercial motor vehicle while under the influence of alcohol   Driving a CMV with a blood alcohol concentration of 0.04% or more; driving under the influence of alcohol, as prescribed by state law; or refusal to undergo such testing.

Drop-off   An uneven highway where new pavement makes part of road higher than the rest, creating a "drop-off" that may be a driving hazard.

Dry bulk tanks   Tanks that have a high center of gravity, which means the driver will use special care, particularly when rounding curves and when entering or exiting a freeway by using an on-ramp or off-ramp.

Dual air brake systems   The truck has two separate air brake systems—the primary system and the secondary system—but only one set of controls.

Dual parking control valves   Some vehicles (mainly buses) have auxiliary air tanks that can be used to release the spring brakes so the vehicle can be moved to a safe place. Vehicles with dual parking control valves have two control knobs on the dash—one is a push-pull knob used to apply the spring brakes for normal parking. The other is spring-loaded in the "out" position.

Dummy coupler   Seals the air brake hose when a connection is not in use.

Dunnage   Loose packaging material.

DUI   Driving under the influence.

Effective braking distance   Distance the vehicle will travel once the brakes make contact with the drum. With good braking technique and brakes perfectly adjusted on good, dry pavement, a vehicle going 55 miles per hour will travel 150 additional feet before coming to a complete stop.

Electron   A tiny particle carrying a negative charge of electricity.

Elliptical   An oval shape sometimes found on "fish-eye" mirrors.

Emergency brake system   The system that stops the vehicle in an emergency situation—usually caused by failure of the braking system. The emergency brake system uses parts of the service and parking brake systems.

Emergency brakes   Stops the vehicle in an emergency situation—usually caused by failure of the braking system.

Emergency equipment   Equipment needed during an emergency. For a commercial motor vehicle, the emergency equipment consists of a fire extinguisher, reflective emergency triangles, fuses (if needed), tire change kit, accident notification kit, and a list of emergency numbers.

Emergency exit   Exit used for emergency purposes only.

Emergency line   Air line between the tractor and the trailer. If the service line becomes disconnected, the emergency line becomes the air supply to the trailer brakes. If the emergency line is broken, it will cause the trailer brakes to lock.

Emergency Response Guidebook (ERG)   Used by fire fighters, police officers, industry safety personnel, and others in the event of an emergency involving HazMat cargo. This book is available through the Department of Transportation.

Employee   Any operator of a commercial motor vehicle, including full-time, regularly employed drivers; casual, intermittent, or occasional drivers; leased drivers; and independent, owner-operator contractors.

Employer   Any person or entity (including the United States, a state, the District of Columbia, or a political subdivision of a state) who owns or leases a commercial motor vehicle or assigns employees to operate such a vehicle.

Endorsement   An authorization to an individual's CDL that is required to permit the individual to operate certain types of commercial motor vehicles.

Endorsements   Optional tests that allow drivers to add permits for certain vehicles or cargo.

Engine compartment   Area where the engine is located.

Engine retarder   Also called "Jake Brake," "Williams Blue OX Brake"—engine retarders allow the engine to be used to help slow the vehicle down, particularly if brake fade occurs on a downgrade.

Engine temperature gauge   Usually marked "Temp" or "Water Temp." This gauge indicates the temperature of the engine's cooling system in degrees.

En route   During travel or on the way.

EPA   Environmental Protection Agency.

Escape ramp   A ramp—usually at the bottom of a down-grade—which drivers may use to stop their vehicle if the brakes fail.

Etiologic agents   Microorganisms (also known as germs) that can cause disease.

Evasive action   Action taken to avoid an accident, hitting debris on the road, or a dangerous situation—often involves swerving, braking, sudden lane changes, etc.

Exhaust system   Required on all motor vehicles and used to discharge gases created by the operation of the engine.

Explosive   Material or a mixture that can explode.

Fail-safe brakes   Also known as spring brakes. The most commonly used emergency brake and/or parking brake system on tractors and buses. They must be mechanical, because air can leak off.

Federal Hazardous Materials Table   Designates which materials are hazardous to transport. They have been designated as "hazardous materials" because they endanger the health, safety, and property of those around them during their transport.

Federal Motor Carrier Safety Regulations (FMCSR)   Governs the operation of trucks and buses by common, contract, and private motor carriers.

Felony   An offense under state or federal law that is punishable by death or by imprisonment for a term exceeding one year.

Field of vision   The area in which you can see in front of you.

Fifth wheel   Controls how much weight is distributed on each axle of the tractor. It is part of the locking device that is used to connect a trailer and a tractor.

Fire extinguisher   Safety device used to put out fires.

"Fish-eye" mirror   Convex mirror, positioned on the side of the truck, usually providing driver with wider view of the back of trailer; makes vehicles and objects appear smaller and farther away than they are.

Fishyback   Carrying trailers and containers by ship.

Flags   Used to mark over-length or over-wide vehicles.

Flammable   Material that can burst into flames.

Flammable cargo   Cargo that can ignite if exposed to a fire or flame.

Flares   Burning signal device—part of safety equipment.

Flash point   The lowest temperature at which a substance can give off flammable vapors that can ignite if the vapors come in contact with a fire or a spark.

Flatbed   Truck or trailer without sides or a top.

Fluid pressure   The nature of fluids is to flow; when they cannot, pressure is created— fluid pressure is used to operate hydraulic brakes.

FMCSR Part 393   Describes parts and accessories needed to safely operate a commercial motor vehicle.

Foreign   Outside the 50 United States and the District of Columbia.

Foundation brakes   Used at each wheel—parts of the brake that don't rotate. The most common is the S-cam drum brake; wedge and disc brakes are less common.

Four-way flashers   Two amber lights located at the front and two amber lights or red lights located at the rear of the vehicle. These are usually the front and rear turn signal lights, equipped to do double duty as warning lights.

Frame   The metal infrastructure of any vehicle—creates the underpinnings to support the rest of the vehicle.

Friction   The rubbing together of two objects which causes resistance.

Front brake limiting valve   Vehicles built before 1975 have a front brake limiting valve control switch on the dash. The valve has two positions—"normal" and "slippery." Putting the valve in the "slippery" position reduces the normal air pressure to the front brakes by 50 percent—and in doing so, reduces the braking power of front brakes by 50 percent.

Front clearance lamps   Two amber lamps located at each side of the front of large buses, trucks, truck tractors, large semi-trailers, full trailers, pole trailers, and projecting loads.

Front identification lamps Three amber lights located at the center of the vehicle or cab. Required on large buses and trucks and truck tractors.

Front side marker lamp Two amber lights located to each side or near the center of the vehicle between the front rear side marker lamps. Required for buses, trucks, semi-trailers, full trailers, and pole trailers.

Front side reflectors Two amber reflectors located on each side toward the front of buses and trucks, tractors, semi-trailers, full trailers, and pole trailers.

Front turn signals Two amber signals located to the left and right front of the tractor. Can be above or below headlights. Required on buses, trucks, and truck tractors.

Front wheel skids (drive wheel skids) The most common type of skid, resulting from over-braking or over-acceleration—can be stopped by taking foot off accelerator. If road conditions are slippery, push the clutch in.

Fuel and fuel system Provides energy to the engine so that it will run.

Fuel injectors Spray the fuel into the combustion chambers.

Fuel lines Carry the fuel from the pump to the cylinders.

Fuel pump Delivers the fuel to the engine.

Fuel tank Holds the fuel.

Fuse Device that completes the electrical circuit and prevents overheating by breaking the circuit, thus reducing the risk of fire damage.

Gas mask A safety device carried in vehicles transporting hazardous materials—in case of an accident, the driver will use the gas mask to avoid inhaling poisonous or harmful fumes.

Gear Pertaining to the transmission. Each gear supplies a certain speed to the vehicle. The lower the gear, the slower the vehicle's speed and the greater pulling power.

Gearshift The stick or lever located inside the tractor that the driver uses to select the gear.

Generator Changes mechanical energy into electricity to power batteries and other electrical systems.

Glad hand Air hose brake connection between the tractor and the trailer.

Glare A condition caused by sun or bright lights reflecting off pavement or a vehicle's glass or metal parts, causing difficulty in a driver's vision; particularly a problem when driving west as the sun is setting.

Groove pattern The area between the tread ribs.

Gross combination weight rating (GCWR) The value specified by the manufacturer as the loaded weight of a combination vehicle. In the absence of a value specified by the manufacturer, GCWR will be determined by adding the GVWR of the power unit and the total weight of the towed unit and any load thereon.

Gross vehicle weight (GVW) Total weight of a single vehicle and its load.

Gross vehicle weight rating (GVWR) The value specified by the manufacturer as the loaded weight of a single vehicle.

Grounding Provides an alternate safe path for an electrical current if the normal path is accidentally broken.

Handhold On buses, what passengers use to hold onto while standing in the aisle.

Hazard Harmful item or situation.

Hazard Class   Indicates the degree of risk associated with a particular material.

Hazardous Material Table   A list of hazardous materials outlining federal guidelines.

Hazardous materials   A group of materials that the Secretary of Transportation judges to pose a threat or risk to safety, health, or property while it is being transported in commerce; the meaning such term has under section 103 of the Hazardous Materials Transportation Act.

Hazardous waste manifest   Any cargo containing hazardous waste must be accompanied by a hazardous waste manifest—and this must be signed by the driver.

HazMat   Hazardous material(s).

Headache rack or header board   Protects the driver from the freight shifting or crushing him or her in an accident or a sudden stop.

Headlights   Two white headlights, one to the right and one to the left, located on the front of the tractor—required on buses, trucks, and truck tractors. Used to illuminate the vehicle to help the driver see and to help others see the vehicle.

Heater   Warms the cab of the vehicle.

High beams   Lights used at night to see long distances. Use only when other cars are far away from you.

High center of gravity   The majority of a load's weight is high off the ground.

Horn   Used to communicate with other motorists.

Hydraulic brakes or hydraulic braking system   Brakes that use fluid pressure to stop.

Hydroplaning   Occurs when water or slush collects on the roadway and the vehicle's tires ride on top of the water, instead of the roadway itself, causing the driver to lose control of the vehicle.

Identification lights   Lights located on the top, sides, and back of a truck to identify it as a large vehicle.

Identification (ID) number   Number used to identify hazardous materials on shipping papers. ID numbers begin with UN—except those loads traveling between the United States and Canada, which are identified by an NA number.

Ignition point   The point at which a flammable substance will catch on fire (ignite).

Ignition switch (or starter)   Supplies electricity to the engine and other systems. When the key is turned, it turns on the accessory circuits. As soon as the engine starts, release the key. If you have a "false start," let the engine cool for 30 seconds before giving it another try.

Inertia   The tendency of an object to remain in the same condition, either in motion or standing still, until it is acted on by an outside force (e.g., applying the brakes to stop a truck).

Infectious substances   May cause disease or death in animals or humans. This includes human or animal excretion, secretions, blood tissue, and tissue components.

Inhalation hazard   A material that can be harmful if inhaled.

Innage   The depth of the liquid loaded in your tank, measuring from the bottom of the tank to the surface of the liquid.

Inspection routine   List of steps you go through to inspect your vehicle—in the same way each time—so that you do not forget a step.

Insulation   Material used to maintain certain temperatures within trailers; particularly important in refrigerated units to maintain cool temperatures.

Intermodal containers (fishyback/piggyback)   Containers sealed by the shipper, transported by boat, and then loaded on trailers for final delivery. Shippers prefer containers because they resist pilferage (theft) and other problems.

Johnson bar   Most tractors have a handle attached to (or near) the steering column—called a "Johnson bar" or "trolley valve"—used to apply the trailer's brakes.

Kingpin   Used in coupling, a hardened steel pin on a trailer that locks into the fifth wheel.

Knowledge Tests   Written tests that a driver must pass in order to receive a CDL or special permits.

Landing gear   Supports for the front of a trailer when it is not attached to a tractor.

Leaf spring suspension   Dampens wheel vibration; all the leaves must be intact to provide this comfort. During inspection, look for missing or broken leaves.

Length and width limits   Limitations on the length and width of a truck or tractor trailer rig. Combinations exceeding these limits must have special permits and travel irregular routes or have a route plan.

License plate lamp   One white light located at the center rear—on buses, trucks, tractors, semi-trailers, full trailers, and pole trailers.

Lights   Help others to see you, help you to see others, to signal intentions (such as lane changes, slow down, or stop), and communicate with other vehicles.

Liquid density   Liquid in a tanker that has a high mass for its volume.

Liquid surge   The movement of a liquid in a tanker, created by the physics of forward motion. When tanker stops, the force of the liquid surge can actually move the entire vehicle several feet forward.

List of Hazardous Substances and Reportable Quantities   A list of hazardous materials that drivers should learn if they consistently haul such materials.

List of Marine Pollutants   A list of materials that are harmful to marine life or—if they enter the water table—or humans.

Livestock   Live animals, such as cattle, hogs, horses, sheep, and goats.

Load rating   Refers to the strength of the tire.

Locking device   Keeps the towed trailer and towing tractor together until you're ready to uncouple them. This locking device is called the "locking jaws" and it locks around the shaft of the trailer's kingpin.

Locking jaws   Another name for Locking Device.

Low air pressure warning signal   On all vehicles equipped with air brakes—signals when air pressure falls below 60 psi.

Low beams   Normal headlight setting used to illuminate the vehicle to help the driver see and to help others see the vehicle.

Manifest   A document describing cargo in the vehicle.

Manual drain   An air tank drain that is operated by turning a knob (or petcock) a quarter turn—or by pulling a cable.

Mirrors   Used to see what is behind and to the sides of the vehicle.

Modulating control valve   This is controlled by a handle on the dash board and is used to apply the spring brakes gradually. The more the handle is moved, the more the brakes are applied. This valve is designed to use in case service brakes fail while driving.

Motor vehicle   A vehicle, machine, tractor, trailer, or semi-trailer propelled or drawn by mechanical power, used on highways, except that such term does not include a vehicle, machine, tractor, trailer, or semi-trailer operated exclusively on a rail.

MPH   Miles per hour.

NA   Initials preceding identification numbers that are used only in shipments between the United States and Canada.

National Response Center   Has the ability to contact the proper law enforcement agency and the proper containment or clean-up personnel. The National Response Center phone number is 800-424-8802.

Net weight   Weight of a package, not including the packing materials.

Night driving   Driving at night.

Noise levels   The concentration of noise.

Non hazardous material   Material that by itself or in bulk does not create any hazard to health or the environment.

Nonresident CDL   A CDL issued by a state to an individual living in a foreign country.

Normal stopping   In a normal stopping situation, you apply pressure to the brake pedal until the vehicle comes to a stop. Pressure is applied smoothly and steadily.

N.O.S.   Not otherwise specified.

"Nose factor"   When carrying livestock, remember that your cargo does have an odor, and you should try to park your vehicle downwind of other vehicles or truckstops to keep everyone happy.

"No zone"   The area to each side of the truck where it is not possible to see approaching traffic.

Odometer   Keeps track of the total miles the vehicle has traveled.

Oil pressure gauge   Gauge that measures oil pressure.

Oil temperature gauge   Gauge that shows the temperature of the oil.

On-ramp/off-ramp   Ramps leading on and off freeways. Some ramps may bank, so it is recommended that you enter and exit a ramp at speeds below the posted speed limit.

ORM (Other Regulated Materials)   These materials are not considered hazardous materials, by definition, but are dangerous when transported in commerce, so they must be regulated.

Out of service order   A declaration by an authorized enforcement officer of a federal, state, Canadian, Mexican, or local jurisdiction that a driver, a commercial motor vehicle, or a motor carrier operation may not continue to operate.

Outage   Space in a tanker that allows for liquid loads to expand. Drivers must know outage requirements for each product they haul.

Overacceleration   Too much power supplied to the drive wheels—driving too fast and not adjusting your speed to the road and traffic conditions.

Overbraking   Braking too hard and locking the wheels, causing a skid.

Overload   More weight than your vehicle can carry or that is legally allowable.

Oversteering   Turning the wheels more sharply than the vehicle can handle.

Oxidizing substances   Substances that react with oxygen.

Pallet   Flat wooden support structure used to group an amount of cargo together for shipping and stacking.

Parking brake controls   In older vehicles, the parking brake will be controlled by a lever. In newer models, the driver applies the parking brakes (spring brakes) using a diamond-shaped, yellow push-pull knob—you pull the knob out to apply the parking brakes and push it in to release.

Parking brake system   The system used when applying the parking brake.

Parking brakes   Brakes used when you park the vehicle.

Parking lamps   Two amber or white lights located just below the headlights on small buses and trucks.

Passenger supervision   Providing passengers information necessary for their safety during trip. This includes movement in the vehicle, storage of luggage, placement of carry-ons, and general behavior.

Perception distance   Distance the vehicle will travel from the time driver sees a hazard and the time the driver reacts (presses the brake pedal).

Permanent tank   A tank that is attached to the vehicle and must be loaded with the vehicle.

Piggyback   Trailers or containers that are first carried by rail.

"Pigtail"   Detachable connections—electrical connections between towing and towed vehicles—made by simply twisting wires together with shielded cables.

Pintle hook   Used in coupling, at rear of the fifth wheel—used to tow trailers.

Pitman arm   A lever attached to the steering box—moves the front wheels back and forth.

Placard   A sign placed on cargo to indicate that the shipment contains hazardous materials. These signs must be visible from all angles.

Plies   Separate layers of rubber-cushioned cord.

Poison   This hazardous material class includes materials that are toxic to humans or so toxic that they pose a health hazard during transportation. The class also includes materials presumed hazardous to humans because of laboratory tests. It also includes irritants, such as tear gas and infectious substances.

Pole trailer/pulpwood trailer   A trailer that is composed of a telescopic pole, a tandem rear wheel unit, and a coupling device used to join the trailer to a tractor.

POP   Performance oriented packaging.

Portable bulkheads   Bulkheads that can be removed from the trailer or moved in different configurations.

Portable tank   The tank can be taken off the vehicle and loaded and unloaded.

Portable Tank Emergency Systems   Systems that will lessen the impact of an accident by automatically sealing the tank.

Post-trip inspection   Driver's inspection of rig after each trip.

Pressure relief systems   Monitor the internal pressure of the tank and prevent the cargo from leaking out while the vehicle is on the road.

Pre-trip inspection   Before you begin to drive, a check of your vehicle to make sure that all systems are damage free and working properly to ensure safe driving.

Projecting loads   Cargo that has projecting items which need flags to warn others of the protruding objects. The load must extend more than four inches from the sides of the truck or four feet beyond the rear of the truck. Flags used to mark projecting loads must be at least 12 inches square and must be red.

Psi   Pounds per square inch.

Psia   Pounds per square inch absolute.

PTO lever   Power take-off lever.

Pullup   Stopping and remaneuvering to the correct position.

Pups   Double trailers.

Push rod   Attached to one end of the slack adjuster.

Pyrometer   Displays the engine exhaust temperature.

Radial ply   Ply that does not cross at an angle but is laid from bead to bead, across the tire. Radial tires have a number of belts and their construction means the sidewalls have less flex and less friction—which requires less horsepower and saves fuel.

Radiator shutters   Outer portion of the radiator; if the shutters freeze shut, the engine may overheat and stop. Remove ice when this happens.

Radioactive   Substances that give off radiation rays that are usually harmful.

Railroad crossing   Where the street crosses a railroad track.

Ramps   Entrances or exits to major roadways; may be slightly graded or banked.

Reaction distance   Time it takes for driver's foot to get off the accelerator and stomp on the brake.

Rear bumper   The protective apparatus that prevents shorter vehicles from running under taller ones. Clearance between the bumper and the ground is no more than 30 inches, measured when the vehicle is empty.

Rear clearance lamps   Two red lights located at the top right and top left of the rear of large trucks and buses, tractors, semi-trailers, full trailers, pole trailers, and projecting loads. These lamps outline the overall width. Not required on smaller vehicles.

Rear identification lamps   Three red lights centered on the top rear of large buses and trucks, large semi-trailers, full trailers, and pole trailers. Not required on smaller vehicles.

Rear reflectors   Two red reflectors located on the lower right and lower left of the rear of small and large buses and truck trailers, full trailers, and pole trailers.

Rear side marker lamps   One red light located on each side of the lower left and lower right rear of the side of buses and trucks, semi-trailers, full trailers, and pole trailers.

Rear side reflectors   Red reflectors located just below the rear side marker lamps—required on buses, trucks, semi-trailers, full trailers, and pole trailers.

Rear tail lamps   Lights located at the rear of the truck—amber in color.

Rear turn signal lamps   Two amber or red lights, each located at the lower right and lower left of the rear of trucks and buses, tractors, semi-trailers, full trailers, pole trailers, and converter dollies.

Rear-end projection   Projection four feet beyond the rear of the truck. Flags used to mark projecting loads must be at least 12 inches square and must be red.

Rear-view mirrors   Mirrors used to see on the sides and behind the vehicle.

Rear-wheel skid   Occurs when the rear drive wheels lock and have less traction, causing the rear of the vehicle to slide sideways. To correct, let off the brakes, allowing the rear wheels to roll again, and turn quickly. When the vehicle begins to slide sideways, quickly steer in the direction you want the vehicle to go.

Reefers (refrigerated units)   Truck or tanker used to carry refrigerated cargo or perishables.

Representative vehicle   A motor vehicle which represents the type of vehicle that a driver applicant operates or expects to operate.

Reservoirs   Air tanks.

Retarder controls   Controls that allow the engine to slow the speed of the vehicle, particularly on a downgrade.

Retest and Marking   Specified by the Department of Transportation, requires a regular testing and remarking schedule for tanks authorized to carry HazMat cargo—usually the responsibility of the carrier.

Return spring   Pulls the brake shoes away from the drum.

Right-of-way   The right of a person or vehicle to go before another.

Rim   Part of the wheel that holds the tire in place.

Roof hatch   Opening in the top of a bus to let air in.

Route plan   Prescribed route prior to the trip, usually when the vehicle is carrying hazardous materials or irregular loads. The driver may use less-traveled roads or comply with times during which hazardous materials may be hauled on certain roadways.

RPM   Revolutions per minute. Read by a tachometer and indicates when to change gears.

RQ   Reportable quantity.

Saddle mounts   A steel assembly that couples a towed vehicle (trailer or semi-trailer) with the towing vehicle.

Safe speed   Posted as the speed limit.

Safe-haven   A location approved for parking an unattended vehicle loaded with explosives.

Safety chains   Usually used in pairs with a tow-bar connection to keep trailers from accidentally separating.

Safety valve   Located in the first tank the air compressor pumps air into. This valve will release excess air and protects the air system from exceeding psi limitations (and possibly damaging the system.)

S-cam brakes   The usual configuration of brakes on modern vehicles. Pushing the brake pedal causes the S-cam to force the brake shoes away from the drum. On releasing the brake pedal, the S-cam twists back, returning the wheels to free motion.

SCF   Standard cubic foot.

Seatbelt   Safety harness that holds the driver into the seat. Seatbelts should always be worn when driving—make sure and put it on before you start the vehicle.

Segregation and Separation Chart   Requires certain hazardous materials be loaded separately.

Selector knob   An air-assisted lever on the gearshift which takes the transmission from low-range to high-range.

Self-reactive materials   Materials that are thermally unstable and that can undergo a strong decomposition and may even detonate without participation of oxygen (air).

Serious traffic violation   A conviction received when operating a commercial motor vehicle for excessive speeding, reckless driving, improper or erratic traffic lane changes, following the vehicle ahead too closely, or a violation arising in connection with a fatal accident.

Service brake system   The system that applies and releases the brakes as you apply and release pressure on the service brake.

Service brakes   The vehicle's main braking system—used to stop the vehicle in regular driving situations.

Shaft of the kingpin   Coupling device on the trailer around which the jaws of the locking device are placed for a secure connection.

Shear section   Will save the important part of a pipe and its attachments, thus preventing a leak.

Shipper's certification   A written statement saying that the cargo was prepared according to the law.

Shipping papers   Documents that include any information that is required by FMCSR Parts 172.202, 172.203, and 172.204.

Shutting down the engine   Actually turning off the ignition and allowing the engine to cool.

Side marker lamps   Two amber lights located to each side or near the center of the vehicle between front rear side marker lamps. Required for buses, trucks, semi-trailers, full trailers, and pole trailers.

Side reflectors   Two amber reflectors located on each side or near midpoint of the vehicle between the front and rear side reflectors of buses and trucks, large semi-trailers, large full trailers, and pole trailers.

Skid control   The ability to control the movement of the vehicle once it has entered a skid. Usually done by steering—never by braking.

Skills Test   The actual driving test to make sure that a driver can operate a trailer or tanker.

Slack adjuster   Attached to one end of the push rod and on the other to the brake cam shaft. When it is pushed out, it causes the brake cam shaft to twist, which will cause the S-cam to turn. This forces the brake shoes away from each other and presses them inside the drum, causing the vehicle to stop.

Slack adjusters   Located on the brake chamber push rod, this adjustment device compensates for brake shoe wear.

Slosh   Term used to describe the action of liquids in a tanker—moving front to back or side to side.

Spare tire   Additional tire used as a precaution in case something happens to the vehicle's tires.

Speedometer   Shows the vehicle's road speed in miles per hour (mph).

Spindle   Another word for axle.

Splash guards (mud flaps)   Rubberized sheaths hanging behind the wheels that lessen amount of water or mud kicked up in back of a trailer or truck.

Spotting mirror   Same as convex mirrors—objects appear smaller and farther away than they really are. Always check and adjust prior to each trip.

Spring brakes   Also known as fail-safe brakes. The most commonly used emergency brake and/or parking brake system on tractors and buses. They must be mechanical because air can leak off. Otherwise, they are the conventional brake chambers.

Stab braking   Apply the brakes as hard as possible, release the brakes when the wheels lock, and when wheels start rolling again, reapply the brakes hard—repeat this process as often as necessary.

Standee line   A line behind the driver's seat of a bus that passengers should stand behind.

State   A state of the United States and the District of Columbia.

State of domicile   The state where a person has his or her true, fixed, and permanent home and the principal residence to which he or she has the intention of returning whenever he or she is absent.

Steer-countersteer   Once you've steered around an obstacle, you will turn the wheel back in the other direction.

Steering   The actual directing of the vehicle's movement—rolling frontward or backward.

Steering axle   An axle that steers vehicle—can be powered or nonpowered.

Steering column   Connection between the steering wheel and the steering box.

Steering gear box   The housing between the steering column that holds the power steering pump to make the wheels turn right and left.

Steering system   The steering wheel, steering column, gearbox, Pitman arms, tie-rod ends, and front axle make up the entire steering system.

Steering wheel   The wheel that allows you to direct the front wheels of the vehicle.

Steering wheel knuckles   Found on Pitman arms and tie-rod ends. Connection allows them to swivel.

Steering wheel lash   Usually caused by hitting an object or hole—causes the steering wheel to lash back in the opposite direction. To prevent injury, keep your thumbs outside the steering wheel when wrapping your hands around it.

Stop lamp switch   Stop lights come on when the brake pedal is applied. The electrical switch that turns on the stop lights is activated by air pressure.

Stop lamps   The same as "stop lights." Located on the back of the tractor/trailer—indicate you are stopping the vehicle.

Stop valves   Located on the loading and unloading outlets of the tank vehicle—stop the flow of the liquid cargo.

Stopping distance   The time it takes for a vehicle to stop.

Storage tanks   Air tanks.

Straps   Proper tiedown equipment.

Streetcar crossing   Where the street crosses a streetcar rail.

Supply pressure gauge   Tells the driver the amount of air pressure (measured in pounds per square inch—psi) in the system. If the vehicle has dual air brakes, there will either be one gauge with two needles or two separate gauges.

Suspension   Springs used to support a vehicle and its axles.

Swinging meat   A side of beef or any other meat that can be extremely unstable when hanging in a refrigerated trailer (reefer).

Tabbed   Same as Tagged—a way of marking shipping papers indicating a portion of the cargo is hazardous material.

Tachometer   Instrument located on the dashboard indicating the number of engine revolutions per minute (rpm). RPM is often used to indicate when to shift gears.

Tagged   Shipping papers marked to show that a cargo contains hazardous materials are "tagged" with colored tags or other special markings.

Tailgate   Slang term for a vehicle following too closely.

Tank vehicle   Any commercial motor vehicle that is designed to transport any liquid or gaseous materials within a tank that is either permanently or temporarily attached to the vehicle or the chassis.

Tanker   Special trailer used to carry liquids or dry bulk loads, such as grains, chemicals, etc.

Tarp or tarpaulin   Material used to cover most freight—tied down with rope, webbing, or elastic hooks.

Television receiver   Device that receives television signals. FMCSR states that a television set must be installed behind the driver's seat or otherwise outside of the driver's line of vision while he or she is driving. The regulation further states that the television set must be placed in such a manner that the driver will have to leave the driver's seat to watch it.

10 o'clock and 2 o'clock position   If the steering wheel were a clock, these two times would be where your hands would be placed.

Throttle   A cable connected to the carburetor, which acts like an accelerator, causing the engine to go faster when the knob on the dash board is pulled out. When pushed in, the throttle will slow the engine.

Tie-downs   A category of chains, ropes, and other implements used to secure cargo.

Tie-rod   Part of the steering mechanism, connecting devices on the steering column to enable the steering column to turn the wheels of the tractor or truck.

Tire chains   Chain grids used on tires to provide additional traction on snowy or icy roadways.

Tire failure   When tires fail due to tire damage or defects.

Tire pressure   Amount of air pressure enabling tires to support their maximum weight.

Tires   Provide traction and reduce road vibration, transferring braking and driving force to the road.

Torsion bar suspension   A steel rod, bar, or arm assembly that acts as a spring instead of a leaf or coil spring to create suspension over the rear tractor wheels.

Total stopping distance   Distance from the time you see the hazard until your rig has stopped—about the length of a football field. If you're traveling faster than 55 miles per hour, you're going to increase the distance it takes to stop. If you double your speed, it will take you four times the distance to stop.

Tow bars   Part of a full trailer that allows the trailer to be coupled to the tractor or another trailer with a locking device and safety chains or a cable to prevent accidental separation.

Tow-away operation   Trucking operation offering towing services to disabled vehicles or to transport several tractors/trucks at one time using one vehicle.

Traction   The ability of your tires to "grab" the road.

Transmission control lever   Another name for Gear Shift.

Transport index   Tells the degree of control necessary during transportation—and the total transport index of all packages in a single vehicle cannot exceed 50.

Tread   Series of tie bars and fillets in the outer covering of the tire to improve traction. Tread depth should be at least 2/32 inch.

Triple   A vehicle carrying three trailers or tankers.

Trolley valve   Most tractors have a handle attached to (or near) the steering column called a "Johnson bar" or "trolley valve." It is used to apply trailer brakes.

Turn to the right   The most difficult maneuver because the driver can't see what is happening to the right of the vehicle.

Turning space   Turn wide at the beginning of the maneuver or, if there is not enough room, turn wide as you complete the turn.

Twins   Disconnecting a trailer or combination of trailers.

U-bolts   Used to hold the springs on the frame and hold the springs onto the axle.

U-joints   Located between the drive shaft and the transmission and the drive shaft and the differential.

UN   The first part of a hazardous materials ID number. If the letters are NA, you know the shipment is traveling between the U.S. and Canada. All other ID numbers begin with UN.

Uncoupling   The act of unhitching the trailer/trailers from the tractor.

United States   The term United States means the 50 states and the District of Columbia.

Upgrade   A steepening of the road, usually found around mountainous terrain or in hill country; the opposite of a downgrade.

Vacuum brakes   Type of brakes usually found on trailers, operated by knob control from the tractor and requiring air tanks to operate.

Vehicle group   A class or type of vehicle with certain operating characteristics.

Vehicle   A motor vehicle, unless otherwise specified. Also, any wheeled contraption, including motorcycles, automobiles, trucks, and tractor-trailer rigs.

Viscosity   The tendency of a liquid not to flow. Low viscosity liquids flow easier than those with high viscosity.

Visual awareness   A driver's constant checks of the right and left rear view mirrors and in front of vehicle to avoid obstacles, accidents, or situations that would endanger the driver and/or the load.

Voltmeter   Shows voltage in the alternator or generator; device registering the amount of electricity being produced that goes to the battery.

Warm up   Allowing the engine and fluids to heat up to normal running temperatures before starting the vehicle.

Weaving   Going back and forth between lanes.

Webbing   Used to hold tarps in place.

Wedge brakes   The wedge is pushed by a push-rod between the ends of the brake shoes. The push-rod shoves the shoes apart and presses them against the brake drum. Wedge brakes have one or two brake chambers.

Weight distribution   Percentage of weight carried on each axle according to how the cargo is loaded.

Wheel   To be inspected with each trip; carries a tire and is attached with lugnuts.

Wide load   A trailer carrying a wider-than-usual load that requires more land width on the highway.

Wig-wag   Another type of low air pressure warning. This is a metal arm located above the driver's sight-line—attached at the top of the windshield near the visor. When the air pressure reaches around 60 psi, the wig-wag will swing in front of the driver's face.

Winch   Device used in loading and tying down cargo; also used to tow vehicles or to move heavy cargo from one place to another.

Windshield wipers   Used to remove precipitation from the windshield.

Work zones   Roads or highways that are under construction.

Index